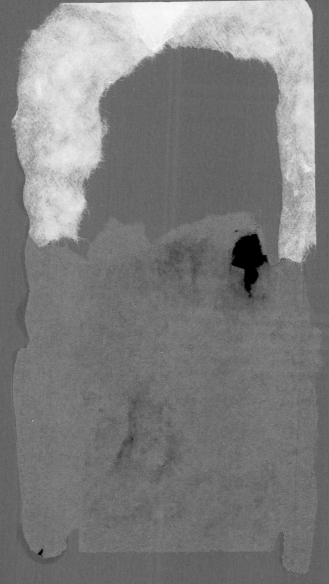

The Baltic Crusade

†

The Baltic Crusade

William Urban

NORTHERN ILLINOIS

UNIVERSITY PRESS

DeKalb / 1975

*Publication of this book was assisted by the American
Council of Learned Societies under a grant from the
Andrew W. Mellon Foundation.*

We wish to thank the University of Wisconsin Press for permission to reprint excerpts from *The Chronicle of Henry of Livonia*, translated by
James A. Brundage, copyright © 1961 by the University of Wisconsin Press.

Library of Congress Cataloging in Publication Data

Urban, William L   1939–
    The Baltic Crusade.

    Bibliography: p.
    Includes index.
    1. Livonia—History. 2. Estonia—History. I. Title.
DK511.L36U7   947'.41   74-12825
ISBN 0-87580-052-1

Published by the Northern Illinois University Press, DeKalb, Illinois 60115
Manufactured in the United States of America
All Rights Reserved

Design and cartography by Guy Fleming

In memory of my great-uncle,
Lawrence Gilbreath, 1894–1964

CONTENTS

ILLUSTRATIONS

P R E F A C E

IT IS AN UNFORTUNATE FACT THAT MOST WRITERS WHO STUDY THE "CRUSADES" discuss only those expeditions to the Holy Land that ended in 1291. This is often due to practical considerations in writing and publishing, but just as often is due to a narrow definition of "the Crusades." However that may be, the crusading movement was not confined to the Near East. Crusades were declared against heretics, pagans, and political opponents, as well as Saracens. They were organized and led by popes, kings, nobles, hermits, peasants, children, and excommunicants. They were organized against enemies in Greece, Spain, Germany, Bohemia, the Balkans, and Russia, as well as in the Holy Land and North Africa—for the purposes of conquest, booty, and revenge, as well as for protection of the holy places.

In short, the crusading spirit and the crusading movement affected every social class and every generation from 1100 to 1500 and virtually every geographic location accessible to Europeans. Nor did the crusades cease to be a factor in European politics with the end of the military expeditions. The Renaissance papacy cannot be understood without considering the financial and political difficulties imposed by the Turkish menace. The Spanish conquest of the New World also exhibited the spirit of the Crusades and lacked only the formality of a papal bull and the assent of historians to be called by such a name. From Clermont to Tannenberg, from the cloisters to the courts, these four centuries were a crusading era.

The Baltic Crusade presents a picture of one part of one crusade that occurred in the distant past in a remote part of Europe but has affected the history of that region into the present century. It attempts to show that this was an important crusade and that the success of the venture depended largely upon political factors in the homeland, that is, Northern Germany and Scandinavia.

Of special relevance to modern times, and of special concern to the author, is the concept of a righteous war, which is certainly to be considered in discussing the Crusades. The crusades in the Baltic region were efforts to protect converts and commerce and to suppress superstition, barbarism, and anarchical tribal warfare. Led by a professional priesthood whose sole duty was the care of souls whom God had placed in their charge, these crusading endeavors were theoretically as humanitarian a venture as one can conceive, when one takes human weaknesses into account. If this was not a righteous cause, there can be no cause worthy of taking up arms in its defense. What came of this noble dream as the years unfolded is the subject of this volume.

The Baltic Crusade

†

1

Northern Germany in the Late Twelfth Century

SKAGERRAK

KATTEGAT

SWEDEN

DENMARK

• Lund

Jutland

Bornholm

• Roeskilde
Seeland

BALTIC SEA

• Stenby

• Odense

NORTH SEA

Ripon •

Lyö •

DENMARK

Rugen

Pomera

NORTH FRISIAN COAST

Schleswig

Schleswig •

• Kiel

Plön

Eider

• Bornhoeved

Rendsburg

Neumünster •

Mecklenburg

Dithmarschen •

Segeberg •

Reinfeld

Lübeck

• Schwerin

Itzehoe •

Holstein

Trave

Ratze-
burg

Hamburg

Mölln •

Stade •

Lauenburg

Frisia

ELBE

Brandenburg

Archbishopric
of Hamburg-
Bremen

Lüneburg

Weser R.

Dannenberg

Oldenburg

Bremen •

Braunschweig

Stedigen •

Verden •

(Before 1180, Duchy of Saxony)

Magdeburg •

Ems R.

Utrecht

Münster

Loccum •

Braunschweig •

Halberstadt

Saxony (Anha

Minden •

Schauen-
burg

Goslar •

Osnabrück •

Lippe

Hildesheim

• Münster

Paderborn •

Marienfeld

Paderborn

Utrecht •

Holland

Gelders

RHINE R.

Westphalia

Denmark and North Germany

Miles

0   25   50   100

0   40   80   160

Kilometers

For most Germans who lived during the middle of the twelfth century, the Baltic was a *mare incognita* of storms and sandy shoals, devoid of sure harbors and swarming with pirates from pagan tribes. Its trade, such as it was, was dominated by the descendants of those Viking sea raiders who had established states stretching, at times, from England to Estonia and from Estonia to the Black Sea. The interests of Germany, like those of Europe as a whole, seemed to be to the south. The Mediterranean, not the Baltic, was the center of the known world in every important aspect —military, commercial, religious—and then as now the Germans, as if by a law of gravity, were drawn to Italy.

Even for the great Emperor Frederick Barbarossa, Italy was of greater importance than Northern Germany. To be sure, much of Frederick's interest centered on his desire to make Swabia, where the Hohenstaufen lands were located, the center of an empire comprising Germany, Burgundy, and Italy (rather than just an outlying province of a weak feudal German state). Revenues from Italy would permit an attempt to create a central authority over the German nobility, and imperial intervention was necessary in unorganized Italy to forestall other ambitious princes. There was no alternative to adventures in Italy, even though this necessarily meant weak imperial influence in North Germany.[1]

Because of the Slavic reactions to German attempts to expand toward the northeast, their common frontier had remained relatively static for many years. Toward the middle of the twelfth century, however, a number of ambitious men began a new movement of political expansion and subsequent colonization. As a result of the work of Henry the Lion, Adolf of Holstein, and Albrecht the Bear, a change came about in the lands north and east of the Elbe that in the course of the ensuing century completely reordered the complex of settlement, commerce, culture, and language along the shores of the Baltic Sea.

The princely houses these men headed became important during the period of disorder following the investiture controversy, when the two great families of Welf and Hohenstaufen contested for the imperial throne. In the course of this struggle the territorial princes enhanced their powers at the expense of the Emperors and saddled Germany with an incomplete form of feudalism, so that damage to German unity, to imperial government, and to the rights of the lesser nobility and peasantry was considerable. The royal government was greatly weakened, and power was exercised by the nobility without responsibility to the state. The result was chaos, as unscrupulous men seized the opportunity to carve out independent states for themselves. The weaker magnates sought imperial protection when the stronger men began to war among themselves, but the appeal served only to accentuate the Welf-Hohenstaufen dispute and to strengthen the position of the stronger princes.

Fully aware of the changes that had come about, Frederick Barbarossa (1152–1190) ceased his opposition to the new feudalism and, instead, sought to harness it to the service of the state. His father a Hohenstaufen, his mother a Welf, this great-nephew of the late Emperor was able to reconcile all the quarreling factions of the unhappy Empire and to restore peace. He conciliated the Welf faction in 1156 by recognizing his cousin, Henry the Lion, as Duke of Bavaria and Saxony, but at the same time he separated Austria from Bavaria to achieve a rough balance in the south and, in hope of doing the same thing in the north, granted Holstein to Adolf of Schauenburg and the North Mark to Albrecht the Bear. In establishing equilibrium between the parties, Frederick hoped to prevent, or at least determine the outcome of, serious disputes in the Empire. Royal intervention would be decisive. Meanwhile, government could be reorganized along feudal lines. Having completed these tasks, Frederick turned his back on Germany and concentrated on Italy.

The prince who profited most from this settlement was Barbarossa's Welf cousin, Henry the Lion, who was described by a contemporary as follows:

This duke . . . was the son of Duke Henry [the Proud] and Gertrude, daughter of the Emperor Lothar. Bereft of his father and mother while still in the cradle, when he grew to manhood he was endowed with physical strength and comely in appearance, but was especially notable for his great intelligence. He was not corrupted by luxury or idleness, but—as is the custom of the Saxons—he rode horseback, hurled the spear, vied with his companions in running, and although he surpassed all in fame yet he was dear to all. . . . This man had . . . received from the emperor the duchy of Bavaria. Learning the character and habits of his men, by his great vigilance and wisdom he soon achieved such fame that, after establishing peace throughout all Bavaria, he became exceedingly dear to the good and a source of great terror to the bad.[2]

And although powerful through his possession of Bavaria, Henry's fame rests upon his activities in Saxony. There, where he had a freer hand, he wrote his name large. By his foundation of cities, his encouragement of trade, and his promotion of settlement, he made changes that endured long after he and his royal English wife were laid to rest in Braunschweig Cathedral.

The other North German princes feared the centralizing policies of Henry the Lion, and not without foundation, for at one time or another all of them had to suffer from his hunger for land and power. Links with England and the control of Goslar were essential to Henry for strengthening his position in Saxony. He felt it necessary, therefore, to control the archbishopric of Hamburg-Bremen, which lay athwart the vital water routes up the Weser and Elbe, which connected these two bases of Welf power.[3]

The prince most threatened by Henry the Lion was therefore the Archbishop of Hamburg-Bremen, who was, for his part, every bit as land-hungry and power-greedy as Henry the Lion—and, furthermore, coveted the lands belonging to that Welf Prince. Indeed, more than a century earlier, during the minority of Henry IV, Archbishop Adalbert had dominated Northern Germany. Because the Emperor Henry III had granted extensive territories to the ecclesiastical princes to counterbalance the secular princes, the Archbishop had acquired great wealth and power; but alarmed by his pride and ambition, the secular and ecclesiastical princes had revolted and, led by the Archbishop of Cologne, had destroyed Adalbert's power and left behind only the dream. It was the dream of resurrecting Adalbert's state that led the Hamburg and Bremen cathedral chapters to elect Hartwig of Stade as Archbishop in 1148. To the day of his death twenty years later, Hartwig fought the Welf at every opportunity.[4]

Unfortunately for Hartwig, his career was marked by a succession of failures. Angered by the settlement of 1156, Archbishop Hartwig refused to attend Court or send aid to the Emperor in Italy. He pleaded the necessity of defending his family inheritance in Stade and his ecclesiastical lands against Henry the Lion—excuses that were hardly acceptable to the hard-pressed Emperor—and when his military resources proved inadequate, Hartwig had to flee Bremen, leaving it in Welf hands. Shortly afterward he found himself on the list of princes reprimanded by the Emperor at the Diet of Roncaglia and, as punishment, lost control of the bishoprics of Lübeck, Schwerin, and Ratzeburg, which went to his enemy, Henry the

Lion, who had supported the Emperor in Italy. Hartwig's attempts to regain imperial favor brought him only more trouble because he was foolish enough to recognize the anti-Pope, Victor IV, just before that prelate died and his party began to collapse. As punishment, Pope Alexander III transferred the Scandinavian bishoprics to the Archbishop of Lund. Even inactivity proved equally vain, because Welf influence over his domains grew steadily. Finally, in 1166, Hartwig led the princes in a desperate revolt against Welf centralization. The resulting disorder displeased Frederick Barbarossa, whose Italian affairs were in crisis, and since he was dependent on the troops sent by Henry the Lion, the Emperor supported his cousin. Thus the revolt collapsed, Hartwig died shortly thereafter, and his successor was so subservient to Henry the Lion that a medieval chronicler, Arnold of Lübeck, says it is better to pass over that period in silence. Hartwig's long, stubborn opposition to the Welf Prince was not without effect, however, for it led to Frederick Barbarossa's recovery of Goslar as his price for mediation in 1168. This created bad feelings between Welf and Hohenstaufen, which worsened with each passing year.

North of the Elbe, the most important prince was Adolf II of Holstein. By continual war against the indigenous Wendish tribes and the Danish King, he had conquered a rich country that he resettled with peasants from Holland, Frisia, and Westphalia. By dint of tremendous personal activity and courage, he defended his conquests up to the last year of his life, and only then, in 1163, was he forced to surrender his newly founded and prosperous city of Lübeck to Henry the Lion. This loss was a terrible blow to the land-rich but money-poor Count, and the recovery of Lübeck was to remain an unfulfilled ambition of the Counts of Holstein for centuries thereafter.

Because of his youth, Adolf III of Holstein was unable to escape the domination of Henry the Lion; and even after he attained his majority, Adolf was unable to attain the independence his family believed to be so essential. Although very ambitious and brave to the point of rashness, Adolf waited for a weakening in the Welf position before attempting to regain his freedom.

The last and most dangerous of Henry's opponents was Albrecht the Bear, who ruled in the North Mark, or Brandenburg. In spite of his advanced age, Albrecht defied both time and Henry the Lion and fought relentlessly against Welf encroachments, until death finally claimed him in 1170. With his passing, the last great prince of the Hohenstaufen party was gone. All Northern Germany came under the influence of the Welf Prince.

To all intents and purposes, Henry the Lion was sovereign in Northern Germany, With his expanded power in Saxony and his domains in Bavaria, it appeared that he was the equal of the Emperor Frederick Barbarossa. So secure was he that in 1171 he was able to leave Germany on crusade to the Holy Land, and this one act, this crusade, symbolizes what the Welf Duke had achieved. He had united Saxony and created a powerful state that could not only support colonization in the east and promote German commercial interests in the Baltic but could also revive the spirit that had been demoralized in the Second Crusade. The achievements of Henry the Lion cannot be ignored. In a distant corner of Germany a certain German unity was formed, and, more important, movements that dominated the following century—colonization, commerce, and crusades—were set in motion. Henry had accomplished so much that even the events that followed could not disrupt the direction he had given German history in this part of Europe.

Why did Henry the Lion have such a far-reaching influence on Northern Germany? The answer is simple: this was a frontier region. When the Wendish crusade of 1147 opened the regions across the Elbe to German colonization, Henry had been the first prince in the field. Consequently, he had won the lion's share of the new lands. Throughout the era of settlement and development he was foremost among the princes in encouraging the foundation of cities and in supporting the efforts of merchants to develop new markets.

In settling the new lands, Henry and the other princes were wary of establishing a strong noble class below them. They saw little need for landed vassals. To attract colonists, they had offered significant concessions, so that most communities were exempt from the traditional obligations. The princes supported themselves and their followers not from the produce of their demesnes but from the taxes of the villages and cities. Therefore the princes needed tax collectors and justices, and these offices could be filled by *ministeriales* as well as by landed vassals.

There were also certain advantages to the use of *ministeriales*. These knights, descendants of free commoners and former serfs, were professional warriors and servants who could be removed at any time, and therefore they could be controlled. Their wealth and position were dependent on their lord, and their social position separated them from the noble vassals; therefore they were more dependable. And if they were killed in battle, they could be replaced from among the rich peasants who had equipped themselves to fight on horseback.

The result of this policy was to create a society in the north of Germany somewhat different from that found elsewhere. Here the prince was supreme, but his powers were limited. His nobles were weak, but most peasants and burghers were submissive to the advocates, who were often drawn from their own ranks. Commerce was more important than farming, and the prince saw to the prosperity of the merchants because he shared in their wealth through the increase in taxes. In short, Henry the Lion laid the groundwork for the Hanseatic society that later developed in the region.[5]

There were, of course, nobles in the north. Some were from old Saxon families, some were princes of very minor rank, some were vassals of local importance, and some were from ministerial families on the way up. A number of them were identified with the House of Welf, and profited from Henry's successes, but most of them saw the Welf policies as a threat to their social position. For this reason numerous nobles took every opportunity to oppose the programs of Henry the Lion, especially those programs that would centralize authority in his hands. When Henry left for crusade in the east in 1171, he took as many of these vassals with him as he could, but dissatisfied men nevertheless remained behind to create minor disorder. In repressing these risings the Welf partisans increased their holdings at the expense of their traditional enemies. As a result, every rising brought a repression that heightened the dissatisfaction of large numbers of nobles.

So dangerous was this dissatisfaction that Henry did not dare go personally to Italy to support Frederick Barbarossa in 1174, when his presence was most needed. As long as the nobles in Northern Germany were angry, he had to remain there and keep watch over them, as he could not require his entire nobility to go again to Italy so soon after their crusading effort. Another reason for his refusal to support his cousin was his growing confidence that he could defy an emperor who was tied down by wars in Italy. When the Emperor asked for reinforcements in 1175, Henry demanded that Goslar be returned as the price of his assistance. Goslar would round out the Saxon holdings, and Saxony would become a kingdom within the kingdom. Frederick Barbarossa, unable to grant such a concession, decided to fight on without assistance. Under such circumstances, the Emperor ascribed his defeat at Legnano to Henry's failure to send aid.

Imperial revenge was not long delayed. Although defeated on the battlefield, Frederick Barbarossa won a victory at the peace table that more than compensated for his losses. And in doing so he cleverly struck at the Welf party. The Emperor agreed to remove bishops who had not been recognized by the Pope from their sees and to restore confiscated Church lands to their proper owners, a move that affected Welf adherents. When the Welfish Archbishop of Bremen received the papal letter announcing his deposition, he suffered a stroke and died, and the vacancy was filled with the imperial candidate. Shortly afterward, several minor Saxon princes declared a feud against Henry the Lion, and although the rising had tacit imperial approval, it was not completely successful. In 1178, therefore, Frederick summoned Henry to Court, where the dispute would be decided according to feudal law. But rather than face a hostile nobility and an angry Emperor, Henry chose to remain in Saxony and defend himself as best he could. Now, however, the ring of enemies was closing in upon him. The Archbishop of Cologne, the Archbishop of Bremen, and the Count of Holstein joined in the attacks, and slowly the Welf Duke was driven back into the narrow confines of Braunschweig, his family land.

> From that time on many evils came on the land, because everyone had risen against the duke, and every hand was against him, and his hand was against everyone. The Archbishop Philip brought his troops on a second invasion . . . and crossed the entire ducal territory with a powerful army, and everyone feared him. Many disgusting and terrible things happened on this invasion.[6]

The contest was still in doubt when the Emperor threw his weight against his cousin. The feudal nobility condemned Henry for failure to perform Court service, and Frederick Barbarossa personally led an army into Saxony. There was little opposition. The Welf vassals deserted to the Emperor, and only a few of Henry's more favored cities offered resistance. Judged by his peers according to feudal custom, the Saxon Duke was deprived of his fiefs and banished from the kingdom for four years. The confiscated estates were divided among the princes who had attacked the Welf Prince most opportunely, and although Frederick Barbarossa did not profit directly, he was rid of a dangerous rival.

The dismemberment of the Saxon duchy not only enriched the princes but brought forth mutual jealousies that had been hidden for many years. The Archbishop of Cologne, who profited more than any other prince, began to develop his Rhenish lands into a powerful base for future expansion. Next was Bernard of Anhalt, the son of Albrecht the Bear, who

9

acquired the title of Duke of Saxony and, consequently, suzerainty over the numerous unruly vassals of the area. The Archbishops of Magdeburg and Bremen, the Bishops of Paderborn and Hildesheim, and the Counts of Thuringia, Holstein, and Lauenburg each seized some lands. But no matter how much territory each prince received, each believed that he deserved more, and the conflicting claims were to be a problem in the future.

Although defeated and exiled, Henry the Lion was not without hope of recouping his losses. He still retained his family lands around Braunschweig and Lüneburg, so that he remained in the first rank of princes. Many vassals and *ministeriales* remained loyal to him, and others might be won over if there were sufficient chance of profit for them. Furthermore, Henry could count on the military and financial support of his Angevin relatives in England, and even the King of Denmark might offer assistance. Lastly, there was the Pope. The papacy, always fearful of imperial success, readily lent aid to disruptive factions in Germany. Opposed to Henry were quarreling princes, who had not yet organized their new territories, and the Emperor, who was in distant Italy. All Saxony was unstable, and when Henry the Lion returned to Germany in 1184 he expected to recover most, if not all, of his losses.

Henry wasted little time before seeking to reassert his hegemony in Saxony; however, he moved too quickly and frightened his enemies. As a result, shortly after he succeeded in placing his candidate in the vacant archbishopric of Bremen the princes voted to exile him again. Henry was not yet ready to fight against such numbers, and therefore he returned to England.

The new Archbishop of Bremen was Hartwig II, a proud, stubborn, ambitious man desirous of restoring his see to its former position of hegemony in Saxony. But this was not consistent with the Welf party's goals, and therefore Hartwig was to waver between the parties in the future difficulties and thereby achieve few of his ambitions, in spite of his many intrigues and wars. Hartwig's failures may be seen as a result of the incompatibility of his goals rather than as incompetence or bad luck, though the latter also played a role in his political misfortunes. His difficulties were sufficiently imposing without the addition of party conflict. His see had been disrupted by a generation of warfare; many advocacies were held by hostile nobles; and the debts could not be covered by the inadequate revenues.

Then as now, lack of revenue was at the root of most administrative problems. If Hartwig could have raised more taxes, many of his problems would have been solved, but neither the citizens nor the peasants were eager for higher taxes; and every attempt to increase them produced more resistance than funds. The problem in the countryside was that most communities possessed immunity from taxes that dated from the time of settlement, when the Archbishops had offered tax remission to peasants who would settle in the marshes and reclaim the bottomlands. Now that they were prosperous, the peasants were also numerous and warlike enough to defend their privileges. Protected by arms and the natural difficulties of the terrain, such independent peasants long remained a thorn in the side of the feudal proprietors along the North Sea coast. Archbishop Hartwig's attempts to coerce the peasants literally "bogged down" in the bottomlands. And his armies' failure to penetrate the swamps left him deeper in debt than ever. An illegal tax on the citizens of Bremen brought an imperial rebuff and fine. Hartwig's only hope seemed to be outside help, and he entered into correspondence with Henry the Lion.

If the Archbishop of Bremen was faced by seemingly insuperable difficulties, he could take some small comfort from the fact that his neighbors were faring little better. The Archbishop of Cologne was opposed by a coalition of minor princes who hoped to limit his power before he became too dangerous. The Dukes of Thuringia and Saxony were feuding, and Holstein and Denmark were on the verge of war. In short, there were many malcontents in the area, and Henry the Lion was the man who could unite them. The promise of money could win over many princes, and with English silver the Welf Prince set a widespread conspiracy afoot.

This time Henry the Lion waited patiently for a propitious moment rather than risk a premature return that might provoke an imperial rebuke. His opportunity came in 1189, when, to conciliate the Pope and to demonstrate the unity of western Christendom, Frederick Barbarossa set out on crusade with the Kings of France and England. North Germans had responded eagerly to the imperial summons, and hardly a person of importance remained behind. Adolf of Holstein, the Counts of Schwerin, the Archbishop of Bremen, and the sons of Henry the Lion all took the cross; knights, burghers, sailors, and peasants joined one or another of the several fleets or bodies of men that were leaving for the east. Once the crusaders had departed, Henry returned to Saxony, and though many of his followers were among the crusaders, he found sufficient welcome in the north to frighten his enemies. Moreover, the frightful and unexpectedly sudden end to the crusade made Henry's invasion of Saxony very dangerous. When Frederick Barbarossa drowned in Asia Minor, the feudal ties that had held all Germany loyal to him were loosed. Consequently, German feudalism faced a crisis, and the heir to the throne, as well as most of the nobles, hurried home to see that their rights and possessions would be maintained. Henry's invasion coincided with the death of the Emperor to bring an end to the crusade and the beginning of a new struggle in Saxony.

By this time, however, Henry the Lion was no longer as fearsome as his reputation. Without foreign assistance, he could not stand against his numerous deadly enemies, and his brother-in-law, Richard the Lionheart, who had assisted his return to Germany, was harassing the Hohenstaufen Emperor by interfering in Sicily. Such tactics, combined with Richard's high-handed arrogance, were to make him hated by his allies in the Holy Land and to lead to his subsequent imprisonment by Leopold of Austria. Because Richard was on crusade and Henry needed more help, the latter turned to his old ally, the King of Denmark.

When Frederick Barbarossa had become King and Emperor in Germany, Denmark was a relatively insignificant state, subject to the Holy Roman Empire and continually distracted by civil war. Denmark's ceaseless feuds, assassinations, and widespread piracy made it appear that the waves of priests sent out by the Archbishops of Hamburg-Bremen had been able to wash only a shallow tide of Christianity about the pagan souls of these Northmen. Proud, independent, warlike, the Danes had contented themselves with subjecting their equally proud and warlike Scandinavian neighbors and extorting tribute from the tribes along the shores of the Baltic. Neither rich, populous, nor well led, they had little influence on affairs in Germany. This was to change, thanks to the efforts of Waldemar I (1157–1182), Canute IV (1182–1202), and the great Archbishop Absalon (1157–1201), when this far-flung kingdom was organized into a state where officials and merchants could cross the seas and travel the roads in safety, where churches could be built and endowed, and where most authority lay in the hands of the King. (Although royal authority was limited by the assemblies of rich peasants who served in the army, the nobility was only in the formative stages of organization; so effective police power rested in the housecarls of the monarch and his officials.) The great Kings, assisted by the Archbishop of Lund, bent their subjects to their will and revived Danish greatness.

As Danish influence grew, it was inevitable that some arrangement be made with the German state created by Henry the Lion. After some initial conflict, the Danes and the Welfs found it more convenient to work together rather than against one another. Both Waldemar I and Henry the Lion sought to establish central authority over their subjects; both opposed the Wendish Slavs and Adolf II of Holstein; both were interested in opening the Baltic for trade; and both wished to throw off the domination of a strong German Emperor. However opposed their ultimate goals, for many years they found it convenient to cooperate in furthering their mutual interests.

When Henry the Lion defied his sovereign, the Danish monarch gave him encouragement but had no wish to involve himself in a military conflict with Frederick Barbarossa. Confronted by an imperial demand that he do homage, King Canute made a different and less humiliating submission: he offered his daughter as a bride for an imperial son. It was during this short-lived period of good relations with the Emperor that Canute replaced the Welf overlordship in Mecklenburg by forcing its Princes to recognize his suzerainty. However, there was not a firm foundation for the alliance of the two royal houses, and the projected marriage never took place. But the Danish King did not need imperial support; indeed, his interests were diametrically opposed to those of the Holy Roman Emperor, and the chaotic situation in the North of Germany gave him ample opportunity to extend his influence there.

When the peasants of Dithmarschen rose against the Archbishop of Hamburg-Bremen, Danish knights came to their assistance, claiming that all lands north of the Elbe were within the Danish sphere of influence and that therefore the King of Denmark would decide all disputes in that area. Henry the Lion and his followers, who had little to lose in this region, gave implicit recognition to this claim in hope of obtaining Danish assistance for the recovery of Saxony.

The interests of Danish King and Welf Prince converged in Holstein, which lay between their domains. Conveniently, the Count was absent on crusade, and thus it was to Holstein that Henry the Lion devoted his energies when he returned from England. His resources were inadequate, however, and the attack failed when Adolf III returned hurriedly from the east and obtained assistance from the Dukes of Saxony and Brandenburg. Henry fled into Denmark, where he hoped to obtain military support for another invasion of Holstein. King Canute, moreover, had reason to intervene. His uncle, Bishop Waldemar of Schleswig, had rebelled in an attempt to seize the throne, and when the canons of Hamburg-Bremen learned that their Archbishop Hartwig II had opted for the Welf party, they shut the city gates on him and elected the rebel Danish Bishop as his successor. This was a real threat to the stability of the Danish throne. But the prospects for a Welf victory seemed so poor that King Canute refused to do more than offer the Welf Prince refuge in his kingdom. It was a wise move. When Richard the Lionheart fell into the hands of Leopold of Austria, the English silver that had held the Welf party together was diverted for his ransom, and the Welfs went down to defeat.

It was the Pope who saved the Welf conspirators from their fate. Knowing that it would be a political blunder to allow the Hohenstaufen party to strengthen itself unduly, the Pope intervened on behalf of Hartwig II and saved his office for him. Bishop Waldemar sailed off to Sweden to continue his rebellion and shortly afterward was captured by his nephew. With Bishop Waldemar in prison, and King Canute ill, Danish affairs quieted down. With Henry the Lion in exile and a strong Emperor on the throne, North Germany was again dominated by members of the Hohenstaufen party. The Welf party survived, thanks to the papacy, but it was weak.

When the chronicler noted baldly that "about this time the old duke Henry of Braunschweig died,"[7] few people cared—only a handful of Welf supporters, such as the one who wrote:

> Now he is taken from us.
> God be graceful unto us
> And soon give us from that family
> Another such to come.
> Who will honor and enrich the world.
> A noble fruit of Braunschweig,
> That was the worthy Henry. . . .[8]

Adolf III of Holstein organized affairs in the north to his own liking, so that in 1196, when another crusade was preached, he could take the cross and absent himself from Holstein for three years. He took many malcontents with him, including Hartwig II of Hamburg-Bremen. At the same time, many sailors and soldiers of Bremen sailed to the Holy Land and established a hospital for injured crusaders. This enterprise developed into the Order of the Teutonic Knights, an organization of great importance in the history of the Baltic Crusade.

The stability of Northern Germany was to be short-lived, however, as the contending factions resumed their rivalry. The Italian policy of Emperor Henry VI began a great duel between the Popes and Emperors, and this revived the Welf-Hohenstaufen dispute in Germany. And though the struggle would be fought on German soil by German magnates, it would be fought for foreign purposes and with foreign money. German unity would be destroyed, and a new power would rule the lands north of the Elbe.

NOTES TO CHAPTER ONE

1. My viewpoint may seem Welfish, influenced by James Westfall Thompson and his *Feudal Germany* (New York: Frederick Ungar, 1966), but I am in general agreement with the views of Geoffrey Barraclough's *The Origins of Modern Germany* (Oxford: Basil Blackwell, 1957), whose position is summarized on p. 193: "Frederick Barbarossa had built well. His efforts and ability and firm grasp of realities had rescued the Empire from the set-backs of the Investiture Contest, which had retarded and perhaps even perverted German development by comparison with France and England. But there were certain problems outstanding, both in Italy and Germany, when he died in 1190." Certainly Northern Germany was one of those problem areas. Frederick's death, and the sudden demise of Henry VI, led to a breakdown in the imperial system. As civil war divided the heartland of Germany, the north was set to drift into the orbit of Denmark, then into virtual autonomy. Whatever one may think of Thompson's Welfish views, from the standpoint of North Germany they are justifiable.

2. Otto of Freising, *The Deeds of Frederick Barbarossa*, trans. Charles Christopher Mierow (New York: Norton, 1966), p. 278.

3. The policies of Henry the Lion resemble, on a regional level, those of Frederick Barbarossa on the national level. His goal was to divide and weaken the independent princes and make them subordinate to his authority. From the financial base provided by the cities (Henry founded his; Frederick fought to conquer his in Lombardy), he expanded his influence over the neighboring states. To assert that Henry the Lion believed in regional autonomy and national development is only to say that he believed in protecting what was his. If he had been Emperor, he probably would have invaded Italy. Certainly his son, Otto IV, adopted the Hohenstaufen program as soon as he had the opportunity. See Austin Lane Poole, *Henry the Lion* (Oxford: B. H. Blackwell, 1912), and Marcel Pacaut, *Frederick Barbarossa* (New York: Charles Scribner's Sons, 1970).

4. The rest of the chapter is taken from Otto of Freising, *Deeds of Frederick Barbarossa*; *Helmoldi presbyteria Bozoviensis Chronica Slavorum*, 3d ed., Bernard Schmeidler and Johann M. Lappenberg (Hannover: Hahnsche, 1937); *Arnoldi abbatis Lubecensis Chronica*, ed. Johann M. Lappenberg (Hannover: Hahnsche, 1868) (hereafter cited as *Arnold of Lübeck*); and *Annales Stadenses auctore Alberto*, ed. Johann M. Lappenberg (Hannover: Hahnsche, 1859) (hereafter cited as *Albert of Stade*). All of these chronicles are found in the *Monumenta Germaniae Historica,*

Scriptores rerum germanicarum in usum scholarum separatim editi. For an English summary, see Wilson King. *Chronicles of Three Free Cities: Hamburg, Bremen, Lübeck* (London: J. M. Dent & Sons, 1914).

5. Thompson, *Feudal Germany*, pp. 292–337. One would think that Marc Bloch's *Feudal Society* (London: Routledge & Kegan Paul, 1961) would put to rest all ideas that feudal practices were uniform, as used to be suggested in "pontifical" texts. It is absolutely essential to an understanding of the Baltic Crusade to remember that feudalism was a growing and changing institution and that it developed differently in different places. Feudal practices in Livonia and Denmark were based upon the practices in Northern Germany, but in each place they evolved so as to satisfy local needs. Therefore, one cannot expect Livonian customs to be the same as those customs characteristic of the classical feudalism of Northwestern France.

6. *Arnold of Lübeck*, from the year 1179.

7. *Sächische Weltchronik*, in *Monumenta Germaniae Historia, Deutsche Chroniken*, ed. Ludwig Weiland (Berlin: Weidmann, 1877), 2: 234.

8. *Braunschweigische Reimchronik*, in *Monumenta Germaniae Historica, Deutsche Chroniken*, ed. Ludwig Weiland (Berlin: Weidmann, 1877), 2: 519.

2

Livonia on the Eve of the Invasions

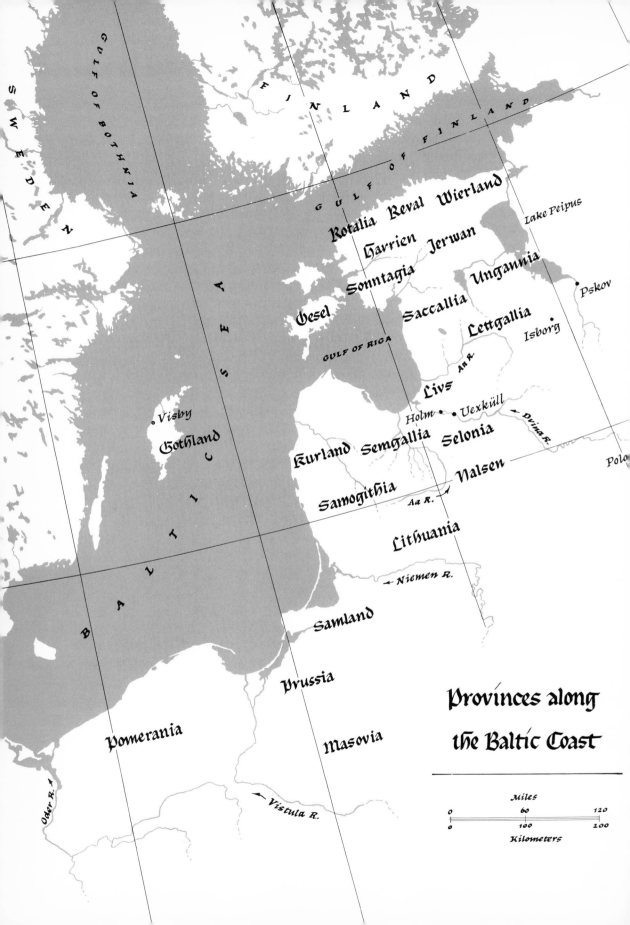

SWEDEN

GULF OF BOTHNIA

FINLAND

GULF OF FINLAND

Lake Peipus

Rotalia Reval Wierland

Harrien Jerwan

Sonntagia Ungannia

Pskov

Gesel Saccallia

BALTIC SEA

Lettgallia

Isborg

GULF OF RIGA

Aa R.

Livs

Visby

Holm Uexküll

Dvina R.

Gothland

Kurland Semgallia Selonia

Nalsen

Polo

Samogithia

Aa R.

Lithuania

Niemen R.

Samland

Prussia

Masovia

Pomerania

Oder R.

Vistula R.

Provinces along the Baltic Coast

Miles
0   60   120
0   100   200
Kilometers

THE WESTERN WORLD KNEW LITTLE OF LIVONIA. ITS INHABITANTS, NOT organized into kingdoms or dukedoms, were little more than victims in the march of conquest and trade that periodically made the Baltic region important to the rest of Europe. These people had rejected the infrequent offer of salvation through the two competing bodies of Christians, the Greek and the Roman Churches, and consequently rejected the culture traditionally borne by them. Hence they lived quiet lives like their ancestors, in which the cycles of birth, marriage, and death, plenty and famine, victory and defeat in war, and the monotony of daily work repeated themselves unnoted by outsiders.

Life was not easy. The cold, dry springs were followed by rainy summers and long, bitterly cold winters. The flat, sandy western coast was often wrapped in fog, and the northern headlands jutted into stormy seas. In winter even the sea froze solidly, halting all sea travel for half the year. From the coast, a rolling plain extended into the interior, where it gradually merged with swamps and marshes to make a frontier with Russia. This plain was occasionally broken by the remains of glacial activity: steep unforested hills, long moraines, wide and shallow lakes. The numerous streams and rivers were broad and shallow, and flooded every spring when the snow melted. Much of the country was covered by forest, with oak and beech predominating in the south and fir in the north; and there were only a few open areas that were fit for intensive agriculture. Even these areas might not have been fit for cultivation if the climate had not been moderated by the Baltic Sea, the salvation of the land, which provided moisture and warmth and linked Livonia to the commercial areas of the west, just as the rivers led to the commercial areas of the east. It was trade that gave Livonia the prosperity it enjoyed, and not the natural richness of the land. The warlike and piratical nature of the natives, however, discouraged merchants from visiting them. According to Adam of Bremen:

> There also are other more distant islands that are subject to the authority of the Swedes. Of these islands the largest, the one called Courland, takes eight days to traverse. The people, exceedingly bloodthirsty because of their stubborn devotion to idolatry, are shunned by everybody.... We are told, moreover, that there are in this sea many other islands, of which a large one is called Estland. It is not smaller than the one of which we have previously spoken. Its people,

too, are utterly ignorant of the God of the Christians. They adore dragons and birds and also sacrifice to them live men whom they buy from the merchants. The men are carefully inspected all over to see that they are without a bodily defect on account of which, they say, the dragons would reject them. This island is said, indeed, to be very near the land of women.[1]

Adam of Bremen was very well informed on geographic matters, but even he connects this little-known area with the legend of the Amazons, with the Cynocephali who had their heads on their breasts. He knew more about Thule and Greenland than about the Baltic. Therefore, if this chronicler—universally acknowledged as our best source—was so woefully ignorant of the lands lying to his northeast, we can easily imagine what the rest of the population was willing to believe. The truth was far different.

The descriptions of the native tribes that have survived are very similar to those written by any civilized reporter about his more savage neighbors. A chronicler of the Teutonic Knights summarized them thus:

There are numerous pagans we are pressing back. One group is called Lithuanians. Those pagans are arrogant, and their army does much harm to pure Christianity. That is because their might is great. Nearby lies another group of pagans, a strong people named Semgallians, who dominate the land around them. They give hardship without relief to those who live too close. The Selonians are also pagan and blind to all virtue. They have many false gods and do evils without number. Nearby is another people named Letts. All these pagans have most unusual customs. They dislike living together and farm alone in the forest. Their women are beautiful and wear exotic clothing. They ride in the ancient fashion. Their army would be very strong if it were all brought together. Along the sea lies an area named Kurland. It is more than three hundred miles long. Very few Christians come by intent to this land, because they will be robbed of life and property. The Oselians are evil heathens, neighbors to the Kurs. They are surrounded by the sea and never fear strong armies. In the summer, when they can travel across the water, they oppress the surrounding lands. They have raided both Christians and pagans, and their strength is in their ships. The Estonians are pagan also, and there are many mothers' sons of them. That is because their land is so broad and so spread out that I cannot describe it. They have so many powerful men and so many provinces full of them that I do not want to talk more about them. The Livonians are also heathen, but we have hope that God shall soon bring them from that.[2]

This last tribe, the Livonians, was the weakest of all and was the first to confront, and fall to, merchants and warriors from the west. They lived scattered along the seacoast and in the Dvina basin, each clan dominated by a chief who held sway from a hilltop fort. Subject to the Letts but also paying tribute to the Russian Prince of Polozk, the Livonians were relatively independent, so weak was the structure of government.

Diverse as these people were and divided by language and mutual hatred, they nevertheless had much in common.[3] Their basic social unit was the extended family, which usually was organized into clans. The foremost male of the family was a "senior" and he met with the other "seniors" or elders to form the tribal council, which was basically responsible for the government. Occasionally one of these landed aristocrats ruled as chief, levying taxes and tolls and commanding the army, but such instances were rare, and authority was limited in all cases. Everywhere the commoners had considerable rights. The warrior class lived by raising cattle and farming, as did the elders, and often possessed sizeable personal estates. The peasant renters were free, and although they probably could not afford to outfit themselves for cavalry warfare, they were an important military class.

Military technique was everywhere primitive. Pitched battles were rare, whereas sudden raids in overwhelming force were common, followed by a swift retreat before the victims could rally. Henry of Livonia described a Livonian-Semgallian-German ambush of a party of Lithuanians that was returning from a raid into Estonia.

> The Lithuanians came with all their loot and captives, who numbered more than a thousand, divided their army into two parts, placed the captives in the middle, and, because of the excessive depth of the snow, marched single file over one path. But as soon as the first of these discovered the footprints of those who had gone before, they stopped, suspecting an ambush. Thus the last in line overtook the first and all were collected in one formation with the captives. When the Semgalls saw their great multitude, many of them trembled and, not daring to fight, wished to seek safer places.[4]

Elsewhere he remarked:

> The Lithuanians were then such lords over all the peoples, both Christian and pagan, dwelling in those lands that scarcely anyone, and the Letts especially, dared live in the small villages. Not even by leaving their houses deserted to seek the dark hiding places of the forest could they escape them. For the Lithuanians, laying ambushes for them at all times in the forest, seized them, killing some and capturing others, and took the latter back to their own country.[5]

Such raids provided the stronger tribes with large numbers of slaves. However, the nature of the land was such that an able-bodied man could easily escape and make his way homeward. Consequently, the raiders often slew the males and kept only the women and children. Perhaps a number of males were sold to slave traders from the Byzantine and Turkish worlds.

It was the danger of such raids that made the wooden stockade or fort so important to the tribes. Located on easily defensible sites, they consisted of logs laid horizontally and bolstered by tower-like bastions. Roofed by wood and bark and covered with clay, they were proof against the primitive siege techniques of their neighbors. Most of the population lived outside the fort, however, in a scattered settlement surrounded by only a weak wall or hedge. They rushed to the fort at the first sign of danger, knowing there would be no attempt to defend the outer wall.

This warfare, constant and cruel, was rarely total. Lightning raids and sudden retreats by mounted infantry, ambushes, and organized flights into the forts were practically the only military skills. In the rare pitched battles, one mob would hack away at another until one would weaken; then the latter would flee for their horses. Casualties were heavy only because of the panic. This type of warfare reflected the limited goals of the tribesmen, who wanted prestige, booty, and prisoners, not land or tribute. The very sameness of the crops, resources, and livestock gave little impulse to economic aggression, and lack of organization hindered political expansion. Therefore the tribes were pitted against one another in eternal but relatively bloodless petty warfare.

As we have seen, the Europeans of the late twelfth century knew little more about these peoples and their petty feuds than they knew of the great ice sheets that had once covered and formed the landscape of this area. Individual traders had searched out and purchased the precious amber and other products of the Baltic coast for thousands of years, yet such knowledge as was gained tended to be kept secret lest it be of advantage to competitors. This changed little when groups of Scandinavian and German merchants and sailors began to make regular visits to Livonia, except that, unable to remain completely silent about their adventures, they invented wonderful and horrible stories of pagan demons, murder rituals, and monsters. Such stories entertained their comrades, impressed their children, frightened the girls who met them in port, and confounded their competitors. The stories also lured adventurers and devout missionaries to the area.

It was the arrival of the merchants in ever larger numbers that upset the

22

traditional system of alliances and tribute by which the eastern Baltic region was governed. When merchants began to visit the tribes regularly, they expected protection and justice, and if the princes and chiefs hoped to retain their valuable taxes and tolls, they had to provide maximum security from robbery and murder. When the native rulers failed in this, as they did, the merchants acted in their own behalf. To secure access to their markets, the merchants became imperialists.

To be sure, the merchants had little interest in imperialism as such. They were interested only in trade, not in conquest and government. But they represented the farthest outreach of the dynamic new society developing in the west, which demanded the products available in the Baltic northeast. The German economy in particular sought the furs, honey, wax, leather, and amber of Livonia, and German merchants set out from the new Baltic ports with iron weapons, cloth, glass trinkets, and probably alcoholic beverages for exchange. The first and most basic requirement for trade was security: a safe harbor for ships, a secure depot for goods, and a guarantee of justice to all traders. They found this at Visby on the island of Gothland, which had the further advantage of being easily reached by merchants from the entire region—Russian, Estonians, Livonians, and Scandinavians, as well as Germans. Waldemar I of Denmark and Henry the Lion of Germany cooperated to secure the sea lanes to Visby, and soon a thriving merchant colony grew up there. Although most goods could be purchased at Visby, many traders wished to visit the mainland, where the prices were lower and the demand for western goods was greater. But that was dangerous, and the merchants clamoured for more protection, usually without much effect. For these reasons they were willing to support any imperialist venture that might further their mercantile interests.

Important as the merchants were in encouraging expansion into the eastern Baltic, the Church was even more important. The medieval Church was ashamed of the fact that the Livonians, Estonians, and Prussians remained pagan, but it was even more concerned with the religious condition of the powerful Russian communities that lay to the east.

The Russians were a multi-national people. Mainly Slavs, but with important minorities of Lithuanians, Finns, Lapps, and various steppe tribes, they lived in the forested region north of the great steppe. At one time their empire had extended to the Black Sea, but Cumans and Patzinaks now ruled along those shores. The vast and thinly populated forest and river country was divided into ten major states, each named after the most important city of the region and governed by a member of the house of Rurik, the royal family purportedly founded by Swedish Varangians who had passed through Russia to trade and raid the Byzantine and Moslem worlds. The great prince Jaroslaw had divided the country among his descendents so that the genealogically eldest was always to rule in Kiev, and those next in line at Novgorod, Suzdal, Smolensk, etc. In practice, however, the princes warred among themselves and lost their authority to their boyars and great cities. Novgorod, which styled itself Lord Novgorod the Great, was from 1196 on a self-governing city republic that elected a member of the house of Rurik as its prince, but denied him real power.

Novgorod, Smolensk, and Polozk were important to Baltic trade because of their control of the portages in the Valdai hill country. A merchant could sail from Visby upriver to these cities, and there exchange his goods for the produce of the south and east. In theory, he could proceed east, but rarely if ever did so. More important than the products of China, Persia, or Byzantium, however, were the furs of the north. The native Russian merchants, therefore, tended to travel the river routes toward the northeast trapping areas, and few sailed out into the Baltic to visit Visby and other ports. Instead it was Gothlanders and Germans who braved the pirates and storms, so the western settlements in Novgorod and Smolensk were much larger than the Russian establishment in Visby. The trade in furs and goods in transit brought wealth to these Russian cities, but much of the wealth was spent in procuring grain supplies. And the princes of the house of Rurik ignored the north in favor of the more populous and important cities of the south.

The Russians were Christians but of the eastern persuasion, having been comparatively recently converted by Byzantine missionaries. Many border regions and rural areas remained basically pagan. But to the eyes of the western visitors, pagan and eastern orthodox practices were equally odious. The Roman Church wished to win over the Orthodox Russians to acceptance of the Pope and Latin rites, thereby uniting a divided Christendom. And while the immediate objective was the pagan tribes along the coast, the churchmen never lost sight of the more important Russian communities in the interior. Also, the Russians were competitors who might convert the pagans in Livonia and Estonia to the Orthodox faith. Already the natives there were tributary to the Russian princes. Impelled by these motives (and by others pertaining to north German politics), the missionary movement to the Baltic region increased greatly during this period.

Where the merchants lacked interest, the Church was willing to press matters, and where the two groups had common interests, something was bound to happen. When the secular powers in the Baltic were convinced that military support was necessary for the expansion of trade and missions, the result was the Baltic Crusade, a form of western European imperialism that was to exhibit many of the characteristics, both good and evil, of the imperialism of more modern times.

That the missionary movement to Livonia eventually assumed an imperialist form should be no surprise. The Christian state often acted as the carrier of the Christian religion by imposing the latter on newly conquered subjects, and even more often Christian rulers supported missions to neighboring lands as a means of extending their influence abroad. This type of imperialism was not confined to princes; archbishops also sponsored missionaries for motives that were as much secular as religious, and "episcopal imperialism" was to be an important aspect of the mission to Livonia.

Because of their role in the conversion of the Danes, the Archbishops of Hamburg-Bremen traditionally exercised great authority over Scandinavian affairs. But after they lost control of the Scandinavian bishops to the Archbishop of Lund, this was no longer true. When Archbishop Hartwig II heard of the pagans of the eastern Baltic, he saw an opportunity to extend his authority over them. By creating a series of suffragan bishoprics in Livonia and Estonia he hoped to replace his losses, and also to forestall expansion in that direction by Lund.[6]

There had been occasional missions to Livonia before the latter part of the twelfth century, but they had always been ineffective. Only the Orthodox Church had made much impact on the natives' paganism, but, even so, conversion was limited to the ruling classes of tribes subject to Russia. This situation was not to change suddenly, but in 1180 an Augustinian monk named Meinhard established a western mission in the Dvina basin.

He came to Livonia with a band of merchants simply for the sake of Christ and only to preach. For German merchants, bound together through familiarity with the Livonians, were accustomed to go to Livonia, frequently sailing up the Dvina River. After receiving, therefore, the permission of King Vladimir of Polozk, to whom the Livonians, while still pagan, paid tribute, and, at the same time, after receiving gifts from him, this priest boldly set out upon the divine work, preaching to the Livonians and building a church in the village of Uexküll. . . . The next winter, the Lithuanians, after having laid waste Livonia, took many into captivity. The same preacher, together with the people

25

of Uexküll, avoided the wrath of the Lithuanians and took to the forests. When the Lithuanians had withdrawn, Meinhard accused the Livonians of foolishness, because they had no fortifications; he promised them that forts would be built if they decided to become and be considered sons of God. This pleased them and they promised and confirmed by an oath that they would receive baptism.[7]

Thus the most important decision in Livonian history was to undergo baptism in return for protection from hereditary enemies. The next year, 1181, stonemasons from Gothland built two stone castles on islands in the Dvina River. Both Uexküll and Holm, as they were named, were easily defensible and easily accessible to merchants from the west. It was only after the completion of the castles, however, that Meinhard informed the natives that he expected them to pay taxes for the upkeep of the castles and the maintenance of the church. Or perhaps he had told them earlier but they had taken it as an outlandish joke by a stranger. Whatever the reason, Meinhard gained few new converts to his small following. Nevertheless, he had sufficient success that Hartwig II of Bremen consecrated him Bishop of Uexküll in 1186 and sent priests to aid him.

Foremost among the new missionaries was Theodoric, a Cistercian monk from Loccum, a monastery near Hannover. Quite possibly young Theodoric was among the monks who had been sent to the new abbey at Reinfeld in Holstein in 1186, the same year that Meinhard returned to Germany for his investment. The Augustinian monastery at Segeberg was less than ten miles from the Cistercian foundation at Reinfeld, and undoubtedly Meinhard visited both Segeberg and Reinfeld in hope of recruiting assistants. With his abbot's permission, Theodoric sailed east with Meinhard to take up the difficult responsibilities of a missionary to the pagans, an event of far-reaching consequence. The Augustinian mission was now augmented, and eventually superseded, by a more militant and aggressive religious order. God's acres would not just be sown but would be plowed, tilled, and reaped. The spirit of Saint Bernard came to Livonia with Theodoric, and through Theodoric it dominated the ensuing thirty years of Livonian history.[8]

Theodoric and several unnamed fellows sought new fields for missionary work. He himself went to a Liv community to the north, where he settled among the natives and raised his own food. However, his farming practices were so superior to the natives' techniques that he narrowly escaped being sacrificed to their gods:

Because the crops in his fields were quite abundant and the crops in their own fields were dying because of a flooding rain, the Livonians of Treiden prepared to sacrifice him to their gods. The people were collected and the will of the gods regarding the sacrifice was sought after by lot. A lance was placed in position and the horse came up and, at the signal of God, put out the foot thought to be the foot of life. Brother Theodoric prayed aloud and gave blessings with his hand. The pagan priest asserted that the Christian God was sitting on the back of the horse and was moving the horse's foot forward; that for this reason the back of the horse had to be wiped off so that God might slide off. When this was done, the horse again put forth the foot of life, as before, and Brother Theodoric's life was saved. When Brother Theodoric was sent into Estonia, he likewise endured from the pagans a great many dangers to his life.[9]

Because the natives were satisfied with their traditional gods and did not think the priests dangerous, they allowed them to preach without harassment. But when the priests began to make converts, and when they threatened the use of force, the attitude changed. Abandoning their skeptical tolerance, the Livs began to look upon the priests and their converts as a dangerous and subversive element.

There can be no doubt that the missionaries threatened the traditional mode of life in Livonia. Bishop Meinhard maintained a small body of paid retainers in his castles and exacted tithes and taxes from his flock to support the garrisons and to maintain his priests. Because Meinhard could tax only those who accepted Christianity, this meant that the taxes on each individual had to be relatively high; nevertheless, as his income was not equal to his expenses, Meinhard was on the horns of a dilemma. The financial burden of Christianity already was such as to discourage converts, and there was little hope of converting sufficient numbers so as to spread the burden, because by remaining pagan one qualified for tax exemption. On the other hand, if Meinhard abandoned the castles and returned to a simple mission supported by foreign funds, he could not offer the military protection that would convert entire tribes at once. As he saw it, the problem was simple: he had promised protection, which required soldiers and castles, and this required money, which was provided by converts. The solution was equally simple: the natives should live up to their bargain and submit to baptism. Unfortunately for Meinhard, the natives had no wish to place themselves under his authority or to pay his taxes. A few probably saw that, in the end, Meinhard would be dominant in the political as well as in the religious

27

life of the community, and indeed Meinhard could not deny this. His object was to establish an ecclesiastical system similar to that in western Europe. Fundamentally, the issue was power, though few—perhaps not even Meinhard—understood this fully. They argued about taxes when the real issue was authority over the tribes.

The implications of Meinhard's position became clearer to the native elders when he threatened compulsory conversion. They did not worry as long as he had no army, but knowing that he might raise an army abroad, the elders forbade him to leave the country. They left him freedom to travel and to preach and did not object to his governing and taxing those who submitted to him freely, but they would not allow him to coerce anyone into the Church or to connive with foreigners against their independence.

The suspicions of the natives were confirmed when Theodoric slipped out of the country and journeyed to Rome to ask for papal assistance. As he had hoped, the Supreme Pontiff approved the use of force against the Livs, and Theodoric returned north to raise an army on Gothland. He expected a quick success because it appeared that the interests of the merchants and the Church coincided, but in fact the merchants were much more interested in punishing pirates than in assisting an elderly Bishop in an armed campaign against good customers. The result was a travesty of the crusading idea.

The expedition was well-planned. Theodoric raised an army from among the German and Scandinavian merchants and persuaded the Duke of Sweden to accompany the army. They planned to sail to Kurland and punish some notorious pirates and then to proceed to the Dvina basin. The plan was good, but its execution was poor; and the expedition went astray at the very beginning. Shortly after leaving Visby, the fleet encountered bad weather, so that it made landfall not in Kurland but in Estonia, where the army decided that one tribe was as suitable a victim as another and thereupon behaved like a band of freebooters. Theodoric was able to bring an end to the fighting and to begin negotiations with the elders for the acceptance of Christianity, but the discussions were barely under way when the Duke of Sweden sailed home, taking most of the army with him. To his chagrin, Theodoric learned that the Duke had been interested only in exacting tribute from the natives and, once it was collected, had no further interest in the expedition. The few serious crusaders who remained behind could entertain no hope of assisting Bishop Meinhard. As a result of the Duke's defection, the army immediately disbanded and returned to Gothland.

Bishop Meinhard, disappointed by the outcome of the expedition, died soon afterward (in 1196), leaving an empty title and a pitifully small number of converts to Christianity.[10]

N O T E S   T O   C H A P T E R   T W O

1. Adam of Bremen, *History of the Archbishops of Hamburg-Bremen*, trans. Francis J. Tschan (New York: Columbia University Press, 1959), pp. 197–98. Swedish authority over the coastal regions dates back to the Varangian era, when Vikings regularly sailed the rivers to the Black Sea and Byzantium. Some historians attribute the foundation of the Russian state to these energetic barbarians. By the time of Adam of Bremen, however, only distant memories of ancient greatness remained to the hapless Swedes. Even the geography is incorrect. Courland (Kurland) is not an island, nor are there any Amazons.

2. *Livländische Reimchronik*, 2d. ed, ed. Leo Mayer (Hildesheim: George Olms, 1963), lines 322–377 (hereafter cited as *Reimchronik*).

3. See Manfred Hellmann, *Das Lettenland im Mittelalter: Studien zur ostbaltischen Frühzeit und lettischen Stammesgeschichte, insbesonders Lettgallens* (Münster: Böhlau, 1954), Reinhard Wittram, *Baltische Geschichte; die Ostseelande, Livland, Estland, Kurland: 1180–1918* (Munich: R. Oldenbourg, 1954), and C. Engel and A. Brackmann, *Baltische Lande*, Vol. 1 of *Ostbaltische Frühzeit* (Leipzig: S. Hirsel, 1939).

4. *The Chronicle of Henry of Livonia*, trans. James A. Brundage (Madison: University of Wisconsin Press, 1961), p. 49 (hereafter cited as *Henry of Livonia*). I have chosen this translation over the Latin edition of Leonid Arbusow and Albert Bauer, *Heinrici Chronicon Livoniae*, (2d ed. (Hannover: Hahnsche Buchhandlung, 1950), because of the numerous quotations I wish to present in English.

5. Ibid., pp. 90–91.

6. The Archbishops of Hamburg-Bremen had lead the missionary effort to Scandinavia since the time of Saint Ansgar (831–865). Under Archbishop Adalbert (1043–1072), Bremen seemed as powerful as a second Rome, but during the Investiture Controversy the northern bishoprics were taken away. Sweden was lost in 1104 beyond recovery, but Norway might still be won back. Georg Gottfried Dehio, *Hartwick von Stade, Erzbischof von Hamburg-Bremen* (Bremen: Diereksen & Wichlein, 1872), pp. 30–32.

7. *Henry of Livonia*, pp. 25–26.

8. Friedrich Benninghoven, *Der Orden der Schwertbrüder* (Cologne-Graz: Böhlau, 1965), pp. 20–23.

9. *Henry of Livonia*, pp. 27–28.

10. Ibid., pp. 28–30; papal approval of the mission was dated 27 April 1193. *Liv-, Est-, und Kurländisches Urkundenbuch*, ed. Friedrich Georg von Bunge (Riga and Reval: 1857–1875), Vol. 1, document XI (hereafter cited as *Urkundenbuch*).

3

Organization of the
Baltic Crusade

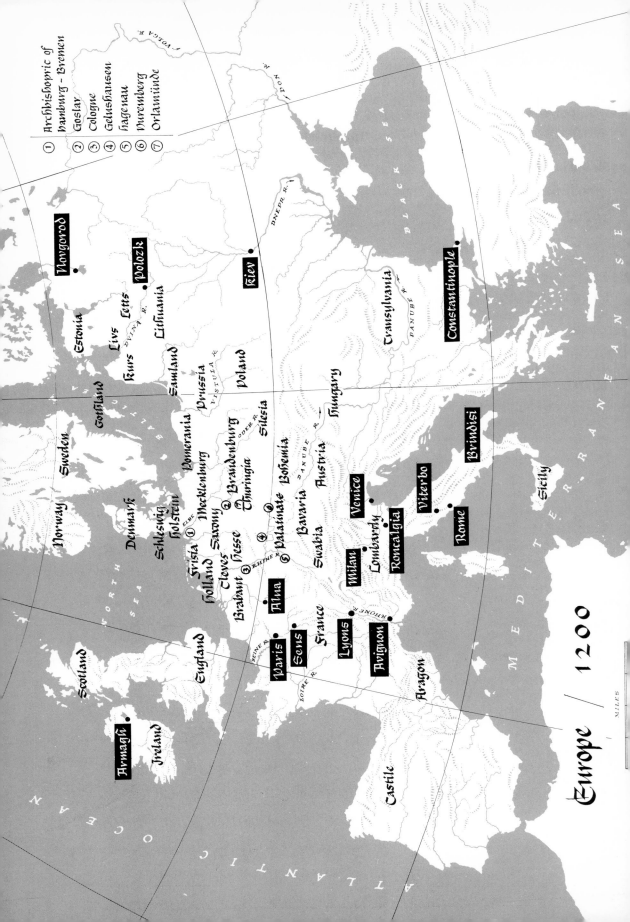

Europe / 1200

Archbishopric of
① Hamburg – Bremen
② Goslar
③ Cologne
④ Gelnshausen
⑤ Hagenau
⑥ Vuremberg
⑦ Orlamünde

ATLANTIC OCEAN

NORTH SEA

BALTIC SEA

BLACK SEA

MEDITERRANEAN SEA

Scotland
Ireland
Armagh
England
Norway
Sweden
Gottland
Denmark
Schleswig
Holstein
Frisia
Holland
Cleves
Brabant
Hesse
Mecklenburg
Pomerania
Brandenburg
Thuringia
Saxony
Palatinate
Bohemia
Bavaria
Austria
Swabia
France
Paris
Sens
Alna
Lyons
Avignon
Castile
Aragon
Estonia
Livs
Kurs
Letts
Lithuania
Samland
Prussia
Poland
Silesia
Hungary
Transylvania
Novgorod
Polozk
Kiev
Constantinople
Milan
Venice
Lombardy
Roncalgia
Viterbo
Rome
Brindisi
Sicily

VOLGA R.
DON R.
DNEPR R.
DVINA R.
VISTULA R.
ODER R.
ELBE R.
RHINE R.
SEINE R.
LOIRE R.
RHONE R.
DANUBE R.

MILES

THE MISSION TO THE EASTERN BALTIC BEGAN DURING A PERIOD OF GREAT upheaval in Germany. There were bitter civil wars, each complicated by papal intervention, and recurring calls for crusaders to the Holy Land. There was also an economic vitality, marked by the increase in the population and the spread of foreign commerce. There was intellectual and spiritual greatness, though other cultures eventually profited most from it. In short, what would otherwise have been a period of greatness became no more than an era of economic progress because of political failures. The Baltic Crusade, caught in the maelstrom of politics, was assured of some success because of the general current of the times and the weakness of its victims, but its progress depended upon the state of affairs in Germany and Scandinavia.[1]

Meinhard had failed in his mission to Livonia because he had lacked the military might to crush the natives. It was obvious to the practical men of that time that force was the only means for the speedy baptism of the populace, and most Christians agreed that—for both spiritual and financial reasons—baptism was absolutely necessary for everyone. Many Germans and Scandinavians, and some Slavs, were willing to earn eternal life by participating in a military expedition to "protect" the Livonian Church, but because of the political situation they were not always available for service abroad. Therefore Meinhard's successors had to take advantage of the times that favored military intervention in the east and somehow survive the less propitious periods.

For seven years the Emperor Henry VI had ruled with a strong and heavy hand; he had reestablished imperial prestige but, in the process, had made many enemies. As a consequence, when he died suddenly in 1197, leaving a three-year-old son as his direct heir, his enemies hoped to undo the work that he and his father, Frederick Barbarossa, had accomplished. However, because they saw the continuity of the Hohenstaufen family as essential to peace and security, the imperial followers in Germany nominated Henry's brother, Philip, as his successor. This brought them into direct conflict with those who sought to take advantage of the crisis for their own purposes.

Because strong Emperors tended to exert much influence in Italy, the interests of the papacy seemed to lie in keeping Germany weak. Certainly

33

the new Pope, Innocent III, believed that Henry VI had been too dangerous. As Innocent saw it, Pope Celestine had tried to reconcile the interests of papacy and empire in areas of irreconcilable conflicts, and Henry had succeeded in encircling the Papal States, a situation that threatened the independence of the papacy. Innocent saw the separation of Sicily from the Holy Roman Empire as a bare minimum for papal safety, and he was determined to accomplish this in any way necessary. Brilliant, ambitious, and forceful, and often considered the greatest of the medieval Popes, he saw the succession crisis as a God-given opportunity to rescue the papacy from the Hohenstaufens. If this had been his sole concern, however, the medieval papacy might have developed in other directions than it did. Not only was he determined to free the Papal States from the danger of secular domination, he was also intent on extending papal influence across Europe. Therefore, even had the German Emperor been willing to give up his rights in Italy, he would still have come into conflict with the Pope, because as the strongest ruler in Europe he would have to face the papal challenge most squarely.

The interests of the English monarch also conflicted with imperial ambitions. Richard the Lionheart saw that members of his Angevin family were being dispossessed by the Hohenstaufen Emperors. He could not ignore the appeals for aid by adherents of the Welf party in Germany and by the Normans in Sicily in the name of his sisters Matilda and Johanna, though perhaps he should have. Richard was not a wise king, but he was proud and chivalrous. Therefore he gave aid to the Welfs, and he encouraged the Sicilians; and such was his hatred for the Hohenstaufens that earlier, while on crusade, he could not resist any opportunity to insult their followers. But Richard also had another motive for mixing in German affairs: he was confronted by Philip Augustus, the Capetian monarch of France. Although Richard had greater resources than his opponent, he could not bring them to the defense of Normandy; as a result, he foresaw the loss of the province unless he found help abroad. Because of the quarrel over Saxony and Sicily, he would obtain little aid from the Hohenstaufens in Germany. Therefore when all was taken into account, it was in Richard's interest to help overthrow the Hohenstaufen dynasty.

Supported covertly and openly by the Pope and the English monarch, the Archbishop of Cologne rallied the scattered adherents of the Welf cause to the support of Otto, the youngest son of Henry the Lion, Richard's nephew. Provided liberally with English silver, he was able to bribe many undecided princes, so that in the early spring of 1198 he could gather a large assembly of princes to elect Otto as Holy Roman Emperor.[2]

Because there were two candidates for the imperial throne, each elected by a large number of princes and each crowned with pomp and ceremony but neither having clear title, it remained for the Pope to choose between them. But Pope Innocent was in no hurry. He delayed making a decision, pointing out irregularities in each election and coronation, and bided his time. There had been procedural error in each case, but this was of less importance than any concessions that might be obtained from the candidates. In particular, he wanted a promise to sever the connection between the German Empire and the Kingdom of Sicily. If this—and more—were not forthcoming, a short civil war in Germany would not harm the cause of the papacy. Innocent III was not a Pope to stand by and wring his hands; he was determined to take measures to force concessions from every monarch in Europe. Germany was a good place to begin, and the disputed election was a good issue.

The issue would not have been settled in Rome, in any case, because neither side would abandon its cause until it had been struck down by the mailed fist of the other side. In the summer of 1198 the Hohenstaufens and Capetians formed an alliance against the Welfs and Angevins, and each German party sought to buy as many supporters as its foreign money would allow. Albert of Stade remarked laconically: "Philip and Otto fought bravely against one another to the great harm of the Empire. Richard, King of England, supported his nephew Otto with money."[3]

The outbreak of civil war in the Holy Roman Empire prompted the German crusaders in the Holy Land to return home as quickly as possible. Among them was an ambitious prelate from North Germany.

> Hartwig, the Archbishop of Bremen, sailed from the Holy Land to Venice and went from there to Bremen. He brought with him relics of the holy Anna and the sword of Peter, the one he had struck off the ear of Malchus with. The pilgrims returned because of the death of the emperor, after they had made a truce with the Saracens.[4]

When Hartwig returned to Europe his first impression was that a Hohenstaufen victory was inevitable, and in May 1199 he joined with other prelates in writing the Pope on behalf of Philip.[5] As he proceeded north, however, he found the Welf strength so formidable that by the time he reached Bremen he was wavering. Nevertheless, he sent troops to support the Count of Holstein against the Danes.[6]

Adolf of Holstein found the situation very serious. Although his domains had not experienced disorder or invasion, he was surrounded by Welfish Princes, and though he could call upon aid from Hohenstaufen-inclined Princes for the time being, he could not expect much help when those princes were threatened by attack. He had chosen sides, but, like most princes of the area, his loyalties were primarily to himself, and—like the others—he hoped that the fighting in the Rhineland would be decisive, one way or the other.

It was in this period, and in the midst of this uproar, that the mission to Livonia was converted into a crusading venture. In 1197, before his departure to the Holy Land, Archbishop Hartwig had invested Berthold, the Cistercian Abbot of Loccum, as Bishop of Uexküll. Berthold accepted his new duties grudgingly, perhaps displeased that Hartwig was stripping the land of soldiers for his own crusade. That meant that Berthold's first venture into Livonia would have only minimal military support.

> He went to Livonia, came to Uexküll, took over the patrimony of the church, and gathered into his presence all of the more important Livonians, both Christian and pagan. He strove to please them with food, drink, and gifts, and said that he came at their invitation and that he had succeeded his predecessor as sole heir. They received him cordially at first, but at the consecration of the cemetery at Holm, some conspired to burn him in the church, others to kill him, and others to drown him. They charged that he came because he was poor. After considering this beginning, he went secretly to the ships and back to Gothland and on to Saxony. He bewailed both to the lord pope and to the bishop, as well as to all the faithful of Christ, the ruin of the church of Livonia. The lord pope, therefore, granted remission of sins to all those who should take the cross and arm themselves against the perfidious Livonians.[7]

Berthold returned to Livonia in 1198 with an army. The natives gathered their forces opposite the Christians, and though they were unwilling to submit to mass baptism, they offered to allow Berthold to stay in the land to compel his converts to remain faithful; but he would be allowed only to persuade, not force, others to belief in Christ. This was not sufficient for Berthold. When the natives refused his demand for hostages, and killed several German foragers, he ordered an attack.

Ironically, Berthold was almost the only Christian casualty. The small

Saxon army was composed of mounted knights who swept away the unprepared natives. But Berthold's horse had bolted, carrying him into the enemy ranks, where he was cut down. The crusaders, after taking a terrible revenge for his death, established small garrisons in the castles and then sailed home.[8]

> The clergy and one ship of merchants remained. Now the wind filled the sails, and lo! the treacherous Livonians, emerging from their customary baths, poured water of the Dvina River over themselves, saying: "We now remove the water of baptism and Christianity itself with the water of the river. Scrubbing off the faith we have received, we send it after the withdrawing Saxons."[9]

Soon afterward the monks were attacked. Unable to go into the fields, they saw their crops perish. At last, hearing that death had been decreed for any priest who remained in the land past Easter, the frightened clergy fled back to Saxony.

Thus it was clear that occasional expeditions were inadequate to the task of subduing the pagans in Livonia, and it was equally clear that it would be a great task to raise a large force for long-term service abroad from a divided and disorderly Germany. When Archbishop Hartwig II looked about for a suitable successor to the martyred Bishop, he looked first among his own relatives, because ties of blood and marriage were even more important in those troubled days than usual. His choice was his nephew, Albert of Buxhoevden, who was a canon in the Bremen Church. The selection was sensible, and nepotism was no argument against him in those days, but rather an argument in his favor. The close relationship between the archbishopric and the crusade was now reinforced by family ties, and with the blessing of the Church, young Albert became Bishop of Uexküll.[10]

Because the crusade was so dependent upon the Archbishop of Hamburg-Bremen, its success was largely determined by the fortune of archiepiscopal politics, which in turn, were determined by the Welf-Hohenstaufen struggle for the crown. At first all went well for the Archbishop. By driving a hard bargain for his support of the Count of Holstein against the Danes, he recovered Stade, the fortress on the left bank of the Elbe, standing on the only high ground between Hamburg and Bremen. Stade also controlled the Elbe traffic and was the center of a rich bottomland filled with crops of grain and fruit. For decades the archbishops had striven to recover it—the essential first step to the recovery of archiepiscopal power such as his distant predecessors had enjoyed. Thus Hartwig's support of the

37

Baltic Crusade was a reassertion of Bremen's traditional role as a missionary center.

The most important man in the north was not the Archbishop, however, but the King of Denmark. Guided by his brother Waldemar, the sickly monarch advanced the Danish banners in several directions at once. He exhausted the Count of Holstein simply by concentrating a number of knights along the frontier and forcing the Count to expensive counter-measures. He drove the Brandenburg Duke out of Pomerania, and sent an expedition to Estonia (of which we know too little). It was not an overtly aggressive policy; the Danes threatened here, then there, and day by day wore down their opponents without committing themselves in the Welf-Hohenstaufen struggle.

Bishop Albert's travels in 1199 illustrate how well he understood these political realities. He traveled overland from Bremen to Lübeck, where he took ship for Gothland, for it was absolutely essential to gain the assent of the Visby merchant communities for any military expedition to the eastern Baltic. Fortunately, they were eager to participate, and 500 of them took the cross to Livonia. Albert then returned to Denmark to visit King Canute, Waldemar, and the venerable Archbishop of Lund. He spoke to the needs of the Livonian Church, and undoubtedly discussed the advantages that Christianity in general, and Denmark in particular, would receive by establishing a bishopric on the banks of the Dvina. It is not stated what Albert promised the Danes, but from the claims that Waldemar later brought forth it seems probable that there was some submission to Danish overlordship, especially in Estonia. Albert then left for Germany, having obtained a vague promise of support that amounted to a friendly neutrality. His next venture was at the Court of Philip of Hohenstaufen, the leading candidate for the throne of the Empire.

> King Philip went to Magdeburg on the day that our Lord was born of the maiden he had chosen as his mother. There went an emperor's brother and an emperor's son, in one garment, although they had three titles. He carried the true sceptre and the true throne. He strode easily in full calm. After him came a high-born queen, a rose without thorns, a dove without gall. All gazed upon them. The Thuringers and Saxons performed court service so that the most fastidious would be satisfied.[11]

It was a glittering occasion, immortalized by Walther's poetry. Not only did the Hohenstaufen adherents appear, but also many Welfish and neutral nobles. Adolf of Holstein, Hartwig of Bremen, and Bernard of Saxony presented themselves. It was at that time that Philip confirmed Hartwig's possession of Stade, disregarding the Welf claims.[12] Then, probably immediately after that business, Hartwig introduced his nephew to the Emperor. Albert, allowed to address the assembled Court, described the proposed crusade, after which he obtained a promise of imperial support. Then he turned to the papal legate, a silent witness of the proceedings:

> In the presence of the king an opinion was asked for as to whether the goods of the pilgrims to Livonia were to be placed under the protection of the pope, as is the case of those who journey to Jerusalem. It was answered, indeed, that they were included under the protection of the pope, who in enjoining the Livonian pilgrimage for the plenary remission of sin, made it equal with that to Jerusalem.[13]

This was what Albert had been waiting for. He may have already visited the Pope personally, for his schedule would have allowed time for a trip to Rome, and most likely he knew that the Pope had approved the crusade. But never could he have announced the decision so effectively as at the Court at Magdeburg. With the support of the Danish King, the Hohenstaufen candidate for the crown, and now the Pope, any noble or cleric who wished to escape the conflict in Germany could do so by taking the cross to Livonia. None would be accused of cowardliness or dereliction of duty but would be praised for such a decision. Bishop Albert was ready to gather his army.

Albert preached the crusade across Saxony and Westphalia. He won over a number of volunteers, most notably Conrad of Dortmund and Hartberg of Iburg, but not as many as he had hoped. Few came from Holstein, where Count Adolf had called up every available knight for service against the Danes, but all in vain—he had to surrender the great fortress at Rendsburg and the land of Dithmarschen in return for a truce. Therefore most of the crusaders were of common or middle-origin. Of these, several hundred Frisians were the most important; these hardy warriors had already made a reputation in the Holy Land, and their skill in sailing and marsh warfare would be much appreciated in Livonia.

The crusaders sailed from Lübeck to Gothland, where the volunteers from Visby joined the fleet, and its twenty-three vessels proceeded to Livonia. Each of these heavy, decked vessels could carry a hundred or more fighting men and their supplies; so Bishop Albert had a respectable army. Its size and the memory of the previous battle were sufficient to prevent the natives from offering open resistance. Still, the Livs fought back; although the population fled into the forests, the warriors attacked single ships and ambushed small squadrons of cavalry. This method was a skillful use of their traditional tactics, but it was not successful. When Bishop Albert proposed a parley, the elders agreed to come.

> Called by the Germans to a drinking party, they all gathered at the same time and were shut up in one house. Fearing lest they be brought across the sea into Germany, they presented about thirty of their better boys from the region of the Dvina and from Treiden to the bishop. He received them with joy and, committing the land to the Lord, returned to Germany.[14]

Because it was obvious that hostages could not do more than maintain a tenuous peace with a part of the Liv population, Bishop Albert had to raise another army. He sent Theodoric to Rome to explain the situation, with specific instructions to obtain permission to organize a second crusading expedition and to prohibit trade between Christians and the unconverted tribes. The Pope obliged him by publishing the necessary documents, and later the Gothland merchants agreed to prohibit trade with Albert's enemies. This assured him a monopoly of the local trade and access to a considerable source of revenue.[15]

When Albert returned to Germany in the fall of 1200 the political situation was not favorable for appeals to crusaders, for there was little sign that the civil war would end soon. The Hohenstaufen forces had failed to take the Welf stronghold at Braunschweig but had captured Lauenburg. There were persisting rumors that Otto's brother, Henry, would desert the Welf cause, but he and other wavering princes remained loyal. There was no decisive battle, and when the long, dark, wet North German winter arrived, all military activities were suspended; and the countryside lapsed into an insecure and deceptive peacefulness.

In spring 1201 the war began anew. In March, Pope Innocent III, having obtained a promise from Otto to separate Sicily from the Empire, recognized the Welf candidate as the duly elected Emperor, which sent a chill through the Hohenstaufen forces.

Adolf of Holstein was in a particularly difficult situation. When the Hohenstaufen army was in the north, near enough to assist him if he were attacked, he invaded Dithmarschen and took it from the Danes. Then he awaited the Danish counterattack, but it did not come. He could call upon Philip to send troops to fight but not to act as a garrison. The Hohenstaufen forces soon moved away and Adolf and his ally, Hartwig of Bremen, were left alone. The Danish tactics could be described as "masterly inactivity," for only after the Hohenstaufen forces had crossed the Rhine did the Danes attack. In the first encounter the Danish vassal, Prince Henry Burwin of Mecklenburg, captured seventy Holstein knights. It was a terrible defeat for Adolf. Albert of Stade summarized the campaign briefly:

> Philip and Otto tested their strength on the Moselle. Canute, king of the Danes, besieged Hamburg, and his brother, Duke Waldemar, crossed the Elbe to attack Count Adolf. Hamburg was taken and Count Adolf had to surrender to the duke.[16]

Bishop Albert sailed from Lübeck for Livonia just as the Danish invasion was beginning, but he had not recruited many "pilgrims," as they were called. He won over two minor nobles, Daniel and Conrad, by promising to enfeoff them with the castles at Uexküll and Holm; but he no longer had much interest in those island stations. He had decided to found a city at Riga, where a natural harbor was formed by the confluence of a small stream and the Dvina River. After building a wall across the narrow stretch of land between the rivers, he moved the cathedral chapter to this site and began the construction of an appropriate building dedicated to the Virgin Mary, who was to be his recruiting "symbol" in the future. What potential crusader could not be recruited to fight for the "Land of the Blessed Virgin?" And as the city was large, he invited merchants and fishermen, regardless of national origin, to settle there permanently. Then, despite the cold and primitive conditions, he set an example by wintering there himself.[17]

It was as well that he did not return to Germany, and perhaps his decision to remain in Livonia was determined by the reports of Danish victories. Soon after Albert had cleared Lübeck harbor, the Danes captured the Lübeck fishing fleet and took the leading citizens as hostages, which eliminated that city as a military asset to the Count of Holstein. Then the Danish forces marched to Hamburg and the other cities, as we have seen, and captured them one by one. Adolf of Holstein temporarily eluded capture by crossing the Elbe, but in the winter of 1200–1201 he returned suddenly to retake Hamburg, after which Duke Waldemar hurried south and besieged the city again. When the Alster and the Elbe unexpectedly froze, Adolf saw that he could no longer defend the city, and he sur-rendered.

It was commonly expected that Waldemar might be content with exacting homage from Adolf and leaving him the governance of his domains, a policy followed by the Danes in Mecklenburg, Schwerin, and elsewhere, but an unfortunate incident occurred which cast doubt upon Adolf's usefulness to Waldemar.

> The Saxons suggested that the count go up to Lauenburg and surrender the castle, after which he could go free with his men. Count Gunzel of Schwerin agreed to help Adolf. Count Adolf took an oath on this and went to Lauen-burg to see if he could convince his men in the castle to give it up and thus let him go free. But there were Dithmarschers, who, when they learned that Count Adolf was in the camp, made such an uproar and would have killed him be-cause he was so often an enemy of their land, that Count Gunzel and the others had to keep him well escorted and protected, as the duke had ordered, and use all their power to keep him alive. When the duke came with his men, [Adolf's] honor was shattered.[18]

The outcome was that Adolf forfeited his lands, and Waldemar decided to replace him.

The Archbishop of Bremen fared little better.

> About Christmas, one thousand two hundred and two years after God's birth, the great prince, King Otto, ordered an assembly of the army. His brother Henry came with a great force. Also Count Simon of Tecklenburg brought many knights and knights' sons to the army at Stade, where they besieged the place closely. They took it and captured Bishop Hartwig of Bremen.[19]

Otto IV imposed a harsh peace upon the Archbishop, stripped him of Stade, occupied Bremen, and filled the advocacies with Welf adherents.

At approximately this moment King Canute of Denmark and his powerful Archbishop, Absalon, passed away. Waldemar succeeded to the throne, and the royal chaplain, Andreas Sunesen, became Archbishop of Lund. Andreas, who owed his elevation both to family prestige and royal friendship, understood that the welfare of his archbishopric was inextricably bound to that of the kingdom. For that reason he was to be a consistent supporter of Danish expansion, especially expansion toward the east, and it is not without justification that some Danish historians call him the "Apostle to Livonia."[20]

King Waldemar understood that continued possession of Holstein depended upon a Welf victory in Germany, and henceforth he was to be more active in the Welf cause. On New Year's Day 1202, Waldemar and Otto IV, each having concluded his seige successfully, met and formalized a family alliance. Thus two decades after the fall of Henry the Lion, the North of Germany passed into Welf and pro-Welf hands.

Isolated by winter and the consequent cessation of travel, the crusaders in Livonia could not have received intelligence of these events. The Danish and Welf occupation of the main recruiting areas and the ports for assembly and departure boded ill for the future of the crusade as planned by Bishop Albert and Theodoric. When Bishop Albert arrived in Lübeck in spring 1202, the importance of all this became clear. He gave up all hope of sending more than a few men east that summer and concentrated on plans for 1203.

While Bishop Albert was absent in Germany, Theodoric remained in Livonia. Nonetheless, they were working together. Bishop Albert was petitioning for permission to embark on certain new programs and was seeking out the men to staff these programs, while Theodoric was putting them into effect, anticipating that permission would be forthcoming. First of all, Bishop Albert sought approval to move the bishopric from Uexküll to Riga, which was easily accomplished. Bishop Albert then obtained permission for his brother Engelbert to leave the monastery at Neumünster to become the prior of Saint Mary's. Secondly, he wanted a Cistercian monastery at Dünamünde, whose location was very important as it would afford refuge to pilgrims (crusaders) and merchants immediately upon entering this area at the mouth of the river, and from the military standpoint, its fortification was needed. A Cistercian abbey, with Theodoric at its head, could provide all this. Moreover, Dünamünde was sufficiently isolated that monastic discipline would not be threatened. Thirdly, Albert wanted to find a crusading order that would provide knights and men for the year round defense of the colony and permit the proper administration and occupation of the castles.

The last two ideas came from the productive mind of Theodoric, that enthusiastic Cistercian who played such a role in initiating the military expeditions to Livonia. This was in the tradition of Saint Bernard, who organized crusades, assisted in the foundation of crusading orders, and spread Cistercian monasteries across Europe. Three times had Theodoric visited in Rome (once in 1199 and twice in 1200), and each time he had taken every opportunity to preach the crusade enroute. His visits to Marien-

feld had won over Abbot Florenz, who made his monks available for assignment to the new monastery at Dünamünde. The research of Friedrich
Benninghoven shows that the foundation of the crusading order was more
complex, but equally the result of Theodoric's efforts.[21]

The crusading order was brought into being by a small group of Westphalian nobles and clergy. Theodoric himself had come from Loccum, a
Cistercian monastery on the middle Weser, and he had returned there for
visits at every opportunity. This had brought him into contact with the
famous comrade of Henry the Lion, Bernard zu Lippe, who had entered the
monastery at Marienfeld and later, against his abbot's wishes, had left
it to become abbot of Loccum. Before entering monastic life, Bernard had
been to Livonia on crusade, probably on the first expedition with Bishop
Berthold. Now, at Theodoric's urging, he encouraged his friends to go to
the defense of the Church in Livonia. His close friend, Abbot Nicholaus
of Hardehausen, who also had a connection with Marienfeld, visited a
number of the Westphalian nobles who were in the first contingent of
knights, and Abbot Florenz of Marienfeld later became the first priest
to enter the crusading order. This small group of Cistercians convinced a
few nobles to take the vows of poverty, chastity, obedience, and war against
the enemies of the Church. Pope Innocent III approved the foundation of
the order, named it the Militia of Christ, and gave it a rule based upon
that of the Templar Order.

Why a new order? Why did they not call upon one of the established
crusading orders? Most likely, Bishop Albert feared competition from
such powerful and wealthy organizations. He would probably have resisted
this new order as well, but his need for soldiers was so great that he ac-
quiesced in the bringing of the Militia of Christ into Livonia. He insisted
only that the master of the order render him an oath of obedience. Other
outstanding questions, such as financial support and the limits of autonomy, were not discussed fully—a misfortune in view of the later difficulties.
The first members of the Militia of Christ (*Fratres Militiae Christi*), who
sailed to Livonia in 1202, soon acquired a more lasting name, derived from
their distinctive costume. Clad in a white mantle with a red insignia—a
cross and a sword—they were called Swordbearers or, more popularly,
Swordbrothers.

The establishment of a crusader foothold in Livonia must be credited
to several men, each with different plans for the future. Hartwig II of

Bremen and his nephew, Albert of Buxhoevden, foresaw the establishment of bishoprics throughout the eastern Baltic region, modeled on those of contemporary Germany where the prelate was a secular prince as well as a religious figure. Theodoric and his Cistercian friends foresaw the forced conversion of the natives and the establishment of monastic settlements across the countryside, each ruling the natives in Christian fashion. Supporting each crusading endeavor were minor knights and merchants, each hoping for eventual salvation and perhaps enrichment in the near future—the knights by booty and office, the merchants by increased trade. Interested, but still neutral, was the Danish Monarch, who looked forward to the day he could lay claim to all Livonia and reap all the rewards with minimum effort. The natives, of course, were not consulted.

NOTES TO CHAPTER THREE

1. Friedrich Koch, *Livland und das Reich bis zum Jahre 1225* (Posen, 1943); Rudolf Usinger, *Deutsch-dänische Geschichte, 1189–1227* (Berlin, 1863); and Richard Hausmann, *Das Ringen der Deutschen und Dänen um den Besitz Estlands bis 1227* (Leipzig: Dincker & Humbolt, 1870).

2. Barraclough, *Origins of Modern Germany*, pp. 204–9.

3. *Albert of Stade*, p. 353.

4. Ibid.

5. *Hamburgisches Urkundenbuch*, ed. Johann M. Lappenberg (Hamburg: L. Voss, 1907), 1: 279.

6. *Albert of Stade*, p. 353.

7. *Henry of Livonia*, pp. 31–32.

8. Ibid., pp. 32–33.

9. Ibid., p. 34.

10. Gisela Gnegel-Waitschies, *Bischof Albert von Riga: ein Bremer Domherr als Kirchenfürst im Osten* (Hamburg: A. F. Velmede, 1958).

11. *Die Gedichte Walther von der Vogelweide* (Berlin: Walter de Gruyter, 1964), pp. 23, 25.

12. *Hamburgisches Urkundenbuch*, 1: 277.

13. *Henry of Livonia*, pp. 35–36. A papal pronouncement had already been issued in October. *Hamburgisches Urkundenbuch*, 1: 280.

14. *Henry of Livonia*, p. 37.

15. Ibid., p. 38.

16. *Albert of Stade*, p. 353.

17. *Henry of Livonia*, pp. 38–41; William Urban, "Saint Mary and the Dragonkiller," in *Marian Library Studies*, 2 (1971): 89–94.

18. Neocorus, *Chronik des Landes Dithmarschen*, ed. Friedrich Christoph Dahlmann (Kiel, 1827), 1: 345–46.

19. *Braunschweigische Reimchronik*, p. 530.

20. Friedrich Münter, *Kirchengeschichte von Dänemark und Norwegen* (Leipzig, 1823), 1: 356–68.

21. Benninghoven, *Schwertbrüder*, pp. 37–74.

4

Denmark and Livonia

WHILE THE CRUSADE IN THE EASTERN BALTIC REGION WAS STILL IN ITS infancy, the life of the tiny bishopric of Riga could have been snuffed out by the natives' rebellion, by Danish hostility, or by the crusaders' indifference; but it survived, and in halting fashion grew even stronger. Because there was never wholehearted support for the venture, the crusader state became a minor pawn in the complicated struggle of German Emperors, Roman Popes, and the monarchs of England, France, and Denmark. Nevertheless, this situation was not wholly disadvantageous for the Rigans.

By the spring of 1203 the King of Denmark had strengthened his grip on the new conquests north of the Elbe. Over the Christmas holiday he held Court in Lübeck, to which his opponents or their representatives had come to negotiate the terms of their surrender. The strongest of these, Adolf of Holstein, obtained his freedom, but only by surrendering the fortress at Lauenburg and leaving his sons as pledge for his good behavior. The weaker princes—Ludolf of Dassel, Henry of Dannenberg, and the others—offered homage to King Waldemar and left hostages as well. This saved their lands, but Holstein was obviously forfeit. Adolf left for his family lands in Schauenburg, hoping the King would reconsider. It was expected that Waldemar would bestow Holstein upon his Welf son-in-law, William, brother of Otto IV, but no decision had been announced.

The suspense was to the advantage of the King. No one would dare displease him for fear of injuring his party's chances—faint though the Hohenstaufen hopes were—that the King might listen to them. So secure did Waldemar consider himself that he consented to release his uncle, Bishop Waldemar of Schleswig, from imprisonment. His captivity (on charges of treason) had impeded an understanding with the papacy over the disposition of disputed territories. Waldemar was probably looking forward to the time when his state would encompass not only Denmark and Northern Germany but also all the lands along the coast of the Baltic Sea, even those now occupied by the tiny bishopric in Livonia.[1]

The import of the Danish victory was clear to the colonists in Livonia, and Bishop Albert anticipated that King Waldemar would soon be interested in the crusader state at Riga. If Waldemar insisted that he render formal homage, like the other minor princes, could Albert refuse? On the other hand, was there any means by which Albert could forestall that possibility? It is all but certain that Albert visited Waldemar during the winter of 1202–1203, and his freedom of travel throughout the Danish domains leads us to believe that an understanding had been reached: the crusade would be a nonpartisan venture and would not infringe upon Danish claims to nearby territories. In return, the Bishop could preach the crusade to Livonia, collect men and monies, and transport them to the east.[2]

If indeed he did so, Bishop Albert was wise to represent himself as an independent agent, a servant of the Church, and to emphasize his usefulness to Danish interests. Had he chosen to ally himself with either the Welf or Hohenstaufen parties, he would have encountered difficulties, for the northern principals of those parties were soon surprised by the Danish Monarch. Everyone had expected that Waldemar would enfeoff his Welf son-in-law with the forfeited country of Holstein. Or—in one of those impulses so common to the time—he might return it to the Schauenburg dynasty. But he did neither. He turned, instead, to his nephew, Albert of Orlamünde, a member of that Ascanian family traditionally friendly to the Hohenstaufens because of their hostility to the Welfs. It was a clever move on Waldemar's part but very unpopular. The Welfs, if they won the struggle for the imperial throne, would not have such a strong hold on the north that they could expel the Danes whenever they wished. If the Hohenstaufens prevailed, this would be a step back into their good graces. Meanwhile neither party could object too strongly, as they were busy with their civil war in the Rhineland.[3]

Though he had obtained permission to preach the crusade, Bishop Albert had only moderate success in doing so. Relatively few warriors volunteered to accompany him. Only the minor nobles Arnold of Meiendorf and Bernard and Theodoric of Seehausen are worthy of mention; the other crusaders were but simple knights and merchants. As Albert found it necessary, as well as desirable, to rely upon his own family, his brother Theodoric became the first of his many relatives to sail to Livonia. In all, sixteen ships, carrying perhaps a hundred warriors apiece, set out on the treacherous voyage. In the chronicler's words,

> Not fearing to undergo prosperity and adversity for God, [Albert] committed himself to the raging sea. As he approached the Danish province of Lyster, he came upon the pagan Esthonians of the island of Oesel with sixteen ships. They had recently burned a church, killed some men and captured oth-

ers, laid waste the land, and carried away the bells and belongings of the church, just as both the pagan Esthonians and Kurs had been accustomed to do heretofore in the kingdom of Denmark and Sweden. The pilgrims armed, wishing to avenge the losses of the Christians; but the pagans, knowing that they were going to Livonia, feared greatly and said deceitfully that they had made peace with the people of Riga. Since the Christians believed them, the pagans escaped their lands for the time being.[4]

But not for long.

After their arrival in Visby, the crusaders learned that they had been duped, and when the Oeselian ships reappeared—probably using Gothland as a landfall on the way home—they set out in pursuit, captured two vessels, and killed about sixty pagans. Bishop Albert then sent the bells, church ornaments, and prisoners, which were found aboard the ships, to the Danish primate, Andreas Sunesen, who was the foremost confidant of King Waldemar. In that way he offered proof that the crusade was indeed in the Danish interest and also ingratiated himself with those powerful men.

As soon as the new arrivals had disembarked, the crusaders, who had been in Riga since the previous winter, made preparations to leave. Bishop Albert was to remain, but he sent his closest associate, the Cistercian brother Theodoric, and a prominent native chieftain, Caupo, with the fleet when it departed. They had urgent business in Rome.

Pressing though his business was, Theodoric could not hurry directly to Rome. Travel was expensive and exhausting, and the duty of preaching the crusade called for as many stops as practical, for it was necessary to bring personal influence to bear on potential crusaders—especially those who might bring a sizable body of troops. Almost certainly the travelers visited Marienfeld, where they conferred with the Abbot about the new monastery at Dünamünde, and then they continued by slow stages to Rome.

Now on his third visit to the Holy Father, Theodoric was well acquainted with Pope Innocent III, and undoubtedly the two men agreed upon the necessity of impressing the Livonian chieftain who had come so far to visit the Pope. Pope Innocent, who welcomed them in a most gracious manner, bestowed lavish gifts upon them: 100 pieces of gold to Caupo and a Bible written by Pope Gregory to Theodoric. Caupo was suitably impressed, and afterward remained loyal to Christianity and his German overlords, even when such loyalty was opposed by his own people.

But neither gold nor Bible, impressive as these gifts were, was the object of Theodoric's visit. He informed the Pope of the progress made by the crusaders and sought his aid in recruiting more soldiers, and especially he asked for papal confirmation of the crusading order that he had founded and Bishop Albert had sanctioned. Probably he was successful, for by the time he returned to Livonia, in September 1204, the Order of Sword-brothers had apparently received papal approval.[5]

The year 1203 passed without much success by the crusaders in Livonia. Indeed, by the spring of 1204 the outlook for the future was bleak. If the knights who had taken the cross the previous year had elected to sail away with Bishop Albert, who had to return to Germany to preach the crusade, the crusaders' foothold at Riga would probably have been lost. These men had no desire to endure another miserable winter in the land, but many were willing to remain throughout the summer. Nevertheless, whether replacements came or not, they would sail for home before winter closed the seas. The civilians of Riga agreed to stay as long as the crusaders, and if the next convoy brought reinforcements, they would remain permanently. It was a tense summer for the Rigans, who were so few in number that a posse of only twenty men was available to pursue cattle thieves, and the tenseness grew as the days shortened and the temperature fell. At last the knights prepared to sail, and it was only as they cleared the mouth of the Dvina that they met Abbot Theodoric, who had come with three small ships loaded with men and supplies. This tiny reinforcement saved the crusade.

The homeward journey of the crusaders is instructive in the terrors of thirteenth-century sea travel:

The before-mentioned knights labored long with their companions in the struggle with the rough sea and at length came to a region of Estonia. The Estonians, wishing to take their lives and their possessions, attacked them with ten pirate ships and twelve other ships. God preserved His people, however. They suffered neither adversity nor sorrow from the enemy; rather, one of the pirate ships was broken to pieces by the Christians, some of the pagans were killed, and others miserably drowned in the sea. They hooked another pirate ship with an iron hook and tried to drag it toward themselves. The pagans, however, wishing rather to be endangered in the sea than to be killed by the Christians, jumped from the ship one by one. While they fell into the danger of death, the other ships departed and escaped. Although Almighty God does not cease to test His elect ones, now placed in various tribulations, like gold in fire, nevertheless He does not desert them entirely, but rather, rescuing them from all evils, puts their enemies in greater fear. They continued in many labors, spending especially many days in hunger, thirst, and cold. Although they had very little food, they received fifty shipwrecked Christians standing on the shore and, mercifully helping them, shared and consumed all their food. And when this alone remained, that they might die of hunger, behold how the dawning visited them from on high. A large merchant ship arrived, gave and sold them food, refreshed the starving ones, and they were filled. They went on, however, and fell into very serious danger, for a storm threw them among some very dangerous rocks out of which they came with great fear and difficulty. They arrived at the port of Visby on the vigil of Saint Andrew [29 November], took on food, and then sailed to the shores of Denmark. Being unable to bring the ship to shore because of the great amount of ice, they left it in the ice and, taking their possessions with them, returned to Germany through Denmark.[6]

It is no wonder that few captains would venture onto the sea from September to May and that the crusaders remained isolated from the homeland for more than half of each year.

In spite of their small numbers the crusaders made headway during the winter of 1204–1205. Under the Abbot's direction, the crusade developed an organization and its own distinctive technique of warfare. Most important, the Order of Swordbrothers took on definite form. Abbot Theodoric must be given credit for the formation of this new crusading order, having envisioned it years before and having contacted friends and fellow clerics in Westphalia on its behalf, and even speaking to the Pope and at last obtaining approval from all parties for its foundation. Most helpful were a group of clerics and knights associated with the monastery at Marienfeld, and particularly his Abbot, Bernard zu Lippe, a famous warrior who had entered the abbey for the good of his soul. With their help he had recruited volunteers, drawn up a formal structure of organization and rules, and transported the new members and their equipment to Riga, presumably in his three ships.[7]

Because crusading orders are so important to the Baltic Crusade, both in Livonia and Prussia, some special thought should be given to their significance. Crusading orders were preferred to secular armies because generally they were cheaper to raise and maintain, better disciplined, and always available (the last consideration being particularly important for a distant land like Livonia, which experienced great fluctuations in the strength of the annual convoys of volunteers, many of whom stayed only

for the summer months). On the other hand, crusading orders were noto-
riously ambitious and were often composed of hotheaded fanatics who
quarreled with everyone and anyone. For these reasons Bishop Albert
distrusted the orders and attempted to limit the power of this new one.
Abbot Theodoric, on the other hand, was a Cistercian, and since the time
of Bernard of Clairvaux that order had been noted for its promotion of the
crusading ideal and the crusading orders.

The Order of Swordbrothers was filled with men of various backgrounds. It is no more possible to give a simple explanation to a thirteenth-
century knight's renunciation of the world than it is to explain individual
actions in the twentieth century, but we can set the personal decisions in a
cultural milieu and from it abstract some general meaning, however little
this may apply to individual cases. The thirteenth century encouraged the
renunciation of the world and its shabby pleasures, extolled the virtues of
the monastic life, and praised any type of service to the Church. The greatest gift a layman could give was the sacrifice of his life on crusade; the
greatest act for a cleric was to retire into the cloisters—the military order
combined these acts and motives. Also, it expressed the new ideals of chivalry in a manner that was not yet equalled by the secular knighthood.
Love of combat, travel, pageantry, and glory were combined with the ven-
eration of the Virgin Mary, the perfect lady and the patroness of the Baltic
Crusade. Religious ideals and societal values converged in the crusading
orders.

There were also, of course, less idealistic motives for entering a crusading order: younger sons whose fathers could not find an heiress for them;
ne'er-do-wells and incompetents seeking an easy life; criminals eager to
evade the law; and old men, repentant of their past behavior, anxious to
escape the flames of hell—all found a respectable haven in their cloisters
and a purpose to life in fighting the Infidel. More important, however, was
the fact that monastic life, which presents such a contrast to present day
comforts, was not an aberrant shock to thirteenth-century initiates. Life
consisted of practice for war, and prayer, and entertainment. Equipment
and food were never lacking, and prestige was high. Women might be a
problem, but need for a woman is often a product of societal pressure, and
that society did not exert the same pressure as ours. Moreover, sex could
be sublimated into war and prayer. All considered, the disadvantages of
monastic life did not weigh so heavily upon those generations as to over-
balance the popular encouragement and support of the monastic vocation,

and especially the nobles' support of the military orders. Moreover, the class that formed the ranks of the Swordbrothers was the *ministeriale* class —knights who were often poor and landless, and hardly the comfortable, pleasure-seeking nobles one might imagine.

Of those who chose the world, many echoed Friedrich von Hausen's plaint to his lady:

My heart and my body wish to part, they who have so long traveled together. My body wants to fight the pagans. But my heart has chosen one lady above all the world. And ever since, I have been troubled because heart and body will no longer agree. My eyes did me this great harm. Only God can decide their quarrel. I thought that I should be freed of this burden when I took the cross in God's honor. In duty, my heart should be with me there. But its loyalty forbids it. I should be a proper living man if my heart would give up its foolish resolve. Now I see well that it cares nothing to what end I come.[8]

The convention of courtly love, which had just come to Germany (perhaps introduced by Henry the Lion's English wife, a daughter of Eleanor of Aquitaine), encouraged this kind of devotion to one's lady. The Germans, however, tended to view love somewhat more grossly than the French; hence the popularity of the *Niedere Minne*, the earthy and suggestive poems of love. But they also produced many *Hohe Minne*, in which the ideal lady is subtly identified with the Virgin Mary, an identification that is very important to the Baltic Crusade, which often referred to the Virgin as "Marîa, die vrowe mîn."[9]

Nevertheless, we must remember that only a small fraction of the population, even of the nobility, opted for the monastic life; and some of those who did lacked real alternatives. One or more sons of each noble were expected to enter the clergy, but most chose the secular clergy, where opportunity for advancement and prestige was greater than among the laity. In general, the richer the family, the more likely it was that the sons would seek a career in the secular clergy, rather than in the monastic clergy.

Those nobles who entered the monastic orders maintained a distinct sense of their class, as one would expect of medieval man. Nowhere in those centuries were men considered really equal; the feeling of class cut across the lines of nationality and religious status. Were it not so, certain aspects of the Baltic Crusade would be much easier to understand; as it was, however, the nobles in the Order of Swordbrothers would have preferred to erect stiffer class barriers than they did. Because the order was but recently formed and lacked prestigious members, it had to recruit from the *ministeriale* class, and the *ministeriale* class, which supplied the bulk of the German knighthood, was still open to wealthy and capable members of the middle and even the lower classes. Its ranks were filled, consequently, by sons of *ministeriales* who were not always of the nobility, though they were knights. Therefore in recruiting rich and powerful initiates the order suffered from all the problems of a proud but upstart organization that is faced with intense competition from its older and more established rivals. Indeed, the Swordbrothers never outgrew their reputation as a "second class" military order.

The rules of the order were based on those of the Templar Order, again the Cistercian influence. Each knightly member took vows of poverty, chastity, obedience, and war against unbelievers; each received a horse, armor, weapons, clothing, and a man-at-arms or sergeant to assist him. He was already trained for war; therefore, once dressed in his white mantle with its red cross and sword, he was ready to fight for his honor and his faith.

A second class was composed of priests, who, though few in number, were highly respected and honored. Spiritual advisors to the Swordbrothers, they alone could hear their confessions and grant absolution. They served in the castles and convents and must be distinguished from the pastors who later were placed in the countryside churches established by the order. Undoubtedly, this class included several men who were responsible for the organization of the order and who were very influential.

The servant class consisted of three branches. Highly trained soldiers, the men-at-arms or sergeants served as mounted warriors and were often armed as knights. The professional infantry operated the siege weapons, garrisoned the castles, and occasionally spearheaded the advancing battle line. The cooks, smiths, bakers, and other servants performed all the tasks necessary to feed, clothe, and house the numerous personnel of the military order. In keeping with its low status, this class wore simple dark clothing that was marked with the sword, the symbol of the order.

It is possible that there was a fourth class of auxiliaries, composed of the nobles and merchants of Riga. They would have supported the order in return for such favors as commercial rights in its lands, participation in its fraternal activities, and burial in its cemetery. Probably a number of knights and soldiers also served in the order during the time they were on crusade.

The head of the order was the master, elected by the order for life. Although vested with complete authority, in practice he consulted either the entire membership at a general assembly or any convent chapter, together with his officers, on all important matters. Under him was a hierarchy of officials: the vice master presided in his absence; the treasurer supervised all incomes and expenditures; the marshal was responsible for all equipment; and the chaplain was probably the chancellor, in charge of all correspondence. On the local level, heavy responsibilities were given to the commanders, who were in charge of the castles and convents of the order, and to the advocates, who administered the territories by collecting taxes, supervising justice, and commanding the militia.

The general assembly, which was supposed to be an annual affair, was attended by all who could be spared from duty. In times of emergency, special sessions were held for the officers and experienced men from the major convents. At these assemblies they made reports, discussed policy, and elected new officials and installed them in office. Occasionally guests were invited. There was great pomp, pageantry, and revelry at these periodic gatherings.

Of the officers, only the master was responsible to the Bishop of Riga; the order itself was an independent religious foundation, responsible only to the Pope, and was determined to remain so—a fact that bothered Bishop Albert, who sought to gather all power in his own hands. As a result, Bishop and order were on a collision course from the very beginning, although this was masked by the weakness of the order in its very early years.[10] At that time Bishop Albert could put perhaps a thousand mailed warriors in the field, whereas the Swordbrothers had no more than fifty or a hundred armed riders—a very small but important addition to the crusaders' strength. The powerful Bishop Albert could therefore please Abbot Theodoric by giving the order lands and responsibilities in Livonia.

By the time the Swordbrothers were well established, the crusaders' arms had begun to reduce the native tribes one by one. The endemic warfare of the natives contributed greatly to this success, as the weaker tribes were always willing to accept Christian aid against the stronger tribes. The crusaders thus held the balance of power, and the heavily armored knights, though few in number, were decisive in battle. The first combat of the Swordbrothers illustrates this situation.

In the seventh year 1205, about Lent, when these tribes are more accustomed to engage in war, the Lithuanians moved against Estonia with a force of almost two thousand men. They descended along the Dvina and passed by the city. . . .

After a few days, Viesthard, a noble of the Semgalls, hearing about the Lithuanian expedition, came hurriedly to Riga and spoke in admonition to the Germans for having permitted the enemy to cross their boundaries peacefully. For now that they had learned the location of the place, they might possibly in the future destroy the city with its inhabitants. Although they did not wish, because of the weakness of their forces, to fight before the bishop's return, Viesthard, being a warlike man, excited them to battle and promised to bring a great many Semgalls to their aid. . . . When the army arrived, the hostages were delivered into the hands of the Germans and, their loyalty thus demonstrated, the Semgalls obtained both help and friendship. For the retinue of the bishop, with the Brothers of the Militia of Christ, and Conrad, a knight of Uexküll, together with a few others who could be spared, went out to the army in a high place where they and the Semgalls awaited the return of the Lithuanians. . . . At length the Lithuanians returned with numerous captives and indescribable booty in flocks and horses, entered Livonia, and proceeded gradually from village to village. At last they turned aside to the fort of Caupo and trusting the peace of the Livonians, spent the night among them. The scouts of the Germans and Semgalls inquired discreetly about their return and announced this to their own army. The next day, some other scouts followed the former and reported that the Lithuanians wished to return through the Rodenpois short cut to Uexküll. When they heard these reports, the whole army rejoiced and all prepared in rivalry for the fight. The Lithuanians came with all their loot and captives, who numbered more than a thousand, divided their army into two parts, placed the captives in the middle, and, because of the excessive depth of the snow, marched single file over one path. But as soon as the first of these discovered the footprints of those who had gone before, they stopped, suspecting an ambush. Thus the last in line overtook the first and all were collected in one formation with the captives. When the Semgalls saw their great multitude, many of them trembled and, not daring to fight, wished to seek safer places. Thereupon certain of the Germans approached the knight Conrad and begged insistently that they go first into battle with the enemies of Christ. They asserted that it was better to go to death gloriously for Christ than, to the confusion of their tribe, to take flight dishonorably. Conrad, with his horse and himself well-armored, like a knight, attacked the Lithuanians with the few Germans who were on hand. But God sent such fear into the Lithuanians and they were so dazzled by the brightness of the German arms that they turned away on all sides. The leader of the Semgalls, perceiving that the Lithuanians were so terrified through the mercy of God, exhorted his men

58

bravely to go into battle with them. Thus the army was assembled and the Lithuanians were dispersed on all sides of the road like sheep. About twelve hundred of them were cut down by the sword.[11]

The Semgallians expressed their pleasure at the victory by massacring the Estonian prisoners they had taken from the Lithuanians and by carting away wagons loads of severed heads for a victory celebration. The loot, mainly horses and flocks, was divided among the victors; but the main reward for the Christians was prestige: they had inflicted an overwhelming defeat on the most feared and hated tribe in the Baltic. Furthermore, they knew that the natives hated one another more than they hated the foreign invader and that they could use this hatred to their advantage.

Although this victory was important, another success also had an impact on the Livonian crusade. In the Middle East, the Fourth Crusade had taken Constantinople in 1204. Contemporaries did not worry that it had been completely diverted from its goal, that it further divided the already antagonistic Greek and Latin Churches, and that it fatally weakened an ancient bastion of Christianity in the east. What was important was the sheer reality of another success, after so many years of failure. Christendom was now united, and the war against the infidels could be resumed without fear of Greek betrayal—the common excuse for defeats that were really due to incompetence, inexperience, and the Saracens' courage. The capture of Constantinople, which gave great impetus to the crusading movement in general, was to result in a greater interest among Germans in joining the crusade against the heathens in Livonia. Nevertheless, the laconic North German chroniclers for the most part contented themselves with the notation that "Constantinople was taken by the Latins."[12]

In Germany, the civil war continued unabated, but fortune now favored Philip of Hohenstaufen. The Welf party was weakened by the defeats inflicted upon its English ally and by desertions. The French Monarch had captured Normandy from King John, and the Pope was pressing demands that John grant more independence to the English Church and offer his kingdom as a papal fief. These difficulties combined with John's unpopularity with the English people, so that he could not continue the financial and political support that had helped keep the Welf forces in the field. In Germany, at the same time, Otto's brother, Henry, went over to the Hohenstaufens. The most serious blow, however, was the defection of the

Archbishop of Cologne, and although Pope Innocent III removed that prelate from office and arranged for the election of a pro-Welf archbishop, the damage had been done. In a major battle near Cologne, Philip of Hohenstaufen routed the Welfs, and had the Pope not sustained his cause, Otto would have been compelled to withdraw from the war.

These developments, of course, had an impact on Northern Germany, and it is worth digressing briefly to observe how cleverly Pope Innocent used local antagonisms to embarrass his opponents. Hartwig, the Archbishop of Bremen, was a Hohenstaufen supporter and therefore had often protested various actions of Welf adherents; in particular, he had quarreled with Henry of Braunschweig and the Archbishop of Cologne. Innocent had ignored these protests until the aforementioned gentlemen changed their party adherence; then the Pope took up the complaints on Hartwig's behalf, ignoring his requests that the quarrels be forgotten.[13]

King Waldemar remained in firm control of his provinces and took advantage of every opportunity to strengthen his position. Faced by opposition from the Counts of Schwerin, he authorized Albert of Orlamünde, who was Count of Holstein, to enforce the royal will. The Counts of Schwerin were humbled, but from this time on they were hostile to the Danish King, a fact of later significance. When Bishop Philip of Ratzeburg refused to submit his election to Waldemar for confirmation, the monarch was not able to remove him from office, but he made life very uncomfortable in Ratzeburg, so that Philip later went on crusade to Livonia. Opposed in Pomerania by the Duke of Brandenburg, Waldemar made a counter move by marrying into the royal house of Bohemia. And his prestige rose even higher when Innocent III forced the King of France to reinstate the Danish Princess Ingeborg as his rightful Queen. Danish power and prestige waxed steadily.[14]

Political developments of the past year had favored his mission, so that Bishop Albert spent the winter of 1204–1205 preaching the crusade in Westphalia, where he found many Welf nobles who were seeking refuge from the party strife. On the one hand, they did not wish to antagonize the Pope by going over to the Hohenstaufens, but on the other hand they did not wish to lose their property by continuing to serve in a lost cause. When Albert pointed out that they could go on crusade, whereby they and their estates would be protected by law and custom, Count Henry of Stumphenhusen, Cono of Isenburg, and many other Westphalian and Rhenish nobles took the cross. Also, many Hohenstaufen supporters were being encouraged by Pope Innocent to leave the country; for example, he ordered Hartwig of Bremen to send crusaders to Livonia, which presumably would weaken the Hohenstaufen party in Saxony; and indeed many volunteered for the crusade. Bishop Albert also recruited his brother Rothmann, who was an Augustinian monk in Segeberg, a monastery that had long been interested in the Livonian mission. With all these factors operating in his favor—the success of the Fourth Crusade, peace in the Danish provinces, the trend in the civil war, and the active support of the Pope—Bishop Albert was able to sail for Livonia with the most formidable army yet raised.

The very size of the crusader force cowed all resistance in the area of Riga and brought the natives firmly under German control. For that reason, it was a joyous winter for the crusaders, and Riga was lively with the pageantry of chivalry. Such entertainment was very popular and one of the main attractions of the crusade. Indeed, the Baltic Crusade laid great stress on the ceremonial aspects of knighthood and chivalry—including drama, such as the play that was designed to instruct the natives in the history of the prophets. When the armies of Gideon and the Philistines charged onto the stage, the natives fled the area in fear of a massacre.

The winter passed quietly, if not comfortably—every winter was terribly cold in Livonia. But danger arose in the spring of 1206, when Bishop Albert was confronted by Russian hostility and native rebellion. The Russian Prince at Polozk had long exercised a vague sovereignty over the Dvina basin which the early German missionaries and traders had recognized in various ways. As the time came to renew these ties, Bishop Albert sent his most trusted aide, Abbot Theodoric, to Polozk with presents for the Prince. Unfortunately, he was robbed en route, and after his arrival was kept in close confinement while the Prince conferred with emissaries from the Livonian tribes. Meanwhile Theodoric, hearing that the Prince was planning to send an army downriver to Riga, managed to send a warning to Bishop Albert. When the Prince learned of this, he summoned Theodoric and questioned him carefully. Theodoric stood up to him courageously and in forceful language presented the German cause. The Russian Prince, as a result, did not launch an immediate invasion but instead sent ambassadors to accompany the Abbot back to Riga and mediate the disputes between Bishop Albert and the natives. Apparently he was acting in an impartial manner, as the overlord of both parties.

At the end of May, however, on the day appointed for the ambassadorial meeting, the natives around Treiden and Holm rose and massacred those

Germans and native Christians who were foolish or unlucky enough to be within reach. Thus mediation was out of the question. Bishop Albert, already distrustful of the ambassadors, now refused to treat with them, choosing instead a military solution to the rising. Within a short time Albert's household troops recaptured the castles, but they needed assistance from the Semgallians and Caupo to suppress the other tribes. They were not completely successful in this, and Albert soon found it necessary to depart for Germany and raise more troops. Meanwhile the natives, still in rebellion, fled to Russia and asked for military aid. This time the Prince was more receptive than he had been before.

Shortly after the crusaders whose term of service had expired sailed for home, the Prince's army came down the Dvina River on rafts to reassert Russian hegemony. The remaining crusaders were surprised by the sudden arrival of the Russian troops but were able to repulse their attack on the castle at Holm. Since this was the Russians' first experience with a western castle and the crossbow, twenty Germans were able to hold the castle for eleven days. Then, news that ships were arriving in Riga caused the Russians to withdraw. This cost the Russians their sovereignty over Livonia, but memory of their hegemony lived on. Except, perhaps, for the commitment to King Waldemar, the crusader state at Riga was now completely independent, a status Bishop Albert was determined to maintain.

King Waldemar, however, had designs on the eastern Baltic. For several years he had planned a campaign against the island of Oesel to avenge attacks on his kingdom by Oesel's notorious pirates, but a more ambitious goal of the expedition is clear. In January 1206 the Pope had granted permission to the Archbishop of Lund to establish a bishopric in Livonia, which the Danish Monarch planned to utilize to extend his rule over the eastern Baltic. Waldemar and the Archbishop landed on Oesel and built a castle on one of the harbors, from which their knights terrorized the countryside. At the end of the summer, when it was obvious that the campaign was a failure, Waldemar burned the castle and went home, but the Archbishop of Lund and the Bishop of Schleswig, the royal chancellor, sailed to Riga. The Archbishop, a noted scholar, spent the winter in Riga teaching theology and preparing the clergy for the spiritual guidance of the recently baptized natives. We would not be far amiss, however, to view this visit as a preparation for subordinating the Rigan bishopric to the authority of Lund and the Danish King. The presence of the Archbishop, the chancellor, and their retinue would also help preclude a Russian attack or native rebellion.

In this same winter the Germans introduced advocates into the Livonian countryside to supervise justice, collect taxes, and organize the militia. They laid heavy taxes upon the rebellious tribes but treated their loyal allies leniently. Unfortunately, however, there were many abuses of justice by the new magistrates, but though we are informed of them in detail, the complaints are in no way different from those raised about magistrates in Germany at this very same time. In short, government was oppressive everywhere, and Livonia was no exception. The crusaders were men, not saints.[15]

When Bishop Albert arrived in Germany he learned that the Hohenstaufen party was close to winning the war; in fact, when Philip of Hohenstaufen captured the Archbishop of Cologne in battle in the early fall of 1206, resistance practically collapsed. Innocent III recognized his defeat and sent two legates to treat with the victor. Philip's rival, Otto IV, commanded a rapidly disintegrating army and offered only occasional resistance as he retreated northward.

It was incumbent upon Bishop Albert to speak to the Emperor as soon as possible, since the Danish threat was now as clear as the Hohenstaufen victory. There was no need for further duplicity. Albert had to win support from Philip of Hohenstaufen or accept Danish overlordship. He made his way across Saxony and Westphalia to Holland, everywhere preaching in the streets and churches, telling of his crusade and its hopes, successes and difficulties, and winning volunteers. Then he returned eastward, finally arriving at Philip's Court (probably the one held in Gelnhausen on 2 February 1207). There the Emperor invested Albert with Livonia as a fief of the Holy Roman Empire and promised him an annual donation from the royal treasury. No money was ever donated, but even the subsequent assassination of Philip could not undo the incorporation of Livonia into the Empire —an important legal check to the claims of the Archbishop of Lund and the Danish crown. (After the Welfs inherited the throne, they did not grant new fiefs to their former ally.) And Bishop Albert, of course, could oppose Danish claims to his homage by protesting that he was no longer a free agent, able to offer fealty whenever he pleased.[16]

We see, therefore, that in these decisive years the colony in Riga met and overcame the obstacles of native resistance, weather, and Russian competition. Bishop Albert had successfully instituted a governmental system, founded a monastery, and created an army of household troops and crusaders. He had also averted submission to the Danes and had won the recognition of the Pope and the Emperor. But much credit must also be given to Abbot Theodoric for stimulating interest in the crusade, for founding the Order of the Swordbrothers, and for guiding the colony through these difficult years. Two men, working for different but complementary goals by different means, had established a crusading state that would permanently change the course of history in the Baltic regions.

NOTES TO CHAPTER FOUR

1. *Arnold of Lübeck*, Ch. 6, para. 17.

2. Adolf Holm makes the unfounded statement that Waldemar forbade crusades to Livonia, which seems most unlikely. See his *Lübeck, die freie und Hansa Stadt* (Bielefeld: Velhagen und Klosing, 1900), p. 22.

3. The Danish-Welf alliance almost collapsed as a result of this. Koch, *Livland und das Reich*, pp. 19–20; Usinger, *Deutsch-dänische Geschichte*, pp. 117–22.

4. *Henry of Livonia*, p. 41.

5. Ibid., p. 43; Benninghoven, *Schwertbrüder*, pp. 53–54.

6. *Henry of Livonia*, pp. 46–47; for the construction of the fort, see Jacob Ozols, "Die vor- und frühgeschichtlichen Burgen Semgallens," *Commentationes Balticae*, 14/15 (Bonn: Baltisches Forschungsinstitut, 1971), p. 3.

7. Benninghoven, *Schwertbrüder*, pp. 54–62.

8. *Medieval Lyrics of Europe*, trans. Willard R. Trask (New York: World Publishing Co., 1969), p. 89.

9. *Reimchronik*, l. 12017. Compare this conception of Livonian monastic life to that in Benninghoven, *Schwertbrüder*, pp. 60–62.

10. Benninghoven, *Schwertbrüder*, pp. 54–62; Friedrich Georg von Bunge, *Der Orden der Schwertbrüder: deren Stiftung, Verfassung und Auflösung* (Leipzig: E. Bidder, 1875). Desmond Seward, *The Monks of War; the Military Religious Orders* (Hamden, Conn.: Shoestring Press, 1972) is superficial and inaccurate.

11. *Henry of Livonia*, pp. 47–49.

12. "Do wart Constantinople van den Latinen gewünnen," in *Sächsische Weltchronik*, p. 238.

13. *Hamburgisches Urkundenbuch*, 1: 300–304; Usinger, *Deutsch-dänische Geschichte*, pp. 131–32; Koch, *Livland und das Reich*, p. 20.

14. Hans Witte, *Mecklenburgische Geschichte* (Wismar, 1909), 1: 145–46.

15. *Henry of Livonia*, pp. 45–68.

16. Ibid., p. 68.

5

Crusader Success in Livonia

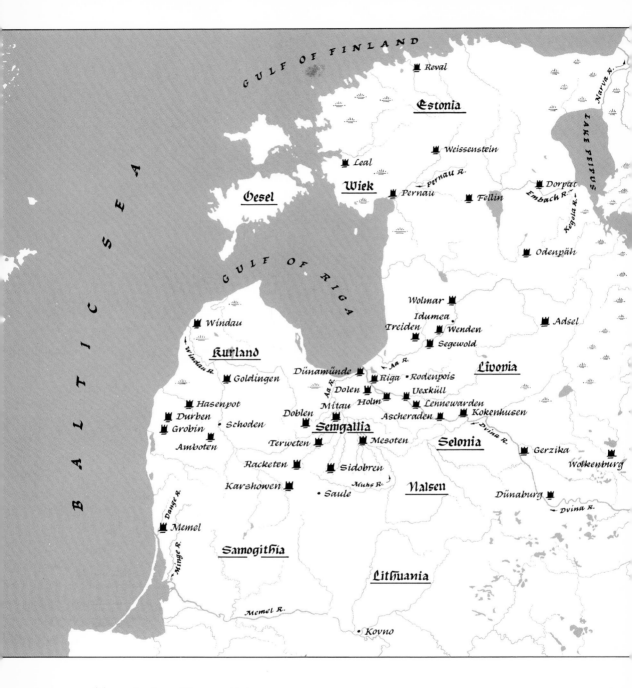

GULF OF FINLAND

BALTIC SEA

GULF OF RIGA

LAKE PEIPUS

Narva R.

Reval

Estonia

Weissenstein

Leal

Wiek

Pernau

Pernau R.

Fellin

Embach R.

Dorpat

Kegola R.

Odenpäh

Oesel

Wolmar

Idumea

Treiden

Wenden

Segewold

Adsel

Livonia

Windau

Windau R.

Kurland

Goldingen

Dünamünde

Aa R.

Riga

Rodenpois

Aa R.

Dolen

Uexküll

Holm

Lennewarden

Hasenpot

Mitau

Ascheraden

Kokenhusen

Durben

Doblen

Grobin

Schoden

Amboten

Terweten

Semgallia

Mesoten

Selonia

Dvina R.

Gerzika

Racketen

Sidobren

Wolkenburg

Karshowen

Saule

Muhs R.

Nalsen

Dünaburg

Dvina R.

Dange R.

Memel

Minge R.

Samogithia

Lithuania

Memel R.

Kovno

BISHOP ALBERT OF RIGA COULD HAVE TAKEN CONSIDERABLE PRIDE IN HIS recent successes. Amid the political feuds of western Europe, he had played each party against the others in a skillful and unobtrusive manner. The result was that by the end of 1206 the crusader state at Riga was firmly established against native attack and bulwarked against Danish claims on its loyalty. Bishop Albert now counted on the firm support of a strong German Emperor against his numerous enemies, and if that support had been available he probably would have triumphed over all obstacles. But, as we shall see, the revival of the Welf-Hohenstaufen dispute slowly sapped his authority and eventually put the crafty Bishop at the mercy of his rivals and enemies.

When the Bishop of Riga returned to his church in June 1207 with a large army, the Danish prelates had already sailed. It is unlikely that Albert wished to meet them anyway; he had no desire to set any precedent or make any promise that might later be embarrassing. In any case, Danish help was no longer needed. Bishop Albert had recruited two counts for this crusade, and the great number of warriors who accompanied him so over-awed the natives that even the Russian vassal, Daniel of Kokenhusen, hurried downriver to assure the Bishop that missionaries would be welcome to preach in his lands. It appeared that Bishop Albert was in firm control, and he passed the summer and fall baptizing natives, building churches, and organizing the local government.

Undoubtedly Albert believed that time was on his side. If he could but delay the inevitable confrontation with the Danes, he would weather any difficulty. The Order of the Swordbrothers, however, chose this moment to ask for one-third of all conquests, future as well as present. They believed this was only just. Although they were not yet numerous (their income was insufficient to sustain more than a few hundred mounted warriors), they were strong enough to be the Christians' mainstay during those winter months when crusaders were few in number. (Many crusaders came only for the summer.) Because they were permanently stationed in Livonia, they could perform valuable, perhaps indispensable service to the crusade, but in order to increase their numbers and wealth they needed more land. They aspired to the power and prestige of the crusading orders in the Holy

Land, where the military orders carried the brunt of warfare against the unbelievers.

It was this ambition that worried Bishop Albert. In the Holy Land such orders quarreled among themselves and with the secular princes, so as to disrupt the crusading effort. Bishop Albert wanted to avoid internal trouble at all costs. Because he did not want a rival in Livonia, he sought to postpone a final decision over the lands, saying that he could not grant what he did not possess but that he was willing to grant them one-third of his present holdings. This, of course, was but a fraction of the expected conquests, and the brothers rejected the offer. The brothers must have believed that if they harassed the Bishop sufficiently, they could force him to comply with their wishes. During the previous winter they probably had long conversations with the Danish officials, and the possibility of using the Danes against the Bishop could not have been overlooked. Also, Bishop Albert had treated with an Emperor who was still excommunicated, which suggested that the crusading order could expect aid from the Pope. Therefore, after some delay, they temporized by accepting the offer to divide the present conquests.

The lands were divided into three parts, of which Bishop Albert had first choice, as well as receiving the part rejected by the order. The Bishop compensated the order for its possession in his territories. The brothers accepted all this but did not agree to foreswear any future claims, and soon carried the case to the papacy. We see, therefore, both Bishop and crusading order playing a double game. Each sought to advance his cause in Livonia by playing politics in the papal, imperial, and Danish courts. Complicated by the long-standing antagonisms between regular and secular clergy, this quarrel created mistrust and even hatred between the two parties that was never cleared away.

Bishop Albert also had difficulties with his own administrators and vassals. Even in the best times there was corruption and rebellion, but in periods of upheaval and absentee government, as in Livonia, they were multiplied.

The bishop sent priests into his parts and left the Brothers to administer their own part. That year a certain pilgrim knight, Gottfried, was also sent to Treiden to administer the office of magistrate in secular law. He went through the parishes, settling the disputes and quarrels of men, collected money and a great many gifts, and, sending a little bit to the bishop, kept most of it for himself. Accordingly, certain other pilgrims who resented this broke open his chest and found nineteen silver marks which Gottfried had realized from property that he had stealthily collected, not counting much more which he had already dissipated. Because he had acted unjustly in perverting judgment and oppressing the poor, in justifying the iniquitous and levying toll on the converts, by the just judgment of God it so happened that, to the terror of other such men, he should incur such a humiliation, and he afterwards died a shameful death, as some report.[1]

(The last phrase is a medieval moralism meaning that he was not punished but should have been.)

More serious was an incident that made an ally into an implacable enemy:

At this time there arose a quarrel between the king of Kokenhusen and Daniel, the knight of Lennewarden. For the king had caused Daniel's men many inconveniences and, although warned, had not ceased his molestation. The armed men of this Daniel, therefore, rising up at night, went hastily with him to the fort of this king. They arrived at dawn and, finding those within the fort sleeping and the watch itself, moreover, less than properly watchful, they mounted the walls suddenly and reached the very center of the fort. . . . They seized the king, among others, cast him in chains, and bringing all the wealth that was in the fort together in one place, they carefully watched it while they summoned their lord, Daniel, who was nearby. He, however, wishing to hear the counsel of the bishop on this matter, made everything known to the people of Riga. The bishop and all his men regretted this very much, for they did not approve of what had been done. The bishop then ordered the fort to be restored to the king and all his wealth to be given back and, summoning the king, honored him with gifts of many horses and many suits of precious garments.[2]

This was a blow to Albert's policy toward the natives. He was losing the confidence of those native nobles whom he had hoped to incorporate into a feudal state, and eventually he would be able to rely only upon foreign knights. Moreover, there was invasion:

On that very Christmas night the Livonians sent messengers to inform the bishop that a Lithuanian army had entered Livonia. Other messengers subsequently followed the first to report on the men killed and captured, on the churches laid waste, and on all the evils which the pagans had brought upon the new church. When the bishop heard these things, he called together the pilgrims, the Brothers of the Militia, the merchants, and all his own men, and told them all, for the remission of their sins, to make of themselves a wall for the house of the Lord and to liberate the church from its enemies. They all obeyed, prepared themselves to fight, and sent to all the Livonians and Letts the following threat: "Whosoever does not come out to follow the Christian army shall be punished by a fine of three marks." Fear filled all and, hearkening to this threat, they met the people of Riga on the banks of the Dvina. They then went together to Lennewarden, assembled within the town, and awaited in silence the return of the Lithuanians. They then sent scouts to investigate their route. The Lithuanians, with all their captives and loot, met these scouts near Lennewarden and crossed the Dvina over the ice at night. The leader of their army climbed the banks, and approached the fort with his companions. He then called the leader of the fort, demanded the whereabouts of the Christian army, and said: "Go, tell the Christians who, two years ago, killed my army as if it were asleep, as it returned from Estonia, that now they will find me and all my men awake." After they had heard this speech, the Christians hastened to the battle of the Lord and followed the enemy at dawn.[3]

It was, of course, a Christian victory—and a perfect model for the strategy subsequently adopted for the defense of the land. In the succeeding years Bishop Albert extended a line of castles along the Dvina, which were watchposts and assembly points for the militia. Rarely was a raiding party intercepted as it entered Livonia, but the heavily laden raiders were always pursued and usually were beaten by the Christian knights and militia. Able to defend themselves for the first time against their traditional enemies, the natives began to respond more favorably to their new masters.[4]

Not all the natives responded favorably, however. For example, King Vetseke of Kokenhusen massacred the German workmen who were rebuilding his castle in stone. He had begun the rebellion the day the crusaders were to have sailed for home, and if contrary winds had not delayed the sailing, the Christians would have lacked the strength to attack him for half a year. As it turned out, 300 crusaders took the cross again, and Bishop Albert hired mercenaries from Gothland, whom he sent back to Livonia. These angry crusaders were more than King Vetseke could face alone, and he fled to Russia. Thus Kokenhusen became a major castle for the crusaders, and such rebels as were captured were cruelly executed.

When Bishop Albert landed in Germany, he learned that strife had broken out in the archbishopric of Hamburg-Bremen. His uncle, Archbishop Hartwig, had died, and the election of his successor revived the old hostility between the two cathedral chapters. The majority of canons in Bremen cast their votes for Bishop Waldemar of Schleswig, as the man most likely to organize resistance to the Danish King. They hoped to restore the archbishopric to its old power and prestige, and this necessitated the expulsion of the Danes from Germany. But the Welf clergy, led by Burchard of Stumphausen, withdrew to Hamburg and held a second election, which Burchard won. This was partly because ages ago the families allied to the Welfs had seized their lands from the archbishopric; consequently, some clergymen feared a revival of archiepiscopal strength that might threaten their family estates. The result was a contested election, and both candidates sent to Rome for confirmation.

Bishop Waldemar probably hoped that the forthcoming settlement between the Pope and the Emperor would include placing a Hohenstaufen supporter in the diocese of Bremen. But in any case he looked upon the archbishopric as only a stepping stone to the Danish throne. Burchard probably expected that any candidate who was favorable to the Welfs and the Danes would be accepted, but he too was disappointed. Despite all the influences upon him, Pope Innocent III refused to confirm either candidate, so both men appealed to arms. Buchard took up residence in Hamburg and captured Stade with the help of Danish knights. Bishop Waldemar was escorted to Bremen by his son-in-law, Bernard of Saxony, and with the help of the peasant army of Stedigen recaptured Stade. Thereafter the war was stalemated. Burchard controlled the right bank of the Elbe and Waldemar the left. The outcome was finally determined not by the candidates and their armies but by an unexpected turn in the Welf-Hohenstaufen dispute.[5]

Everyone had known that the fighting in the Rhineland would be decisive and, therefore, each party had tended to ignore the conflicts elsewhere, such as the Danish-Welf successes in the North earlier and now Waldemar of Schleswig's victories. But few had suspected that the far-off struggle would be so protracted or that Cologne would become the key to the war. The defection of the Archbishop of Cologne to the Hohenstaufens had almost wrecked the Welf cause at one point, but papal intervention rescued the situation. The Pope could not maintain the Welf position alone, however, and at last Cologne was lost. Otto IV retreated to Saxony, then to Denmark, and finally to England. Unable to resist any longer, he recognized the Hohenstaufen as the rightful Emperor. In return for his submission he received the hand of the victor's daughter in marriage.[6] "Then everything was again upset: 'King Philip came to Bamberg. There the Duke of the Palatinate, a Wittelsbach, slew him by guile. He was buried there. Later he was taken out and carried to Speier, where he was reburied.' "[7]

Philip's assassination made Otto the Emperor. The Hohenstaufens, though victors in the civil war, were not willing to resume the bloodshed. Earlier they had made a peace with Otto, now they preferred to negotiate with him to see if he would guarantee their winnings. Otto, most amenable to Pope and nobles, promised everything that was necessary, so that his election and coronation followed quickly.

King Waldemar of Denmark was not pleased by the turn of events. He saw a strong Emperor as a threat to his possessions and trusted the Welfs no more than he did the Hohenstaufens. Therefore he ceased his support of the pro-Welf candidate for the archbishopric of Hamburg-Bremen, whereupon that candidate resigned. This did not mean, however, that he supported his hostile uncle, Waldemar of Schleswig, who was unacceptable to the Pope in any case because he had entered Bremen against the Pope's expressed command. If he could not install a pro-Danish prelate, King Waldemar would see that the vacancy in Bremen remained unfilled. His enmity was confirmed as, week after week, the minor German princes from both parties approached the new Emperor with pleas for assistance against the Danes.

Otto IV, however, had no interest in a war with Denmark. He was less German than English (Norman English, or French) by birth and training. The Angevin heritage was very strong, and if anything can be said about that family, it is that they always thought on a grand scale. Otto IV was like his cousins in this respect. If ever there was a Welf program for Germany, Otto IV did not believe in it. His model for the Empire was not Welf but Hohenstaufen, but few realized it as yet. Otto, who was not a man to prejudice his prospects by talking too much, allowed everyone to believe that their plans were his plans, and they were taken in—Pope and princes. Everyone, that is, except the wily King of Denmark.

When the princes assembled in Halberstadt in September 1208 for the formal election, they expected imperial help against the Danes. All the powerful magnates of the north were present to offer fealty, including such former enemies as Bernard of Saxony, Herman of Orlamünde, and Adolf of Schauenburg. By the time of the next meeting, in May, they were disabused of their hopes. It was in vain that Bernard of Saxony cried, "How long must your revenge keep you occupied in the East? You have what you wanted. It is time to go north!"[8] Instead, Otto went south.

The northern princes could not fight the Danish Monarch alone. Consequently, several of them followed Otto into Italy, and as late as the year

1210, Bishop Philip of Ratzeburg, Adolf of Schauenburg, Adolf of Dassel, and Henry of Schwerin were still at his Court.[9]

The turn of events was not favorable for Bishop Albert. His uncle, the Archbishop, had always looked favorably upon his crusade. But now Hartwig was dead, and the archbishopric was torn by civil war. Philip of Hohenstaufen, who had favored Bishop Albert, also was dead, and his throne was occupied by Otto IV. The situation could have been even more serious, but the Danish King was busy in Sweden, and the Count of Holstein was occupied by rebels. Bishop Albert was not important enough to distract them, and therefore he could still preach his crusade without interference. But the future, clearly, promised a day of reckoning, which Bishop Albert could postpone but could not avert. He would have to come to terms with the Danish monarch, which meant Danish overlordship.

Although Bishop Albert sent little immediate aid to Livonia, affairs in that region prospered. The government, though still inexperienced and undoubtedly corrupt, was strong enough to suppress native dissent. More important, it provided military victories over the traditional enemies of the Livs and the Letts. The prospect of revenge and booty on one hand and the memory of Estonian and Lithuanian butcheries and enslavement on the other were sufficient to guarantee the loyalty of the Livs and Letts to their new Christian rulers. Also, there were more German knights in the country, and the natives had not yet devised a means of neutralizing their effectiveness or emulating their skill. The Order of Swordbrothers was growing in numbers, and more crusaders were willing to winter in Livonia. Riga contained more comfortable buildings, and starvation was no longer a danger.

The crusaders also had an ideal: Bishop Albert's self-serving manipulation of the Virgin cult. This most popular of all medieval cults undoubtedly won many volunteers to the Baltic Crusade because Livonia was dedicated to the Blessed Virgin. Several years later, Albert explained to Pope Innocent III:

"Holy Father, as you have not ceased to cherish the Holy Land of Jerusalem, the country of the Son, with your Holiness' care, so also you ought not to abandon Livonia, the land of the Mother, which has hitherto been among the pagans and far from the cares of your consolation and is now again desolate. For the Son loves His Mother and, as He would not care to lose His own land, so, too, He would not care to endanger His Mother's land."[10]

It was an easy step from Saint Mary's Cathedral to the land of the Blessed Virgin, and a very clever pretext to persuade devout men to enlist under his banner.

Bishop Albert had need of many good men, as the chronicler showed: "At this time the Rigans and the Christians who were in Livonia desired peace, but it did not come; they were seeking good things, and behold, trouble!"[11]

In the summer of 1208 the Semgallians proposed a raid into Lithuania. Those responsible for the government of Riga decided against the venture, but so many crusaders insisted upon participating in it that the authorities gave them permission to do so. Fifty knights—a very considerable force—went to Semgallia to join in the attack, but they had much to learn about native tactics. When the Semgallians learned that the Lithuanians were ready to fight, they fled as quickly as they could, for native tactics were to fight only unprepared foes, preferably women, children, and old men. The Germans did not understand this, having been raised by a different model of personal courage and espousing very different battle tactics. Consequently, when their allies fled, the Christians formed a solid body and stood their ground against the much larger Lithuanian army—but only a few of them survived. The moral was not lost on the Rigans.

> Praying to heaven, all the elders and discreet men decided that thenceforth they ought not to confide in the multitude of the pagans, nor ought they to fight with pagans against other pagans, but that they ought, hoping in the Lord, to proceed boldly against all the tribes with the now baptized Letts and Livonians.[12]

Abbot Theodoric, the most influential figure in the circle of men who ran the crusader state, saw that the possibility of success was greater to the north and east than to the south. Also, the Swordbrothers had been advancing northeastward from their territories along the Livonian Aa River into Lettgallia. If Bishop Albert thought that in dividing the land he had passed undesirable and indefensible territory upon the brothers, he was mistaken; as we shall see, he had little interest in advancing in that direction where he would inevitably collide with the Danes. The Estonians, it turned out, were more vulnerable than anyone had imagined, and Theodoric, who had played a part in the foundation of the Swordbrothers, doubtlessly encouraged the knights' aggression, even though it threatened to involve all the crusaders in a desperate war with the natives. The arrival of

Abbot Florenz of Marienfeld to consecrate the new abbey at Dünamünde probably reinforced Theodoric's influence and weakened that of the Rigans who adhered more strictly to Bishop Albert's instructions.

Bishop Albert's men, particularly his brothers, still retained control of policy, but only barely. Events were moving too swiftly, and the Bishop's strong hand was needed. As time passed, the Swordbrothers tended to become more and more independent. They saw an opportunity to convert the Lettish tribes around Wenden—a territory that had not yet been divided—and resented the efforts of episcopal officials and relatives to thwart them. The Bishop's men feared that the Swordbrothers would simply occupy the lands and refuse to give the Bishop his share, and that giving aid to the Letts would involve all the Christians in war with the Estonians at a moment when all resources were needed along the Dvina River.

The Swordbrothers themselves were divided as to whether they should submit to the orders of the absentee Bishop. However, the faction advocating immediate war with the Estonians at last won control and, removing the leader of the opposing faction from command at Wenden, began to attack those Estonians who refused to recognize their rule over the Letts. Bishop Albert's officials intervened and negotiated a truce of one year's duration, at the end of which Bishop Albert should be back in Livonia. He could settle the situation at such time, presumably in his own favor.[13]

This solution hardly satisfied the Swordbrothers. The faction that wished to defy the episcopal officials was apparently led by Berthold, the new commander at Wenden. The faction that wished to submit was apparently led by Wickbert, the former commander. As Wickbert's influence declined, he lost hope in his prospects and fled to the protection of Bishop Albert's men.

> Abhorring the fellowship of holy living and disdaining the Militia of Christ, [Wickbert] came to the priest of Idumea, said he wished to await there the arrival of the bishop, and wished to obey the bishop in all things. The Brothers of the Militia, Berthold of Wenden and certain other Brothers and servants, followed this Brother as if he were a fugitive, seized him in Idumea, led him back to Wenden and threw him in chains.[14]

Wickbert was released later, but his influence was completely shattered. Later, after Bishop Albert returned, Wickbert murdered Master Wenno and the chaplain with an ax and took flight. "They caught him quickly in the neighborhood and put him painfully on the rack. No one said much for him, and in that the Germans were good folk. Be he knight or servant, they put him to death as people should traitors."[15]

Subsequent to this, however, Berthold failed to be elected master. Perhaps the Swordbrothers were shocked by the whole business and realized that Berthold was not guiltless, though that was not to excuse Wickbert's actions. A more moderate knight, Volquin of Naumburg, became master. Volquin had a difficult task: to satisfy the demands of Berthold's faction without antagonizing Bishop Albert, which perhaps was impossible. Under the circumstances, Volquin had as much success in the years to come as could be reasonably expected. Wellborn, well connected, and possessed of numerous personal virtues, he was universally respected. This respect was his main asset, and since the order lacked prestige, it was all the more important.[16]

When Bishop Albert returned to Riga in March 1209 he was given even sadder news than the murder of Master Wenno: his brother Engelbert, the prior of Saint Mary's, also was dead. Engelbert, whose activities are rarely mentioned in the sources, was Albert's most dependable official, and he could not be replaced. Even though his successor, John of Scheida, served loyally and well in the years to follow, no one could be trusted like a reliable relative. That left only Theodoric and a brother-in-law, Engelbert of Thisenhusen, who appeared shortly afterward.

Bishop Albert brought with him a numerous army and several important nobles from the area of Magdeburg. To one of those nobles, Rudolf of Jerichow, he gave half the income of Kokenhusen as a tax fief. Rudolf occupied the castle, a third of which went to the Swordbrothers (dividing the premises and the incomes of castles was common in Livonia) and made it into a strong point for the defense of Livonia against the Lithuanians. Later, Engelbert of Thisenhusen married the daughter of the former King, which, in addition to his relationship with Bishop Albert, provided a more conventional feudal claim to possession of the castle.

Important though Kokenhusen was, standing not far from the point where the river changes from a northerly to a westerly flow, it could not monitor the main Lithuanian invasion route into Lettgallia and Russia. Gerzika, about forty miles southeast by river, was the key to that route. Traditionally, the Prince of Gerzika was forced to play a sharp game, balancing the Russians against the Lithuanians and, more recently, placating the newly arrived Germans. Since the Lithuanians were now his strongest neighbors, he tended to favor them, which was unacceptable to Bishop

Albert, who led his men in their deepest penetration of the interior and captured Gerzika. But the Bishop had no wish to destroy the city; he allowed his soldiers to sack the houses and the churches (the citizens were of the eastern persuasion), but he restrained them from unnecessary slaughter. He ordered that the prisoners be kept as hostages and sent word that the ruler could return and seek terms, which he did. Bishop Albert then made a proposal:

> "If you will avoid henceforth association with pagans and, accordingly, not destroy our church through them and, at the same time, not lay waste, through the Lithuanians, the land of your Russian Christians; if, moreover, you will grant your kingdom in perpetuity to the church of Blessed Mary, in order to receive it back from our hand, and rejoice with us joined in peace and harmony, then, when these things have been done, we will restore the queen with all the captives to you and always furnish you faithful aid."[17]

The ruler of Gerzika accepted these terms, thereby becoming a vassal of the Bishop. As a token of the agreement, Bishop Albert gave him three banners, and the ruler swore loyalty to Albert. Although the attempt to convince the native nobles to accept a feudal role failed completely, Albert's persistence indicates that his conception of the new order was not that of a Livonia run by foreigners for foreign benefit but that of a feudal state with the Bishop of Riga as lord and the native nobles as vassals.

Further indications of Bishop Albert's ambitions can be adduced from his Estonian policy. Not interested in expansion to the north or northeast, he sought to restrain the Swordbrothers from attacking the Estonians. He saw no profit in such an attack. Probably Estonia was already promised to King Waldemar, so that if Albert succeeded in conquering the area, he would have to surrender it. Better, therefore, to let King Waldemar fight his own battles and to use the crusaders to establish Christian control along the Dvina. Nor was he interested in fighting the Estonian tribes in Ungannia, because they were tributary to the Russian city of Pskov—and Bishop Albert had arranged to marry his brother Theodoric into the ruling house of Pskov.[18]

Because Albert's policies were so directly opposed to the ambitions of the Swordbrothers, a fundamental conflict lay ahead, as the Swordbrothers disregarded episcopal commands and continued to press into Estonia. Nor were they alone in such endeavor.

King Waldemar of Denmark also was interested in Estonia. His predecessors had exercised hegemony over the entire eastern Baltic, and his ambition was to establish a similar empire. Consequently, he dominated Northern Germany, involved himself in expeditions to Pomerania, Prussia, and Sweden, and kept a close watch on events on the eastern shore of the Baltic. Thus his interest was wholly Baltic. Several years earlier, to curry favor with Pope Innocent III, he had promised to take the cross, but when the Pope reminded him of his obligation, Waldemar had set it aside with the plea that he could not leave his kingdom. The disorder in Germany was too dangerous. When that excuse was no longer valid, the Pope pressed the matter very strongly, and when he placed the Danish kingdom under papal protection so that no one would dare attack it in the absence of the monarch, Waldemar had to make some pretense of fulfilling his vow. Instead of making the long journey to Jerusalem, however, he undertook an expedition to Samland to punish some pirates. Because the crusade to Livonia had equal rank with the crusade to Jerusalem, this fulfilled his crusading vow in a technical sense, but it was primarily part of a continuing Danish interest in a Baltic empire.[19]

Despite the efforts of the Danish Monarch and the crusaders and the merchant communities, the seas were still not safe for Christian commerce, and when Bishop Albert and the crusaders sailed for home in the spring of 1210 they encountered Kurish pirates. About thirty knights and many commoners died in the ensuing combat; the Christians in the large ships sailed away leaving the dead, wounded, and drowning to the pagans.

The surviving crusaders returned to a scene of turmoil. Waldemar of Schleswig, sustained by the peasants of Stedingen and the citizens of Bremen, still maintained control of the left bank of the Elbe. Only once had he wavered—when, depressed by the apparent hopelessness of his situation, he had resigned. His retirement was of short duration, however, because the Bremen canons selected Gerhard of Oldenburg as his successor. This had been followed by widespread protests by those who feared the ambitions of the house of Oldenburg, the traditional enemy of Stedingen and Bremen, and Waldemar had been recalled. He agreed to continue the resistance against the Danes, the Pope, and now the House of Oldenburg as well.[20]

In theory, the Emperor was to intervene in crises such as this and, with the help of the princes, to restore order in a just manner. But Otto IV could not intervene, as he was in Italy, and his deputies in Germany had little influence. Moreover, the princes were distracted and confused by Otto's actions, and none had the talent or respect needed for leadership at this time. No one had foreseen the renewal of the struggle between the Emperor and the Pope. Otto was a Welf, and the Welfs were what modern historians refer to as a state's rights party. Having been a papal ally for years, he had suddenly taken up the Hohenstaufen program. In Northern Germany, shortly after his excommunication, this manifested itself in Otto's urging Waldemar of Schleswig to continue his feud against their common enemies. One result of this was that "Welf" and "Hohenstaufen" became labels of little meaning and were replaced by pro- and anti-Danish parties.

Princes of both parties, who were now identified with Otto's cause, were in a predicament. They had nothing to win and much to lose from the renewal of hostilities and therefore sought a safe refuge. Some of them, such as the Bishops of Verden, Ratzeburg, and Paderborn, declared their intention to accompany Bishop Albert on his next crusade, and thereby they escaped the impending crisis.[21]

From Saxony Bishop Albert had traveled to Rome, and on 20 October—shortly before the excommunication of the Emperor—he had an interview with Pope Innocent III at which Master Volquin of the Swordbrothers was present. Although each presented his argument on the division of the lands, the Pope refused to make a decision without further study. He was interested in unifying the crusaders, if possible, and in preventing either party from seeking aid from the Emperor, and any decision would have antagonized either Albert or Volquin; therefore the decision was postponed. The Pope then warned the Bishop to shun the evil influence of Waldemar of Schleswig; rather, he should support Gerhard of Oldenburg. Bishop Albert probably suggested that he would have fewer difficulties if he were entirely free of obligations to the Archbishop of Bremen; and apparently the Pope agreed, because he not only declared that Bremen was to have no authority over Riga, but he granted the Bishop of Riga the right to found bishoprics and monasteries and to change his cathedral chapter from the Augustinian to the Praemonstratensian rule. These were steps toward independence. So eager was Albert to forward these reports to Livonia that he sent messengers overland through Prussia that very winter.[22]

When Bishop Albert returned north he found the princes in arms against the Danes—Brandenburg, Saxony, Bremen, and Schwerin having combined against King Waldemar. But Albert could not afford to offend

Denmark, and he remained neutral in word and deed, if not perhaps in thought. Besides, these princes were overmatched. He therefore concentrated on gathering his crusaders together for the voyage east.[23]

During the Bishop's absence, Livonia had been ravaged by war. The natives, previously divided by traditional hatreds, had begun to unite and cooperate against the westerners. The Estonians came down from the north, the Lithuanians moved up from the south, and some Livs rebelled while the Kurs sailed in from the west. The latter almost captured Riga, but the city was saved because, while the Germans were trying to forget their quarrels over land in the face of the common danger, Caupo and the Livonians came to their aid. Liv hostility to the neighboring tribes and loyalty to the new religion were more important than any independence that might be gained. Moreover, a crusader defeat would have meant only a change of masters, and therefore the Livs remained loyal. Even so, the situation was desperate, and only by combining their strength were the Christians able to defend their castles against the numerous attacks. The most serious defeat occurred when a crusader force was ambushed on the road to Wenden, and many Christian captives suffered martyrdom. Finally, the onset of winter forced the attackers to lift the sieges and return home.

Stung by these setbacks and threatened by renewed attack in the spring, the Christians decided to secure their northern flank during the winter. They already had alliances with the Prince of Pskov, and now another alliance, with the Prince of Polozk, brought further Russian assistance for an attack on the Estonians. Bishop Albert's brother-in-law, Engelbert of Thisenhusen, directed the attack on Fellin, the stronghold of the Saccalians.

> The pagans would listen to nothing about God or the Christian name. They rather threatened war and donned the arms of the Germans which they had seized at the gate of the fort during the first engagement. On the heights of the fort they gloried in these arms, they prepared themselves for war, and with their shouting they jeered and mocked at the army. Russin and the Letts, however, having taken all the captives and slaughtered them, threw them into the moat and threatened to do the same to those who were in the fort. The archers, meanwhile, killed many men and drove them all back to the stronghold, while other men built a tower. The Livonians and Letts carried wood and filled the moat up, from bottom to top, and pushed the tower over it. The Letts and ballistarii went up on the tower, killed many men on the battlements with arrows and spears, wounded many, and for five days a very great battle raged. The Estonians strove to burn down the first pile of wood by casting a great

deal of fire from the fort onto the carts. The Livonians and Letts threw ice and snow and put it out. Arnold, a Brother of the Militia, labored there day and night. At last he was hit by a stone and crossed over into the brotherhood of the martyrs. He was an extremely religious man and was always praying. He found, as we hope, that for which he prayed. The Germans built a machine and, by hurling stones night and day, they broke down the fortified places and killed men and innumerable beasts of burden in the fort. Since the Estonians had never seen such things, they had not strengthened their houses against the force of such missiles. The Livonians added dry wood to the pile of wood up to the plankwork. Eylard of Dolen climbed up on top. The Germans followed in arms, removed the planks, and, on the inside, found another wall which they could not get through. The men of the fort gathered up above and forced the Germans back by throwing stones and logs. The Germans came down, brought flames to the fort and set it on fire. The Estonians pulled apart the flaming planks and the burning timbers of the wall and dragged them away. On the next day, when the burning was over, they replaced everything, and the survivors nerved themselves once again for the defense. There were, however, many corpses of the slain in the fort, there was a shortage of water, and nearly everyone was wounded, so that now they gave out. On the sixth day the Germans said: "Do you still resist and refuse to acknowledge our Creator?" To this they replied: "We acknowledge your God to be greater than our gods. By overcoming us, He has inclined our hearts to worship Him. We beg, therefore, that you spare us and mercifully impose the yoke of Christianity upon us as you have upon the Livonians and Letts." [24]

This was a significant victory, for Fellin controlled all Saccalia, but it was not an unconditional victory. The Estonians surrendered hostages and accepted priests, but no garrison was introduced into the fort. And the war continued with the other tribes.

The Estonians were pressing the war into Livonia when Bishop Albert arrived in the spring of 1211. They were besieging Caupo's fort at Treiden, but not too closely at first because of the crossbowmen who had been sent from Riga. At length, however, they began serious efforts that threatened to carry the defenses. This violated the tradition of native warfare, but the Estonians saw that the Germans were a real danger to their independence and that they had to strike quickly before the invaders became even stronger.

Although their assumptions were correct, the Estonians had waited too long. Bishop Albert had brought the Bishops of Ratzeburg, Verden, and Paderborn, Count Helmold of Plesse, and the famous warrior Bernard zu Lippe with him; and each was accompanied by large forces. Realizing that the loss of Caupo's fort might be ruinous to the Christian cause, because Caupo was the most loyal supporter the Christians had, Bishop Albert marched his forces out at the earliest moment.

They donned their weapons, put the trappings on their horses, and with their infantry, the Livonians, and their whole company made their way to the Aa. They crossed the Aa, went on through the night, and approached the pagans. They arranged the army and instructed it for the war. The infantry they sent ahead on the major road which leads to Wendendorf. The knights, however, followed on the road which leads to the right. The infantry marched cautiously and in orderly fashion. When morning broke they came down from the mountain and saw the fort and the pagan army, and the valley was between them. Immediately they beat joyfully upon their drum and enlivened the spirits of their men with their musical instruments and their song. They called down God's mercy upon them and swiftly hurried towards the pagans. After crossing a little stream they halted for a moment to collect themselves in a group. When the pagans saw them, they were terrified by the unmistakable prospect. They ran, got their shields; some of them rushed to the horses, others leaped over the barricade, and they all assembled in one group. They troubled the air with their shouts and came out in a great multitude to meet the Christians, throwing a shower of spears upon them. The Christians caught the spears with their shields, and when the pagans had run out of spears, the Christians drew their swords, marched closer and commenced the fight. The wounded fell and the pagans fought manfully. The knights saw the strength of the pagans and suddenly charged through the center of the enemy. The trappings of the horses threw terror into the enemy. Many of them fell to the ground, the others turned to flight, and the Christians pursued those who fled. They caught them and killed them on the road and in the fields. The Livonians from the fort went out with the ballistarii and met the fleeing pagans. They scattered them on the road and enveloped them. Then they slaughtered them, up to the German lines. They pursued the Estonians so that few of them escaped and the Germans even killed some of the Livonians as if they were Estonians.[25]

Other units cut off the retreat by land and by sea. Indeed, the slaughter was so tremendous that it would be many years before a native force would again dare to meet the Christians in open battle. Now the way was open to expand into Estonia and, willy-nilly, Bishop Albert had to allow expansion in that direction. However, he was careful not to lose control of the situation in Estonia. If he gave permission, the Swordbrothers would sweep in with the crusaders, as the orders had done in the Holy Land and as the

Teutonic Knights would attempt to do in Hungary. Fully aware of their ambitions, Albert took steps to constrain them.

His first and shrewdest move was to appoint the Cistercian priest, Theodoric, as Bishop of Estonia. Theodoric, one of the founders of the Sword-brothers, was perhaps more responsible for their foundation than any other individual. And he had been their constant supporter. But as Bishop of Estonia he would have responsibilities that would run counter to the ambitions of the order. Also, he would have to deal with the Danish King, perhaps taking some of the pressure off Bishop Albert. This appointment left the important post at Dünamünde vacant, but Albert filled it with the seasoned warrior Bernard zu Lippe, who had entered the Cistercian order a few years previously. Despite his great age, Bernard remained active, and he could cope with any difficulty. A warrior who had earned a great reputation in the previous generation, he held no fear of pagans or crusading orders. Moreover, on crusade in Livonia also, was his son and namesake, the Bishop of Paderborn. The Bishop then negotiated anew the tithe with the native tribes, promised the Gothland merchants safety, justice, and financial stability, and confirmed the division of the lands with the Sword-brothers. When all this was complete, he left the government in the hands of the Bishops of Ratzeburg, Verden, and Paderborn and sailed back to Germany to raise more crusaders.[26]

In the following winter, 1211–1212, the crusaders made a decisive discovery in military strategy: they learned that winter was the best season for warfare. All of their subsequent campaigns were based on this elementary discovery. In Saxony the winters were long and wet but relatively mild, snow covered the ground only a few days each year, and persistent mist and light rain made the ground soggy and the roads impassable. This combination of wet and cold endangered the health of those who remained away from shelter for extended periods. Fighting on horseback under such conditions was difficult, and if knights took advantage of the occasional freeze to sally out, a sudden thaw could disconcert them considerably. Consequently, North German knights tended to spend the long winter evenings in their drafty houses and castles awaiting the return of spring.

In Livonia, on the other hand, a continental climate prevailed. The winters were much longer and colder, the ground and rivers froze, and the air was dry, so that winter was often more suitable for cavalry operations than summer. The swamps froze, the winter underbrush was less bothersome, and the natives had more difficulty hiding in the snowy forests. Thus the knights took the lessons of the previous winter to heart and began a systematic campaign to break the back of Estonian resistance. More than 4,000 German crusaders—infantry and cavalry—used the frozen rivers as highways into the heart of hostile territory.

The success of the crusaders' operations caused their Russian neighbors considerable anxiety. The citizens of Novgorod responded to the Estonians' appeals for aid, but their army remained in Estonia only a short while and withdrew without accomplishing anything. More significant, however, the citizens of Pskov, who were subjects of Novgorod, overthrew their Prince and his German son-in-law and sent help to their Estonian neighbors (whereupon other Estonian tribes, taking advantage of the absence of the army, attacked Pskov and pillaged it). But though the Russian intervention failed in its basic intent—to drive the westerners out—it succeeded in forestalling the German hope of establishing Theodoric as Bishop of Estonia. When Bishop Albert returned to Livonia in the spring of 1212 he sought a truce with the Russians and brought an end to the fighting. Although he forced the Prince of Polozk to recognize his independence from any feudal ties such as might be claimed from years past, Albert could not obtain immediate control of Estonia, and this delay was to prove fatal.[27]

We might understand Bishop Albert's policy better if we remind ourselves of his goals. He wished to govern by means of officials who would be responsible to him and through minor vassals as well—preferably native princes but also some German nobles—who would serve as *ministeriales*. He would entrust all important positions only to members of his family or to prudent clerics. He made his brother Engelbert prior of Saint Mary's, married his brother Theodoric to a daughter of the Prince of Pskov, and after the revolution gave Theodoric and Prince Vladimir important posts in Livonia. This was common practice in Northern Germany, not an innovation, and was certainly understood by men like Bernard zu Lippe, whose family was notorious for its nepotism. Having thus placed trustworthy men in positions of command, Albert conciliated the natives by offering them protection and justice and by allowing them to govern themselves as long as they recognized the supremacy of the Bishop, paid their taxes and tithes, and followed the Christian religion. In short, Albert wanted a strong, independent feudal state, organized along western lines but conforming to native practices wherever necessary.

This policy was challenged by the Russians, by the Order of Swordbrothers, and by the Danes, who in a sense were the most dangerous, for

84

in 1206 the Archbishop of Lund had obtained papal authority to supervise all missionary activity in the Baltic region. The Russians also wished to rule Livonia, but inasmuch as they could not provide security to the natives they were a declining influence, although militarily they remained a great threat. The Swordbrothers were a lesser threat at first, but in the end were the most dangerous: they were too strong to crush and too active to ignore. Besides, their cooperation was needed.

As Bishop Albert could not afford a civil war, he sought to prevent the order's becoming more powerful. This policy only antagonized the order, and the two factions clashed on issue after issue, such as their basic disagreement over the policy toward the natives. Bishop Albert, in hope of winning the allegiance of the native tribes, offered redress to grievances against the intolerant knights, and thus when the Livs rose against the order in 1212, he was able to quell the disturbance easily. But however popular Albert's program with the natives—and it was not always popular—he was to have much trouble with his competitors: the Danes, the Russians, and especially the Swordbrothers.

Bishop Albert had heard many complaints against the Swordbrothers, and it was always the same story: the knights believed in conversion by the sword and could not understand the process of conversion by persuasion. The Bishops, however, could not have corrected the increasingly self-reliant order even if they had wished to. Although Bishop Albert promised to correct the injustices to the natives around Segewold, he did not move quickly enough to prevent the unrest from developing into violence. Bishop Philip of Ratzeburg and Albert's brother Theodoric were sent with the prior of Saint Mary's to Segewold to investigate, but the situation soon became one of open rebellion. Because the rebels were advocating a return to paganism, Bishop Albert felt compelled to support the Swordbrothers, and thus the episcopal army marched north.

The rebels stoutly resisted the attacks on their forts, but the German forces filled the moats or ditches and moved wooden towers to the wall, attacking the rampart and the base at the same moment. The rebel commander was slain on his own rampart by an arrow while talking peace, and other elders were seized during another conference.

At length they gave up, raised Blessed Mary's standard on high, and bowed their necks to the bishop. They humbly besought him to spare them and promised that they would immediately accept the neglected faith of Christ, that they would henceforth observe the sacraments faithfully, and that they would never again call to mind pagan rites. The bishop had pity on them. He forbade the army to sneak into the fort or to kill the suppliants, or to deliver the souls of so many to hell fire.[28]

As punishment, their taxes were doubled. If Bishop Albert was willing to deal with the natives in such a rigorous manner, it should be no surprise that his officials were even harsher.

Albert sailed back to Germany in the spring of 1213, having bound the crusaders by truces with all the neighboring peoples. He had left Bishop Philip of Ratzeburg in charge of affairs, and although few soldiers came to Livonia with the Bishop of Münster on crusade, all took heart by anticipating a larger force in the next year.[29]

The Order of Swordbrothers also had a dream of an ideal state. Like the orders in the Holy Land, the brothers wished to be independent of any outside power and thus free to govern and expand their lands as they saw fit. Their public ambition was the same as Albert's: the conversion of the natives. Their private ambition was perhaps the same: the exercise of power. But their methods differed widely. To become independent, they had to overcome the resistance of the Bishop, and this could be done only with outside help; so the Swordbrothers began to involve themselves in international politics. They visited the Pope and asked that he remove their lands from the supervision of the Bishop of Riga. Unsuccessful in this, they went to Emperor Otto IV, who granted their request and declared their lands to be an independent fief of the Empire. Otto was not particularly interested in their problem, except that it meant an easy acquisition of adherents to his cause, and perhaps anticipating further imperial help, the crusading order began to draw away from the papacy.

Innocent III was not a Pope who could be defied or ignored with impunity. Perhaps the strongest Pope in the history of the Church, he had humbled the monarchs of France, England, and Spain, had fought German Emperors to a standstill, and had launched crusade after crusade in every direction. Under his urging, the crusading movement reached its apogee—in the Holy Land, Egypt, Constantinople, southern France, and the Baltic. (In 1212 even the children went on crusade.) When Innocent finally decided to remove the Welf Emperor, it was but a short time till his candidate, the Hohenstaufen Frederick II, crossed the Alps and rallied many Germans to his cause. Nevertheless, since victory required taking and holding many castles and cities, no quick decision could be obtained. In fact, it was not the Hohenstaufen army that finally defeated Otto IV but rather that of King Philip Augustus, for it was the French victory at Bouvines in 1214 that knocked both the Welf and Angevin forces out of the war. Otto lost his crown, and King John of England barely saved his.

As Frederick II moved northward the princes requested his assistance in driving the Danes from Holstein, Mecklenburg, and Pomerania; but Frederick came to an understanding with King Waldemar that left those lands under permanent Danish control, which angered and dejected the northern Princes. Some, such as the Counts of Schwerin, swallowed their pride and submitted to the Danes. Others continued to plot a war of liberation, without imperial help, similar to that fought by their fathers against Henry the Lion thirty-five years earlier.

Pope Innocent's impressive display of power in overthrowing the Welf Emperor caused the Swordbrothers to reconsider their allegiance, and soon they were back at the papal court in Rome. As Albert was busy in Germany, Bishop Theodoric had to cut short his visit to Holland and hurry to Rome to answer the charges the Swordbrothers had brought against the Bishop of Riga. The Pope had already ordered Abbot Bernard zu Lippe to defend the interests of the crusading order against Bishop Albert, but when Theodoric informed the Pope that he had been duped, the Pope sternly warned the knights against future deceptions. Theodoric represented Albert's cause faithfully, and the Pope ordered every prelate in the north to send priests to Riga to assist in the conversion and guidance of the natives; he also reconfirmed Riga's independence of metropolitan control. Bishop Theodoric then traveled north to Lübeck, where he, Bishop Albert, and the representatives of the Swordbrothers took ship for Riga.

When Bishop Philip of Ratzeburg heard that the Danish King was still dominant in North Germany, he decided to remain in Livonia rather than return to Rome with Bishop Albert to attend the Fourth Lateran Council. He and Bishop Theodoric would go later. Meanwhile they would attend to affairs in the crusader state so that Bishop Albert could sail back to Germany and from there travel to Italy.

The first problem that arose was a question of treason. Bishop Philip, who was in charge of Livonia during Albert's absence, had condemned the Prince of Gerzika for his failure to perform court service; he had not once visited the Bishop. More suspicious, his father-in-law, who had been captured by the Swordbrothers on his return from a visit to Novgorod, had committed suicide in prison, which was construed as a confession of treason. Bishop Philip had therefore summoned the Prince to court to explain these matters, and when he failed to comply with the summons, Philip ordered the knights to attack Gerzika, which they occupied. The Prince fled to Russia, but would later continue the fight against the Germans.

Also, Bishop Philip had a war on his northern frontier, where the crusaders had customarily dealt cruelly with the natives, but where the natives were even more cruel to one another. When the Swordbrothers took a large native force to Rotalia that winter (1214–1215),

> they found all the men, women, and children, and everyone, large and small, in the villages, for they had not been forewarned of the army's approach by any rumors. In their wrath the soldiers struck them and killed all the men. Both the Livonians and Letts, who are more cruel than the other nations, like the servant in the gospel, did not know how to show mercy. They killed countless people and slaughtered some of the women and children. They wished to spare no one in the fields or in the villages. They stained the streets and every spot with the blood of the pagans.[30]

This was typical of a Baltic campaign. There was little warning and practically no possibility of escape in wintertime. There was the surprise, then the slaughter, and then the march of the prisoners—soon to be slaves of the crusaders and their native allies—back into Livonia. Then came the retaliation.

Early in 1215 the Estonians from Oesel, Rotalia, Saccalia, and Ungannia invaded Livonia by land and sea. Part of their plan, to block the mouth of the Dvina, was frustrated only by the chance arrival of a Count of Oldenburg-Wildeshausen and Bishop Albert's two brothers in two cogs at the same moment that a force from Riga was attacking the pagans. Elsewhere, the Livs and the Letts evaded the Estonians' attacks by fleeing into the forests and forts. As the Estonians retired, the Christian natives gathered for an attack upon Ungannia and Saccalia.

> They entered Ungannia, despoiled all the villages, and delivered them to the flames. They burned alive all the men they could in revenge. . . . They burned down all the forts, so that they would have no refuge in them. They sought out the Ungannians in the dark hiding places of the forests and the Ungannians could hide from them nowhere. They took them out of the forests and killed them and took the women and children away as captives. They drove off the horses and flocks, took many spoils, and returned to their own land. As they returned, other Letts again met them on the road and they marched into Ungannia. What the former had neglected, the latter performed.[31]

88

To read further in this long and blood-soaked passage is unnecessary—the Saccalians and Ungannians sued for peace and offered to undergo baptism and pay tribute; the other tribes also broke off hostilities. The atrocities of war change little throughout the ages, and the descriptions of border warfare in Livonia are equaled by other accounts throughout the world; but in few areas has the intensity of warfare endured so long. This same description fits almost every campaign that was waged in this area by Christian or pagan in the next several hundred years.

In the summer of 1215 Bishops Philip and Theodoric sailed for Lübeck en route to the great council in Rome and found affairs in Northern Germany surprisingly stable. Somewhat earlier, King Waldemar of Denmark had been surrounded by a hostile coalition of minor princes and, instinctively, had attacked the most dangerous, his uncle, Waldemar of Schleswig. But his attack on Stade was disrupted by the intervention of a Welf Prince, and Waldemar had to withdraw across the Elbe. The outlook grew bleaker when, shortly thereafter, Otto IV returned north and promised to support the Princes in their war of liberation, and at first all went badly for the Dane. Unfortunately for the princes, shortly after Otto captured Hamburg, the Welf Prince had to break off operations and hurry south to Magdeburg. King Waldemar then took the offensive and captured Stade and, after a long siege, Hamburg. The collapse of the coalition and his subsequent agreement with Frederick II left Waldemar secure in the north.

Another result was the end of the war in the archbishopric of Bremen. Faced by overwhelming odds, Bishop Waldemar's supporters went over to Gerhard of Oldenburg and the citizens of Bremen, and the peasants of Stedingen won reasonable concessions, perhaps because Bishop Waldemar was continuing his resistance from nearby Frisia. After he inspected his diocese, however, Archbishop Gerhard learned that his victory was not as valuable as he had expected. Not only had the archbishopric been devastated by a long and costly war (Bishop Waldemar had liquidated most of the church assets to pay for the war), but Archbishop Gerhard, of course, had anticipated paying his own heavy debts from the assets he would acquire from Bishop Waldemar. Also, he had to maintain an expensive army to ward off the remnants of the Welf forces still in the area. To pay his creditors he had to levy new taxes and reclaim his lost properties, but how he could do this without antagonizing his subjects was an insoluble problem.[32]

War in the north, in any event, was no longer particularly important in the early years of the thirteenth century, at least in comparison with the universal fervor for the crusade in the Holy Land. Even the Danish vassal, Albert of Orlamünde, wrote the Pope that he intended to take the cross. Accordingly, all attention was drawn to Rome, where hundreds of prelates began to converge for the Lateran Council of 1215, including Bishops Philip and Theodoric who sailed from Riga that summer.

Shortly after leaving the Dvina they encountered stormy weather that drove their nine ships into a harbor on Oesel Island, and bad weather prevented the crusaders from sailing away before the natives had blocked the harbor with sunken vessels. They were surrounded by hostile tribes, and more enemy ships came daily from all the nearby peoples, so that soon they were greatly outnumbered. Their ships escaped destruction by fireships because, perhaps, fervent prayer brought a shift in the wind and hard labor put out the fires. Then the Christians hauled their vessels between the sunken hulls and out of the harbor by advancing the anchors step by step on small boats, dropping them, and pulling the vessels forward on the anchor ropes, while the natives attacked the small boats and each day engaged the fleet in a seafight. Above the shouting and the clashing of weapons the chanting of the Mass continued unabated. After three weeks their food was exhausted, and still the winds were unfavorable. Finally, on 22 July, the winds changed and the crusaders sailed to Gothland. Bishop Philip, who meanwhile had fallen ill, continued the exhausting journey south into Italy; but it proved too much for him, and he died in Verona.[33]

The Lateran Council was the greatest assemblage of churchmen in the memory of living men, and its subjects of discussion were worthy of the time and expense involved. Among other important topics, Pope Innocent III proposed a new crusade. The Emperor Frederick II was to lead it, and all secular quarrels were to be laid aside for four years so that all who wished could participate. To finance the crusade the Pope proposed an income tax of five percent on all members of the clergy, except the Cardinals and the Pope, who would contribute ten percent. Agreement was soon reached, and it was decided that the fleet would sail from Brindisi in June 1217.

Bishop Albert did not miss this opportunity to profit from the general enthusiasm. In November he spoke about the crusading movement in the Baltic, describing the trials and tribulations of war in the cold and distant northeast. He told of its past successes, and of its hopes for the future, and pleaded that his crusade not be neglected by the Church fathers. The Pope responded by recognizing Livonia as the Land of the Virgin Mary and by issuing a call for a new crusade to Livonia. Albert then hurried north to the Court of Frederick II, and in January or March 1216 spoke to the Emperor at Hagenau. Frederick II gave him encouragement and promised assistance to his crusade.

The crusaders had gathered, as usual, in Lübeck and, as soon as the weather permitted, Albert sailed with the annual contingent. When they arrived in Riga he learned that war with Russia was imminent, the Germans having expanded into parts of Estonia that were traditionally tributary to Russian Princes and the Estonians having appealed for Russian assistance. Thus the Russians and the Germans prepared to fight for control of the Estonian tribes that lived between them. Already there had been border raids, and outright war was in the offing.

Threatened with invasion by thousands of Russian troops, Bishop Albert's supporters had tried to conciliate the Swordbrothers by territorial concessions so as to form a united front against this most formidable enemy. Bishop Albert agreed and came to terms with the crusading order: he would retain one-third of Estonia, the Swordbrothers one-third, and Bishop Theodoric the remaining one-third. Having reached this agreement, the Christians invaded Saccalia and Harrien with the intent of subduing the region before the Russians could intervene in force. Soon thereafter, the Pskovians invaded Ungannia, ravaged the land as a warning against submission to the Germans, and returned a captured Rigan merchant with their declaration of war. (Merchants were generally considered neutral in these matters; indeed, the Rigans considered robbery much more reprehensible than the murder of their subjects!) The Germans, in turn, captured the Russian tax agents in Ungannia and held them until the Prince of Novgorod arranged for their release. Presumably, both sides agreed to allow merchants to conduct their business regardless of the political situation, and that policy was continued in the future.

The crusaders built a castle at Odenpäh to secure southern Ungannia. When the Pskovians complained about this intrusion into their territories, the Swordbrothers gathered a large number of Ungannians and invaded Russia.

On the feast of the Epiphany [6 January 1217], when the Russians are accustomed to occupy themselves more with their feastings and drinking, they divided their army among all the roads and villages. They killed many people, took captive a great many women, and drove off many horses and flocks. They took much loot and, having revenged their injuries with fire and the sword, they returned rejoicing to Odenpäh with all the loot.[34]

The Prince of Pskov called upon the Novgorodians for assistance, and together they invaded Ungannia, drove the Swordbrothers back into Odenpäh, and besieged the castle for seventeen days. The Germans estimated the size of the Russian force at 20,000. Certainly the Russians had many men, perhaps too many, because their supplies were insufficient. The garrison might have held out indefinitely if Volquin and Berthold of Wenden had not joined with Theodoric, the Bishop's brother, in an attempt to raise the siege. Their 3,000 troops were badly beaten and driven within the walls of Odenpäh as the siege resumed. The Germans, having exhausted their supplies, were starving inside the castle, and the Russians were starving outside. At last the Russians proposed that the Germans abandon the castle to the Russians and return to Riga unhindered. A truce was decreed and the Germans marched out. The Prince of Pskov violated the agreement by seizing Theodoric, his son-in-law, but the rest of the army escaped without incident.

Bishop Albert sought to turn this truce into a general peace, but the Russians informed him that they were determined to destroy his state. It appeared that Estonia was lost, and that even Livonia was threatened, when in the spring of 1217 Bishop Albert sailed to Germany to recruit more soldiers. The Russian attitude to all this is indicated in the *Chronicle of Novgorod*, which describes the entire campaign in very few words but devotes many paragraphs to obscure civil wars.[35]

Fortunately, 1217 was a good year for raising crusading armies. Innocent III had been issuing notice after notice of the crusade to the Holy Land, but he had not neglected Northern Germany. He ordered the bankrupt Archbishop of Bremen to make his required contribution of five percent of his income, and so pressed the nobility that many of them took the cross for the Holy Land. As the Pope's life drew to a close, he became increasingly insistent about fulfilling crusading vows and again warned Archbishop Gerhard to make his monetary contribution to the crusade. As a result, many people from that area, especially the poorer people, answered his summons. Meanwhile Bishop Theodoric was preaching the crusade, thereby continuing the practice by which the Bishops of Livonia recruited crusaders for the conquest of their sees.[36]

The Pope's insistence that everyone fulfill his crusading vows embarrassed Count Albert of Orlamünde, who suddenly learned that many of his vassals had volunteered to undertake the journey to the Holy Land. He had already taken the cross himself, but the vow often did not specify a particular date, and he had planned to make his crusade in Livonia. Naturally he wanted his vassals to accompany him. He wrote the Pope, asking that his vassals be allowed to fulfill their vows in Livonia, and Pope Honorius III, Innocent's successor, granted his request. By the spring of 1217 Count Albert was ready to sail. Though we cannot be certain of his motive for making this crusade, it seems to have been connected with the plans of his Danish overlord to establish a foothold in Estonia. Also, it was very important that Albert be able to return speedily to Holstein. For northern nobles, as well as for German merchants, it was much more convenient— and cheaper—to crusade in Livonia than in Palestine.[37] Thus while one crusade sailed for Damietta and disaster, another crusade sailed for Livonia.

A new phase of the Livonian crusade had begun, as Bishop Albert was no longer in full command. He had relied upon imperial help and native vassals, and both had failed him. His household forces were insufficient, even when augmented by the native militia. The Swordbrothers had become too powerful, and he could neither suppress them nor survive without them. The Russians threatened to destroy his state, and at long last the Danes were coming to make good their claims on Estonia. Indeed, Bishop Albert's command of the situation had somehow slipped away, and now he was practically at the mercy of his enemies.

N o t e s   t o   C h a p t e r   F i v e

1. *Henry of Livonia*, p. 70. This is very similar to misgovernment in the archdiocese of Hamburg-Bremen; see *Hamburgisches Urkundenbuch*, 1: 319.

2. *Henry of Livonia*, p. 76.

3. Ibid., pp. 72–73.

4. William Urban, "The Organization of the Defense of The Livonian Frontier," *Speculum* (July 1973): 525–32.

5. Footnote in *Hamburgisches Urkundenbuch*, 1: 320–21; Usinger, *Deutsch-dänische Geschichte*, pp. 134–45; *Albert of Stade*, p. 355.

6. *Braunschweigische Reimchronik*, p. 537. She died a week after her marriage, however.

7. *Sächsische Weltchronik*, p. 238.

8. *Arnold of Lübeck*, Ch. 7: para. 15.

9. Usinger, *Deutsch-dänische Geschichte*, p. 149.

10. Henry of Livonia, p. 152.

11. Ibid., p. 79.

12. Ibid., p. 81.

13. See Benninghoven, *Schwertbrüder*, pp. 95–97.

14. *Henry of Livonia*, pp. 88–89.

15. *Reimchronik*, pp. 710–16.

16. Benninghoven (*Schwertbrüder*, pp. 98–104) identifies the new Master as Volquin II of Naumburg. His family was closely connected to the noble houses of Lippe and Schwalenberg, to the Cistercian Abbot of Hardenhausen, and to Bishop Albert. His son Widekind later became Grandmaster of the Teutonic Knights, and his other son Louis also was a member of that order.

17. *Henry of Livonia*, pp. 92–93.

18. Ibid., p. 120.

19. Fredrich Christoph Dahlmann, *Geschichte von Dännemark* (Hamburg: Friedrich Perth, 1840), 1: 360–61; Koch, *Livland und des Reich*, p. 32; Hausmann, *Das Ringen des Deutschen und Dänen um den Besitz Estlands*, pp. 3–4; *Urkundenbuch*, 3: document no. XVa; Paul Johansen in his *Die Estlandliste des Liber census Daniae* (Copenhagen: H. Hagerup, 1933), p. 107, says that this event indicates the Danish interest in Prussia, but he contends that Waldemar had no interest in Kurland, Semgallia, or Lithuania.

20. Usinger, *Deutsch-dänische Geschichte*, pp. 151–69; *Hamburgisches Urkundenbuch*, 1: 341; *Albert of Stade*, p. 355.

21. *Henry of Livonia*, p. 96.

22. Ibid., pp. 108–9; *Urkundenbuch*, 1: document no. XVI. Later, in 1213, Bishop Albert was freed from all metropolitan claims. *Urkundenbuch*, 1: no. XXVI; Koch, *Livland und das Reich*, p. 43.

23. Usinger, *Deutsch-dänische Geschichte*, pp. 164–65.

24. *Henry of Livonia*, pp. 105–6.

25. Ibid., pp. 111–12.

26. Ibid., pp. 113–14; Benninghoven, *Schwertbrüder*, pp. 116–17; Koch, *Livland und das Reich*, p. 43.

27. *Henry of Livonia*, pp. 117–23.

28. Ibid., p. 128; for a more detailed analysis of Livonian feudalism as it developed later, see Astaf von Transehe-Roseneck, "Zur Geschichte des Lehnwesens in Livland," in *Mitteilungen aus dem Gebiet der livländischen Geschichte*, 18 (1903).

29. *Urkundenbuch*, footnote, 3: 40.

30. *Henry of Livonia*, p. 138.

31. Ibid., p. 145.

32. *Albert von Stade*, p. 356; Wilhelm von Bippen, *Aus Bremens Vorzit: Aufsätze zur Geschichte der Stadt Bremen* (Bremen: C. Schunemann, 1885), p. 124.

33. *Henry of Livonia*, pp. 147–51.

34. Ibid., pp. 157–58.

35. *Chronicle of Novgorod, 1016–1471*, trans. Robert Michell and Nevil Forbes, Camden Third Series, Vol. 25 (London, 1914), p. 58.

36. Friedrich Georg von Bunge, *Livland, die Wiege der deutschen Weihbishöfe* (Leipzig: E. Bidder, 1875).

37. Hausmann, *Das Ringen der Deutschen und Dänen um den Besitz Estlands*, p. 9; Usinger, *Deutsch-dänische Geschichte*, pp. 194, 440.

6

Danish Intervention and the Conquest of Estonia

THE RINGING DECLARATIONS OF THE FOURTH LATERAN COUNCIL ON BEHALF of the crusading movement and the subsequent decision by the University of Paris that evasion of the crusading obligation was a mortal sin forced many princes to fulfill the vows they had taken many months or years before. This was important for Livonia because, at last, the Danish King and his vassals set out with large forces against the pagans in the eastern Baltic. The first of his men to sail east was Albert of Orlamünde, the Count of Holstein, who took a small army with him in the summer of 1217. Also voyaging with him was Bernard zu Lippe, Abbot of Dünamünde and a noted warrior of another generation. Their families had been on opposite sides of the Welf-Hohenstaufen struggle, but now that was past history, suitable for fireside recitation but unrealistic in the present conditions. Their immediate goals were exactly the same—the conquest of Estonia, but beyond that each man had his own plans. Count Albert had feudal obligations and political agreements that put him in conflict with Bishop Albert. Therefore his crusaders came as a welcome reinforcement, but he also brought a dangerous challenge to episcopal control over Livonia.

As the situation stood, Bishop Albert, who remained in Germany, had little choice but to accept any crusader who was willing to sail east and to send him off joyfully. The Russian threat was greater than ever because the Prince of Novgorod and the Prince of Pskov had promised to bring a large army in September to join the 6,000 Estonians from Rotalia, Harrien, Wierland, Reval, Jerwan, and Saccalia, who were already assembled near the Lettish frontier. Knowing they had little hope of defeating the enemy forces once they had joined together, the crusader leaders decided to march north with all their armies and attack the Estonians before the Prince of Novgorod arrived. They raised about 3,000 troops from the crusaders, the Swordbrothers, the episcopal household, and the natives (the contingents being about equally divided between Saxons and natives) and carefully proceeded north so as to avoid ambush. Master Volquin was in command, and his army marched in battle formation to the hilly and wooded country around Fellin, where it captured several Estonians and forced them to divulge information.

Learning that the Estonians were numerous and eager for battle, Volquin divided his forces into three formations: the Saxon knights and their followers (both mounted and infantry) in the center and the Letts and the Livs to the left and right respectively. When each unit was in position, he gave the order to move forward. They had not progressed far up the road when the Estonians came out of the wood, mounted and in three bodies of troops.

The Saxon knights charged and broke through the Estonian formations opposite them, scattering the enemy in all directions. The native troops on the wings met stiffer resistance, but the Letts overthrew their opponents and killed the foremost Estonian chieftain. Only the Livs suffered a defeat; they had taken up the pursuit of the Estonians in the center, who were fleeing the Germans, and had exposed their flank. Consequently they were taken in the rear by the Estonian wing opposite them and routed from the field. Within minutes the center rallied to the support of the Livs and drove the last Estonians from the field, but the damage had been done: Caupo had fallen. The victors pursued the fugitives into the wood and killed many of them there, so that perhaps more than a thousand perished in that afternoon's fighting. After tending to the wounded and dead, the Christians divided the 2,000 captured horses and all the weapons and other booty equally among themselves.

The crusaders mourned the death of Caupo, their faithful friend who had done so much for Christianity in Livonia and without whose aid their mission most likely would have failed long ago. Probably his tribesmen mourned him as well. Two decades earlier they had been the most despised of all the tribes, victims of attack from all quarters, but for several years now they had been on the offensive, repaying their enemies for their terror and enriching themselves on the booty. Their chief had been admitted to the councils of the Christians and entrusted with military commands. Their tribal prestige had never been so great.

The Estonians also mourned. Their tremendous battle losses were such a blow to their tribal morale that they offered no opposition to accepting Christianity and surrendering hostages. Each tribe came forward, accepted the crusaders' conditions, and agreed to pay a tax to Bishop Albert in perpetuity, after which they were left in peace. The Russians did not come to their aid.

Count Albert, however, was not satisfied with the surrender of the tribes along the Livonian frontier. Because the maritime Estonians, notorious pirates and old enemies of the Danish kingdom, remained strong and vigorous he proposed an expedition to Oesel and began to make prepara-

tions for the attack. The other crusaders, however, had little interest in
such an expedition because the island lay in the Danish sphere of influence.
Knowing it was Danish policy to subject all the land along the Baltic,
whether pagan or Christian, to King Waldemar, the crusaders from Riga
saw little reason to fight such fierce warriors when there were other conquests to be made. They were more interested in the interior provinces of
Estonia, which they had already divided up among themselves. Naturally,
Albert of Orlamünde, a Danish vassal, viewed all this differently, and he
proceeded through the fall and winter with plans for his attack (alone if
necessary), until the melting of the ice made a foot-army crossing to Oesel
impossible. As a compromise the united crusaders turned their attention
to Rotalia and Reval and forced the natives to accept baptism, surrender
hostages, and pay tribute.

The crusading vows were fulfilled when spring arrived, and Count
Albert sailed for home accompanied by Abbot Bernard. When they met
King Waldemar and Bishop Albert in Schleswig to discuss the progress
of the crusade, Count Albert no doubt informed his lord that it would be
easy to extend Danish control over Estonia, and Livonia as well; all that
was necessary was to have troops and princes in the area to "defend"
Danish interests. This must have been welcome information, but King
Waldemar already had means of bringing Bishop Albert to heel. Because
the Danish monarch controlled the German ports and important recruiting areas, as well as the sea lanes, he could stop the flow of crusaders to
the east and thereby undo two decades of work. He need not even act
directly; he could "allow" the Archbishop of Bremen to hinder the movement of crusaders through his lands and through Lübeck. Thus Bishop
Albert was forced to choose between submission to the Danish King and
the destruction of the crusade.

It may seem that the Archbishop of Bremen had acted unduly harshly
in preventing crusaders from sailing to Livonia, but he had been provoked
by Bishop Albert's independent ways; relations between the Rigan prelate
and his superior were not what they had been when Albert's uncle had
been archbishop. The long civil war in the Bremen diocese was responsible
for much of the misunderstanding because in these years, when Bishop
Albert needed all the assistance he could get, little had been available from
Bremen. Now that the war was over, Archbishop Gerhard still had severe
financial troubles and pleaded the excuse of poverty in refusing Albert's
requests for money and troops. It is possible that Bishop Albert had dis-

cussed the situation with the Pope and had complained about the lack of cooperation; certainly he looked forward to the day when he would be free from subordination to Bremen. Nevertheless, the Pope probably acted on political considerations rather than Albert's complaints in transferring the Riga bishopric to the care of the Archbishop of Magdeburg. The latter had played a significant role in the Hohenstaufen victory and was traditionally responsible for the missions to the east. This was the final provocation, and Archbishop Gerhard of Bremen reacted by restricting the preaching of the crusade and the embarkation of crusaders from Lübeck. He would disrupt the crusade, if necessary, to recover the loyalty of the Riga Bishop.[1]

Bishop Albert had no choice except to turn to King Waldemar. In the company of Count Albert and Abbot Bernard, he went to the King and humbly asked for his assistance. Once agreement had been reached that Estonia, and presumably Livonia as well, would be subject to Denmark, the King announced that the ports would be opened to the Livonia crusaders. Bishop Albert did not sail to Livonia in 1218, but he sent a small force under the command of the dean of the Halberstadt Church. Sailing with that fleet, significantly, was another Danish vassal, Henry Borewin, the Slavic Prince of Mecklenburg.

These reinforcements were sorely needed by the crusaders in Livonia because of the possibility of Russian attack. The Russian army had not appeared the previous year, but now a great Russian army marched into Estonia; and the crusaders had ample warning because the Russians had sent agents ahead to mobilize the Estonian forces. Although few Estonians joined the invasion force, the news reached the crusader army.

> The Russians spent the whole day crossing the river which is called the Mother of Waters and they came toward the Livonians. Our scouts returned to us suddenly and said that the army of the Russians was approaching. We rose up quickly and arranged our army so that the Livonians and Letts would fight on foot and the Germans on their horses. When our army was in order we marched toward them. When we had reached them, those of our men who were first forthwith sped toward them and, fighting with them, turned them to flight. They pursued the Russians vigorously and captured the banner of the great king of Novgorod, as well as the banner of two other kings, and killed the men who carried them. They fell here and there along the road and our whole army followed them until finally the Livonians and Letts, who were

running on foot, dropped out. Each of them then mounted his horse and followed after the Russians. The fleeing Russians, about two thousand in number, came to a little stream, crossed it, and halted. They gathered their whole army together and beat their drums and sounded their pipes. King Vladimir of Pskov and the king of Novgorod went around the army, encouraging them to fight. The Germans, after they had forced the Russians as far as the river, also halted, for they were unable, because of the multitude of the Russians, to cross over the river to them. The Germans gathered on a little knoll by the river, awaiting the arrival of their men who were following. They arranged their army a second time, so that some on foot, some on horses stood opposite the Russians. Whatever Livonians and Letts came up the little knoll by the river, where the battle lines were formed, when they saw the size of the Russian army, immediately drew back. Each one of them fled after the other one, seeing the Russian arrows coming at them.[2]

Less than a hundred horsemen stood against a force estimated, by the chronicler, at 16,000—a figure not beyond belief. They defended the crossing for the remainder of the day, but this chivalric action could not hold back such a large army for long. The Russians penetrated to Wenden and ravaged the area with little hindrance for several days. The crusaders and their native allies withdrew into the castles, sallying out only occasionally to harass small groups of marauders. In the end, it was not crusader resistance but news of a Lithuanian attack on Pskov that caused the Russians to retreat, which was followed by Lettish raiders who took such revenge as they could.

The Russian chronicler of Novgorod did not think it was an important campaign. He says simply that the Russians went there, fought with the enemy's outposts, besieged its objectives for two weeks, and returned safely.[3] Not long afterward, Russian emissaries came to discuss peace.

Since the maritime Estonians had joined the Russians in attacks upon the Livs and Letts, it was natural that the crusaders made an attack in reprisal as soon as possible. In February 1219 the German and Slavic crusaders raided the province of Reval, where the cold was so intense that many died of exposure and frostbite; but nevertheless the raid was a great success, as many prisoners and flocks fell into Christian hands. The crusaders returned and divided the loot among the participants.

Instead of facing the prospect of defeat at the hands of the Russians, the crusaders now looked forward to the conquest of the Estonians. They had already cowed those pagans, so that open resistance was abandoned, and great armies were gathering overseas to deliver the decisive blow. Bishop Albert had convinced numerous warriors to take the cross to Livonia, most notably the Duke of Saxony, Albrecht of Anhalt, the advocate of Magdeburg, Burchard of Querfurt, and Rudolf of Stotle. Also, King Waldemar, who had made preparations to bring a huge army across the Baltic, summoned numerous vassals, including the Archbishop of Lund, the Bishops of Schleswig and Roeskild, and Wenceslaus, the Slavic Prince of Rügen. Also accompanying him was Theodoric, the former missionary and abbot, now nominal Bishop of Estonia, who could hope to receive lands in Estonia only if he attached himself to the Danish Monarch.

The crusaders were agreed that Bishop Albert's force would proceed to Riga and operate in that region. Meanwhile King Waldemar would land on the coast and occupy the lands that were needed to control the water route from Gothland to Novgorod, which was used by the growing number of international merchants. As it happened, however, Bishop Albert and his followers either did not or chose not to understand the implications of the royal claims to Estonia. Misunderstandings would arise from this in the near future that would plague the crusaders for many years to come.[4]

King Waldemar brought a great army to Estonia, and although contemporary estimates of its number are completely fanciful, he may well have had several thousand troops with him. Falsely believing that the natives had given up all hope of resistance, the Danes spread their camp near Reval and began to build a great castle that would serve to secure their conquest. Such presumption almost cost the King his life, for the Estonians gathered their entire force (one or two thousand warriors) and made a surprise assault on the Danes, breaking into their encampment at several points and cutting down the crusaders. They made a special effort to murder the King but mistook the tent of Bishop Theodoric for the royal pavilion and slew the Bishop instead. The Danes were fleeing in every direction, pursued by the vengeful natives, when the Slavic troops of the Prince of Rügen came to the rescue, rallied the Germans and Danes against the attackers, and drove them back so fiercely that the battle became a massacre. Before the fighting ended, more than a thousand natives had perished. The Danish claim to Reval was confirmed by the seal of victory. King Waldemar did not remain long in Estonia. He completed the castle at Reval, installed his chaplain as Bishop of Estonia, and sailed away before the onset of winter. The Danish Bishops remained there to baptize the natives and instruct them in the faith, and undoubtedly many troops remained there with him.

The death of Theodoric marked the end of a phase of Livonian history. For two decades this dedicated Cistercian had labored for the Church, building missionaries and monasteries in this distant land and defending them with crusades and a crusading order. Now, the conquest almost complete, Theodoric was no longer needed. Not even Bishop Albert was needed, though it would be harder to remove him from power. (It was ironic that a Cistercian, a member of the most puritanical of all the orders, should die from having been mistaken for the splendidly arrayed King of Denmark.)

While the Danes were occupying the north, Bishop Albert's crusaders were busy in the south. Already the Semgallians from Mesoten had approached the Rigans, asking for aid against the Lithuanians and promising to undergo baptism in return for protection. Bishop Albert was well aware of the strategic location of Mesoten, which was located on a tributary of the Semgallian Aa only a short distance from the Dvina, where a castle would protect the Christian flank near Riga and permit easy access to Semgallia. Because of the swamps and forests between the Aa and Dvina, it would be difficult to establish another base closer to Riga; therefore Albert decided to accept the offer, knowing full well that it meant war with the other Semgallian tribes. Indeed, he had made his plans before he left Schleswig. At the Court of the Danish King he had invested Abbot Bernard zu Lippe as Bishop of Semgallia, and that noted warrior would have the responsibility of defending his new see.

Because of this commitment to the Semgallians at Mesoten, the crusader army that gathered in Riga in 1219 did not expect to march to Estonia. Only a few troops had been sent to Mesoten, however, when news came that the Russians from Pskov had invaded Lettish territory. The Swordbrothers and the Bishop's men hurried north but arrived too late to fight the Russians. Leaving the natives to raid Pskovian territory in reprisal, the crusaders' leaders decided to continue their march north and subject the few remaining independent tribes in Estonia. Once there, they allowed their native allies, including many Estonians, to burn and slay as they wished; and these wild troops killed the males, enslaved the women and children, and drove away the livestock, until the elders came to seek peace. Thousands had died, but all the other mainland Estonians now hurried to seek the baptismal font. Overwhelming force and terror "christianized" these areas of Estonia, areas claimed by the Archbishop of Lund and the Bishop of Reval on behalf of King Waldemar but now occupied by the Rigans.[5]

The problem of ownership had to be ignored because, while the crusader forces were occupied in the north, Mesoten had fallen into paganism again. After its neighboring tribes ambushed a ship bearing crusaders to the fort and massacred the crew and passengers, the garrison had abandoned the fort and fled back to Riga, pleading a lack of supplies and manpower to maintain themselves. Of course, the natives had thereupon reverted to paganism and had renounced the crusader alliance. As long as significant numbers of crusaders were in Estonia, Bishop Albert could not force these Semgallians to return to the fold, but once the Swordbrothers and native troops returned to Riga, he could plan an expedition into their lands.

Bishop Albert had large forces at his disposal for a winter campaign, which was the best time of year to cross the many swamps and rivers of Semgallia. In February 1220 he gathered together his household troops and vassals, the Swordbrothers, and the forces led by Duke Albrecht of Saxony, totaling about 4,000 German troops, and an equal number of Liv and Lettish warriors. This army advanced to Mesoten and commenced a regular siege.

They seized the village which was thereabouts and took off spoils and besieged the fort, making war upon it for many days. Some of them built a tower, others put up the paterells, others used the ballistas, others built hedgehogs and began to dig at the ramparts from below. Still others carried up wood, filled the moat with it, and pushed the tower across it, while others began to dig beneath its shelter. Many of the Semgalls in the fort were hit by stones and were wounded by arrows, while many were killed by the lances of the Livonians and Letts from the tower. The rebel mob did not cease fighting back at this. At last the larger machine was put up and great rocks were cast at the fort. The men in the fort, seeing the size of the rocks, conceived a great terror. The duke took charge of the machine, shot the first stone, and crushed the enemy's balcony and the men in it. He shot a second one and dislodged the planks and logs of the rampart. He discharged a third one and pierced and shattered three large logs in the rampart and struck some men. After seeing this, the people in the fort fled from the ramparts and sought safer places. But since they had no refuge, they asked for quarter so that they could come down and make their plea to the bishop. . . . They were told that they must give up the fort and everything in it in order to keep their lives.

These terms displeased them. They returned to the fort and the fight waxed fiercer than before. All the devices of war were introduced. The knights protected themselves with their armor and went up the ramparts together with their duke. They wanted to take the summit of the fort, but they were still pushed back by those half-alive men in the fort. After this, much wood was piled up in heaps and set on fire and the treacherous knaves were smitten by every means until, at last, in exhaustion, on the following morning, they gave up.[6]

Only a few had come out of the fort, however, when another band of Semgallians appeared in the rear of the crusader army. Most of the troops hurriedly formed a line of battle, but some of them stayed behind and massacred the prisoners. As it happened, the newly arrived Semgallians and Lithuanians saw that the crusaders' strength was too great to fight and hurried away, and when the crusaders returned to the fort they learned that, because of the massacre of the prisoners, the surviving Semgallians had resolved to fight to the death. The siege was resumed to its inevitable conclusion. The few survivors lost all their property and were scattered among the small villages. The fort was destroyed, and in its place Bishop Bernard built a new castle, which would be the military and administrative center of his diocese.

This was not yet the end of the warfare in the winter of 1219–1220, however. Returning to Riga with their loot, the crusaders rested two weeks and then collected their armies again. They were needed in Estonia, where the pagans from Oesel, having crossed the hills and swamps separating Jerwan from the maritime provinces, were attacking the new converts. Not knowing exactly where the pagans were, the Christians divided into three armies, each marching on a different road into Estonia—the Livs on the left, the Germans in the center, and the Estonians on the right. When the German column had approached to a point where it could see smoke rising from the burned villages, the knights donned their armor and advanced. The fighting was fierce, but the crusaders were greatly assisted by the bravery of the native troops, and especially by the captured native women, who, though unarmed, assaulted the Oeselians from the rear. Attacked from all sides and badly outnumbered, the Oeselians were routed; more than 500 of their warriors lay dead on the battlefield as the survivors fled homeward. It was a victory of all the crusader forces, foreign and native alike.

The crusaders now considered themselves master of interior Estonia.

They had won the region by force of arms, had baptized the natives, and had established their right to levy taxes and to raise troops from the tribes. But they did not understand that these regions had been pledged to King Waldemar, and when the Danish Bishops asked that the hostages be sent to them, they refused to do so. Master Volquin in particular was annoyed, because he had understood his order would receive one-third of Estonia, and only now was he informed of arrangements that might reduce its share. He protested to his new friend, the Duke of Saxony, but with little success. The Duke might sympathize; he might promise aid in the future; but at the moment he could only advise that the knights submit to the Danish demands.

Angered by Bishop Albert's supposed trickery, the Swordbrothers sent Rudolf of Wenden to speak to the King. Rudolf was the head of the faction of the order that had long opposed cooperation with Bishop Albert, and, ambitious and alert to all possibilities, he understood that King Waldemar might favor the order over the Bishop if the situation was fully explained to him. Rudolf succeeded in his mission: the Swordbrothers offered their service to the Danes, and in return the King gave them Saccalia and Ungannia—an act that excluded Bishop Albert from Estonia. Nevertheless, Albert continued to send priests into the disputed provinces to baptize natives and collect hostages and taxes. He also sent a messenger overland (through Kurland and Samland) to his brother Herman, an abbot in Bremen, to ask the Archbishop of Magdeburg for Herman's consecration as Bishop of Estonia. The Rigans (i.e., the citizens, merchants, various churchmen, and natives) disapproved of the policies of each of the contending parties and forced the Swordbrothers to renounce their agreement with the King and return to the original division of the land, but they could do little about Bishop Albert. As a result of all this, the conquest of Estonia revived the quarrel between Bishop Albert and the Swordbrothers and sharpened the danger of conflict with Denmark.[7]

Bishop Albert was not present at these discussions in Riga because he had already sailed for Germany with the crusaders (perhaps in the same fleet with Rudolf of Wenden). When he arrived in Lübeck in the late summer of 1220 and learned that Archbishop Andreas of Lund, who had long been in Estonia, had complained to the King about his actions, he hurried to Rome—perhaps fearing arrest and hoping to plead his case before the Supreme Pontiff. Danish diplomats followed after him to represent the King.

The interview was bitterly disappointing for the Rigan prelate. The Pope listened politely but gave him no encouragement. He declined to raise Albert to archiepiscopal rank (the best method of freeing him from domination by Lund or Bremen) and did little toward ending the blockade at Lübeck against crusaders to Livonia. Bishop Albert then went to the Emperor and was turned away again, this time with the advice to make peace with the Danes and wait for better times. After returning to Germany, he conferred with various men who also advised him to submit to Waldemar, so that early in 1221 Albert and his brother Herman, now Bishop of Leal (Western Estonia), decided to do just that.[8]

It had indeed been foolish to oppose the Danish King at that moment, for never had the fortunes of the monarchy rested on so firm a foundation. Waldemar commanded the loyalty of all the Danes, governed much of Northern Germany through vassals, and was in effect lord over even greater regions by virtue of his strong army and navy. The Swedes obeyed his wishes; the young Princes of Brandenburg looked to his leadership; Count Gunzel of Schwerin surrendered half his lands as dowry to a royal Danish bastard; and the Swordbrothers and others in Livonia had offered Waldemar homage.[9]

If his troubles had been confined to the Danish Church and Monarch, Bishop Albert could have submitted with more grace, but he was plagued by the ambitions of the Swordbrothers and Bishop Bernard zu Lippe. The grievance of the Swordbrothers was that Bishop Albert was withholding land from them, thus preventing them from assuming the independent status they craved. Having already gone over to the King, they looked forward to rewards for their loyalty. The challenge presented by Bishop Bernard was more complex, as he had entered the Church after a long and active life and had many friends and a numerous and active progeny. Shortly after he had become Bishop of Semgallia, one of his sons was elected Archbishop of Bremen, and once again a family connection existed between the archbishopric and Livonia. This time that connection might threaten Bishop Albert's independence in Riga, because the new Archbishop, Gerhard II—like his predecessor—prevented the preaching of the crusade and the embarkation of pilgrims to the east. Was Gerhard acting on behalf of Bremen or the zu Lippe family? Bishop Albert had to assume that the zu Lippe family represented a danger to himself and his crusade, and because that family was friendly to the Danish monarchy it was all the more dangerous.[10]

Transplanting the zu Lippe interests to the east was not beyond contemplation. For many years now peasants, burghers, and impoverished knights had been streaming eastward to take cheap land and improve their lot. Slavic and Danish Princes invited these hard-working, hard-fighting taxpayers in such numbers as to overwhelm the native population. And the Rigans were issuing similar invitations to settlers. Far-sighted princes could see opportunity for great enrichment and advancement. And, just as Henry the Lion had fought over Saxony and the trans-Elbe region in the twelfth century to make himself great, so might Bernard zu Lippe carve out a state even farther east. Against the Danes and the Swordbrothers and Bishop Bernard, the Bishops from the Buxhoevden family were helpless. Bishops Albert and Herman could watch the settlers move east and could listen to the restive nobility of Northern Germany, but, display their crusading bulls as they wished, without Danish permission they could not return to Livonia with the army of five hundred to a thousand crusaders needed to defend and extend their states.[11]

In March 1221 they went to King Waldemar and made total submission, surrendering not only Estonia but Livonia as well. The only concession they obtained was that their decision would have to be properly ratified by their vassals, allies, and subjects in Riga, a concession the King could hardly fail to grant as it was a basic principle of feudal law. Now that Albert and Herman had humbled themselves properly, King Waldemar bowed to the papal requests that he reopen the port of Lübeck and allow crusaders to sail to Livonia. Shortly thereafter, Bishop Albert departed with a very small fleet. Only one important noble accompanied him, the Count of Homburg, the other pilgrims being simple knights and clerics. Bishop Herman, who had offended King Waldemar and Archbishop Gerhard by going to Magdeburg for consecration as Bishop of Estonia, was not allowed to sail to Livonia.[12]

Actually, there had not been a total blockade of crusader traffic to the east. Count Adolf of Dassel, a minor noble who had an important relative (the imperial chancellor), had been in Livonia during the winter of 1220–1221, and King John of Sweden had established a short-lived foothold in Estonia in the summer of 1220. King John, who had succeeded King Eric in 1219, had brought the Duke of East Gothland, several Bishops, and a large army to Leal, where he built a castle, garrisoned it, and then sailed away. Because the Germans were to the south and the Danes to the north, the Swedes believed their position was safe; but it was not. A castle at

Leal, threatening the warlike Oeselians, practically invited attack, and early one August morning in 1220 the long ships of the nearby islanders landed there and disembarked a large army. Soon the pagans had set fire to the castle, forcing the garrison outside, where a massacre ensued. They killed over 500 Swedes, including the Duke and a Bishop, and allowed very few to escape. Shortly afterward the Oeselians besieged Reval for two weeks, threatening even that stronghold. Because of such setbacks, the Rigans welcomed Bishop Albert on his return in May 1221.

King Waldemar was a clever politician and a forceful ruler, but lately his successes had followed so closely upon one another that he had become overconfident. In the full knowledge of his power and authority, he did not expect any serious resistance to his rule, especially from the Rigans, who were dependent on the lifeline across the Baltic. But the Rigans resisted. The churchmen, citizens, and native tribes rejected Bishop Albert's agreement with the King, declaring they would risk losing all before they would submit. When the Archbishop of Lund heard of this, he invited a delegation to visit him in Reval to discuss the matter. Archbishop Andreas, the Danish primate, was a skillful and honest churchman, as well as a Danish patriot, and he brought the disgruntled German crusaders to a policy of cooperation by promising to intercede with the King on their behalf. Bishop Albert and the Swordbrothers returned home, reasonably satisfied with their proposed settlement of the Estonian claims, but when they learned that Waldemar had sent an advocate to supervise the government of Riga, they were alarmed—and the Rigans became furiously angry. Refusing to recognize the advocate's authority, they ignored him; and when he decided to leave, they refused to give him a ship or pilot to take him to Gothland. His voyage home was uncomfortable and dangerous, beset by contrary winds and currents. Knowing that the King would not tolerate this insult, the citizens, merchants, and natives called an assembly at the episcopal castle at Treiden to discuss action and take oaths to oppose the Danish King and all other enemies.

"All other enemies" meant the Swordbrothers. The crusading order remained true to King Waldemar because, even though they had been forced to renounce their treaty with him regarding the division of Estonia, they saw themselves as the favored vassals of the Danish Monarch, sure to receive rich grants of land and authority. For this reason they refused to join the other Rigan estates in the protest, and even arrested some of the native elders, preventing them from attending the assembly. Such mistrust was created that the Bishop and his followers refused to send aid to the Swordbrothers when a Lithuanian and Novgorodian army invaded Livonia that summer in retaliation for Christian raids into Estonia and Russia. Inasmuch as these raids were by-products of the Swordbrothers' occupation of Saccalia and Ungannia, which was exacerbating relations with the Rigans, the Rigans did not consider it their fight. Why should they assist the Swordbrothers? Only the Count of Homburg, who was free to serve as he pleased, went to the help of the knightly monks, but his aid was insufficient to ward off invasion. The Lithuanians and Novgorodians plundered certain areas and then withdrew back into Russia, followed by native raiding parties of Livs, Letts, and Estonians, who took full revenge for their losses. As this was the last dangerous Russian invasion for many years, the crusaders were freed from this threat and were able to concentrate on their internal quarrels.[13]

Quarrel though they would and resist though they might, the German crusaders in Riga could not withstand the Danish monarch forever, because King Waldemar seemed to move from success to success with ridiculous ease. Early in 1221 he extended his control over the Archbishop of Hamburg-Bremen. For a long time the royal wishes had been so respected by the canons in Hamburg that Archbishop Gerhard was unable to govern the factious chapter; as a result, bitter quarrels had divided his church— quarrels that could be traced to Danish influence. Already, therefore, the Archbishop was weak; and he was to get weaker. When the citizens of Bremen rebelled against new taxes, broke the chain that blocked traffic on the Weser, and forced the Archbishop to come to terms, the Danish vassal, Count Albert of Orlamünde, forced the unfortunate prelate to destroy the important fortress at Harburg, opposite Hamburg. Beset by these rebellions, by papal demands for contributions to the crusade to the Holy Land, and by other serious financial problems, the Archbishop could not resist the Danes. He was angry but impotent. In the spring of 1222, Waldemar sailed for Estonia, confident of victory there as well.[14]

> The king of Denmark, too, after collecting a great army, came with Count Albert to Oesel and began to build a stone fort. The Danes went out to fight against the Oeselians and, alone, they were not strong enough. But Count Albert and his men came to their aid, turned the Oeselians to flight, and killed many of them, while the rest fled. The venerable bishop of Riga also came with the master of the Militia and his Brothers and with certain Livonians and others who had been sent from Livonia to the king of Denmark in Oesel.

The king rejoiced at their arrival. He spoke to them about the gift by which Livonia had been given to him. They would not agree with him, but rather all unanimously dissented, as they had been instructed by all the people living in Livonia. They besought him to desist from troubling Livonia and to allow the land of the Blessed Virgin to remain free. After taking counsel with his prudent men, therefore, the king at length restored Livonia and everything pertaining to Livonia to the bishop with complete liberty. He abandoned the royal rights in Saccalia and Ungannia to the Brothers of the Militia and all spiritual rights to the bishop. He added that they should render perpetual fealty to himself and that they should not refuse their aid to his men, both against the Russians and against the other pagans. They promised their aid faithfully and forever, both to him and to his men.[15]

This compromise, in the summer of 1222, ended the series of Danish victories—military and political. But it was not a serious setback and could be turned to Waldemar's advantage later. He still controlled the sea lanes; he had universal recognition of his rights to Livonia; and the Bishop and the Swordbrothers had sworn fealty to him. Furthermore, he had weakened the position of the Riga Bishop by granting extensive lands to the Swordbrothers and by encouraging their independent ways.

Master Volquin and his brethren now possessed an immense territory in the center of the new conquests, bounded on the north by Danish lands and on the south, east, and west by Bishop Albert and Bishop Bernard. They controlled Lettish and Estonian tribes through a chain of castles (Riga, Segewold, Wenden, Fellin, Odenpäh, and Dorpat) and a network of advocates and priests. Their Estonian holdings gave them twice the land area and, therefore, twice the potential income of the Bishop to support their army, and there were the warlike natives as well. So the Swordbrothers looked forward to a glorious future. But all was not secure as appeared. The natives were not reconciled to foreign rule; the Russians were jealous; Bishop Albert and the Rigans were hostile; and, in the final instance, the Brothers' security rested on King Waldemar, who had not left a large garrison in Estonia. Soon the structure of their state, imposing but basically unstable, came crashing to the ground.

The first sign of danger came from Oesel. As soon as the crusader fleets departed, the Oeselians had gathered to besiege the Danish castle. Ordinarily the castles had proved impregnable, and the crusaders had probably looked upon the disaster at Leal as a result of typical Swedish thickheadedness rather than pagan skill or valor, but the natives were no longer as backward in the military arts as they had been two decades earlier. They were becoming skilled in the use of machines of war, some of them copied from the weapons used by supposedly pro-Christian tribes on the mainland; and they employed them most successfully against the unprepared castle garrison on Oesel, so that within five days the Christians sued for terms and surrendered. Bishop Albert's brother, Theodoric, and a number of hostages were left as pledges for peace, the others went to Reval, and the castle was leveled to the ground.

Knowing that as long as any crusader remained in Estonia they were not safe, the Oeselians sent messengers to the mainland tribes, exhorting them to fall on their foreign magistrates and murder them. In January 1223 the other tribes responded with a bloody massacre of the garrisons at Fellin, Odenpäh, and Dorpat. Perhaps as much as a third of all the Swordbrothers perished in these bloodbaths or were captured, and there was a tremendous loss of supplies and munitions. Certainly it was a terrible blow to the crusading order, as only 700 of its 1,200 German troops survived. The natives also appealed to the Russians, asking immediate aid against the remaining Christian strongholds, and meanwhile converged on Reval, intent on reducing this Christian castle.[16]

Because of their staggering losses, the Swordbrothers could not rush to the assistance of the beleaguered Danes in Reval, although they well understood that they could not recover their lost territories without strong Danish support. Not even Bishop Albert could wish the Danes ill in this situation. Therefore, everyone was much relieved when the Reval garrison sallied out and dispersed the besiegers. But the Swordbrothers' elation turned to depression when the news arrived from Denmark that the King was a prisoner of the Count of Schwerin. The protector and ally of the Swordbrothers was in the hands of his enemies and could send no aid to Estonia.

The Swordbrothers had made many enemies in the past years and now would have to pay for their arrogance and ambition. Their territories under constant attack, their numbers too few to defend themselves properly (much less recover the castles in Estonian hands), they needed immediate help. Only the Rigans could save them, and so, swallowing their pride, the knights sent Master Volquin to beg for assistance and accept whatever conditions might be set forth. Bishop Albert was in Germany, but his administrator, the experienced prior of Saint Mary's, called the estates together to ask their advice. As one voice they demanded that the order recognize the territorial settlement by which one-third of the conquests fell to the Bishop of Riga, one-third to the Bishop of Estonia, and one-third to the Swordbrothers. It was a great sacrifice for the Swordbrothers; but a third of Estonia was much better than nothing, and they agreed to these terms.

The Rigans dared not gloat too much over their competitors' bad luck. In view of the seriousness of the uprising, it was luxury they could not afford. Raising an army as quickly as they could, the Rigans advanced north. It was not a large army, however, and though the Rigans took many prisoners, they were unable to recapture any of the castles. Returning to Livonia, they beheaded their captives as an act of revenge and warning. Little could be done until the next fleet of crusaders arrived, but they looked forward to that time because they expected it to bring a very large army.[17]

Bishop Bernard arrived in the spring of 1223 with a large army. He had been two years raising this force, which he planned to use in Semgallia to conquer the remainder of his see. Now, of course, he had to turn north instead, and the princedom that the zu Lippe family probably dreamed about had to be postponed. And as he had but one more year to live, the postponement was fatal to his family's ambitions. The bishopric in Semgallia was to remain small and insignificant for many years to come.

By the time Bernard arrived in Riga the crusaders had fought a Russian force on the Sedde River, apparently successfully. However, most of the frontier areas remained vulnerable to Russian and Estonian attacks, which equaled in ferocity the attacks the Letts had made upon Russia and Estonia in previous years. Bishop Bernard set forth with 8,000 warriors to reconquer the rebellious provinces of Estonia.

The crusaders marched to Fellin and beleaguered its German-built castle. Because of the castle's superior design and the natives' newly found skill with ballistas, the attack could not be pressed quickly. The ballistas, towers, and paterells were less effective in reducing the castle than the heat, disease, and exhaustion of the native defenders.

Since the heat was, indeed, exceedingly great and there was a multitude of beasts and men in the fort, and they were perishing from hunger and thirst, there was a great pestilence because of the excessively great stench of those who had died in the fort and the men began to get sick and die. The rest who remained were not strong enough to defend themselves and gave themselves, still alive, and all their belongings into the Christians' hands.[18]

The crusaders then hanged those Russians who had come to the aid of the pagans. This was less important in deterring Russians from entering the war, however, than a distant battle on the Kalka River.

Because the Mongols annihilated a large army of Russians near the Kalka in 1223, the northern states felt obliged to send as much help south as possible. As the *Chronicle of Novgorod* uncertainly notes:

> That same year, for our sins, unknown tribes came, whom no one exactly knows, who they are, nor whence they came out, nor what their language is, nor of what race they are, nor what their faith is; but they call them Tartars. ... God alone knows who they are and whence they came out. Very wise men know them exactly, who understand books; but we do not know who they are, but have written of them here for the memory of the Russian Knyazes and of the misfortune which came to them from them.[19]

As a result, the Novgorodians and Pskovians, sent only an inadequate army into Estonia. The Russians did not go to the aid of the Oeselians but contented themselves with reprisals on the nearby provinces that had surrendered to the Germans. Perhaps also they feared the plague that was ravaging the countryside, or perhaps they were not equipped for a long campaign, but whatever the reason they did not intervene decisively. They left only a few small garrisons in the nearby forts, and this was not adequate. By failing to take strong action, the Russians forfeited their hegemony over eastern Estonia.

The Swordbrothers, though more than decimated by the rebellion, moved forward alone to recapture Dorpat, the key to the province of Ungannia, but their forces proved inadequate to the task. Because the castle was held by Vetseke, the former King of Kokenhusen and contained a large garrison of Russians and Estonians who used it as a base for raids into Lettish territory and Saccalia, it was important that it be recaptured. Also, because the Danes were Christian allies, the Brothers sought to render assistance to their beleaguered castles. The Swordbrothers' activities in the north made it clear to all that they still held to their alliance with King Waldemar and were awaiting only his release to recover their lost territories. The only fault in the knights' reasoning was that King Waldemar did not regain his liberty for many months; and by pursuing an independent course of action, they risked the hatred of Bishop Albert, Bishop Herman, and the other Rigans.

King Waldemar had become overconfident and arrogant and these faults precipitated his downfall. To be sure, he had reasons for self-confidence: his navy controlled the Baltic, his army dominated Northern Germany and Sweden, and his vassals ruled loyally and without difficulty. Although he was not a renowned crusader, he enjoyed the favor of the Pope and the Church. His enemies were weak and divided. Still, he was not secure, and when the Pope asked him to go on crusade to the Holy Land, time and time again he refused, pleading his many enemies as an excuse. He may not have believed that himself, but his enemies in North Germany were to be his destruction.[20]

Jealousy and fear were not the only emotions that plagued the minor princes along Waldemar's southern frontiers; revenge and outrage were equally important. The princes viewed the Danish intrusion into the Kingdom of Germany and the Holy Roman Empire as an insult. If they had been able to convince any of the Emperors of the need for war against Denmark, they would have thrown Waldemar out of Holstein and Mecklenburg long ago; but of course the Emperors had been too busy in Sicily, and the princes were too weak to succeed alone. Nevertheless, armed coalitions had several times opposed the Danish Monarch and gone down to defeat, each time acquiring new grudges that were suitable for instigating another war. Such a grudge was nursed by Count Henry the Black of Schwerin, who some years earlier, with his brother Gunzel, had fought against Waldemar unsuccessfully. After his defeat and submission, Count Henry had left for the Holy Land on crusade and been absent several years, leaving his lands to his brother's administration. Count Gunzel, as it happened, had but one child, a daughter of marriageable age, whom King Waldemar forced to marry a royal bastard, and after the young couple died, the King seized half of Schwerin as the inheritance of their infant son. Not content with half of Schwerin, Waldemar occupied the remainder when Count Gunzel died. Thus it is not hard to imagine the anger of Count Henry the Black when he returned and found his family dishonored and practically dispossessed. His grievance was such that, in revenging himself, he destroyed the Danish empire.

Henry the Black could not resist the Danish might openly or alone. He had few knights, fewer friends, and almost no base of power. Consequently, he pretended to swallow his pride and asked Waldemar to confirm him in possession of such lands and rights as remained, whereupon Waldemar invited him to the royal encampment on the island of Lyö, a favorite hunting spot just off the mainland. The Count of Schwerin then plotted one of the most daring schemes of the epoch: he would kidnap the King from the very midst of his retainers.

Proud and arrogant because of his continued successes, his wealth, and his power, King Waldemar had no fear of Henry the Black, or any other enemy. In May 1223 he was in the center of his kingdom, on an island surrounded by royal vessels in a sea that was practically a Danish lake, and numerous royal bodyguards and vassals protected him every moment. It was a festive occasion, with hunting, feasting, and much drinking—too much drinking in fact. When Waldemar invited the Count to the wassail, both men drank late into the night, and in the early hours of the morning the drunken knights stumbled back to their tents, and everyone fell into deep slumber—everyone except the Count of Schwerin. Calling his men together, he gave them their final instructions and sent them on their assigned tasks. Henry the Black led the main party of conspirators to the royal encampment, where the King and his eldest son slept, and rushing out of the darkness, they overwhelmed the watchmen and penetrated the royal tent. There was considerable noise and excitement, as the King resisted, but he and several bodyguards were at last captured, and many others were slain. Henry's raiding party then fled into the woods, regrouped and made for the ships that other raiders, loyal to Schwerin, had secured for their escape from the island. Within a few hours they were on the mainland, hurrying through the lands loyal to Waldemar toward Dannenberg, where the friendly count would confine the prisoners safely. As news of the deed flew through the countryside on the wings of rumor and good tidings, most people were breathless at the audacity of the Count of Schwerin, knowing what reprisals he would suffer from his rashness. Few thought that he would get away with it.[21]

The Danes were taken aback. Who would take charge of the government? Who would revenge the King and kingdom? Not only was the Crown Prince also a victim of the kidnapping, but no other high official was available to give orders. Archbishop Andreas had resigned his post, and his successor at Lund had not yet been confirmed; the Bishop of Roeskilde was on a pilgrimage to Jerusalem. Without proper leadership, the Danes could do little but grumble at German treachery, as did one chronicler: "We have seen how the Germans rarely or never are successful or victorious except through treason and fraud, which come to them naturaly, as is shown in the capture of the two kings and in other matters.[22]

Their attempts to obtain the King's release through the Emperor and the Pope failed. The Emperor had no real interest, except that he deplored treason, and the Pope did not dare use excommunication because it would be ineffective. The Bishop of Würzburg, who was first ordered to begin negotiations, died inopportunely, and the Archbishop of Cologne, who was next assigned the task of forcing the Count of Schwerin to give way, was himself killed while resisting kidnappers. Consequently the grandmaster of the Teutonic Knights, the imperial chancellor Herman of Salza, conducted the negotiations. Seeking every advantage for his Emperor, he did not hurry the proceedings.

The months passed, and Count Henry ignored the demands that he release his captives. Despite a preliminary agreement on 4 July 1224, he kept the King imprisoned and defied the Pope and the Emperor alike, because Waldemar's release meant his own destruction. In August and September the Imperial Court was held in Bardewick and Nordhausen, with young King Henry presiding on behalf of his father, Emperor Frederick II. All the great princes, lay and secular, assembled there. Count Albert of Orlamünde represented the Danish interests. Opposed to him were Count Henry of Schwerin, Count Adolf of Dassel, Count Henry of Dannenberg, and Count Adolf of Schauenburg, son of the former Count of Holstein. The negotiations for ransom were laborious and slow because the Count of Schwerin asked an impossible price—in essence, that the Danes renounce all lands south of the Eider to the Emperor and pay 40,000 marks in ransom to Count Henry. The Danish representatives could not obtain better terms because Henry feared to release the King for any price. And although he signed the agreement on 4 July, the Count of Schwerin did not release the King. It was obvious to all that the Danish Monarch would be a prisoner for many months to come, and therefore there was a rare oportunity to attack the Danish kingdom, an opportunity that might not come again for many years. Even the aged Bishop of Schleswig briefly emerged from his cloister at Loccum for another attempt to seize the Danish throne.[23]

Bishop Albert and his brother Herman were in Germany at this time, preaching the crusade. To them, the Danish fall from greatness must have seemed heaven sent; Waldemar, who had been their great enemy, could interfere no more. They visited him in his Dannenberg prison and obtained his permission to return to Livonia, and even to install Bishop Herman in his Estonian diocese. They sailed for Livonia in the spring of 1224 with many crusaders and were welcomed joyfully by the Rigans.

The news of the Danish debacle had spread throughout the country, and even the Swordbrothers understood the full implications of the new situation. When Bishop Albert explained the new division of Estonia—he was to receive the maritime provinces in the west, Herman was to receive Ungannia, and the Swordbrothers were to retain Saccalia—they did not demur. They accepted their share, and although secretly they resented the treaty, they armed themselves to assist the others in occupying their lands.

Bishop Albert, once again in command, summoned all his vassals and allies for an attack on Dorpat, the Russian base in Ungannia. The Swordbrothers, the merchants, the citizens of Riga, the natives, and the episcopal retainers joined the crusaders in the siege of that well-fortified castle, which lasted many days and cost many lives. The besiegers filled in the ditches, set huge fires against the walls, and brought up towers and engines of war, while the Russians and Estonians fought back with every means at their command. The noise of instruments, songs, clashing shields, and shouting continued day and night through the smoke and dust around the battlefield. When, at last, the largest tower approached the wall, the defenders broke down part of their burning ramparts and sent incendiary wheels down on the wooden tower, but the crusaders warded off these attacks and finally assaulted the breach. Bishop Albert's half-brother, John of Appeldorn, was the first upon the ramparts, and the castle fell soon afterward. The defenders fought to the last, asking no mercy and receiving none. Of all the men in the garrison, the crusaders spared only one, as a messenger was necessary to report the outcome to his Russian lords.

The battle had an important effect on the natives' attitude, convincing them at last of the crusaders' prowess. The Oeselians freed Albert's brother Theodoric, and the maritime tribes came to pay their long-delayed tribute. The Ungannians surrendered to Bishop Herman, who began to parcel out fiefs to loyal supporters, notably John of Dolen, Helmold of Lüneburg, and his own relatives, Engelbert of Thisenhusen, Theodoric, and Rothmar. Even the Russians came to make peace.[24]

Bishop Albert appeared to be, once again, the dominant figure in Livonia. Only a few years before, his future had been indeed bleak, as King Waldemar, Bishop Bernard, and the Swordbrothers had threatened to ruin him altogether. Now one of them was captive in Germany, one was dead, and the other was sullen and impotent. If only he could acquire the title "Archbishop of Riga" and complete the subjugation of the crusading order, he would be invulnerable to external or internal attack—the vassals, *ministeriales*, mercenaries, and German-trained native militia could defend the frontiers, and the taxes would pay for the upkeep of a large military and clerical establishment. But there were numerous problems with the Sword-brothers, the citizens of Riga, the international merchant community, and the native tribes; and it was urgent that he come to an agreement with each of these groups before the Danish kingdom recovered. Believing it was impossible to work out solutions in time by means of normal channels, he asked for papal help. Only a papal legate could cut through the many difficult problems and impose his decision on the recalcitrant. The Pope agreed to send a former vice-chancellor, Bishop William of Modena, one of the most capable and honest men of his generation. The legation of the Bishop of Modena began a new era in Livonian history, as the Danish era in Livonia closed.[25]

King Waldemar was not released from his prison cell until December 1225. The Pope had demanded punishment of the Count of Schwerin, voicing fear that his act would set a precedent and thereby threaten the stability of every throne in Christendom, but he found that many nobles and churchmen sympathized with the Count and therefore refrained from using excommunication or interdict out of fear it would be ineffective. In November 1225 the imperial chancellor, Herman of Salza, worked out an agreement for Waldemar's liberation that was almost exactly like that of a year earlier: Waldemar would sail on crusade to the Holy Land before August 1226 with at least 100 ships; all lands south of the Eider would be returned to the Empire; Waldemar would offer homage to the Emperor; and five relatives would be given to the Count of Schwerin as hostages for ten years, together with a ransom of 45,000 marks.

This treaty had hardly satisfied the princes of the north, who had joined together against the Danish vassals and decided to reach a better decision on the field of battle. The premature sally by the Bishop Waldemar of Schleswig had failed, but in January 1225 Archbishop Gerhard of Bremen, Count Henry of Schwerin, Prince Henry of Mecklenburg, and Count Adolf of Schauenburg (heir of the former Count of Holstein, who had recently married the niece of Archbishop Gerhard) had defeated Count Albert of Orlamünde and Count Otto of Lüneburg, the Welf nephew of the captive King, at Mölln, capturing the former and routing the latter. Within a few weeks Holstein was again in the hands of the Schauenburg dynasty, as one by one the cities and castles surrendered to the victors. Only then did the princes consider it safe to release King Waldemar.[26]

Although the fighting was not yet over, an era had come to end. No longer was Denmark the invincible power, dominating Northern Germany and Livonia. No longer were the Danish vassals, Albert of Orlamünde and the Swordbrothers, in command. But the new era was not to be as happy as the newly liberated peoples expected. Their joy would fade as a new round of war and civil conflict began. The strong Danish rule was replaced by anarchy, and the crusade to Livonia suffered as a consequence.

Notes to Chapter Six

1. *Urkundenbuch*, 1: document no. XLI; Leonid Arbusow, *Grundriss der Geschichte Liv-, Est-, und Kurland* (Riga: Jonck und Poliewsky, 1918), pp. 26–31; *Henry of Livonia*, pp. 160–65.

2. *Henry of Livonia*, pp. 167–68.

3. *Chronicle of Novgorod*, p. 60.

4. *Henry of Livonia*, p. 170–75.

5. Ibid., p. 178.

6. Ibid., pp. 180–81.

7. Ibid., pp. 182–87.

8. Ibid., pp. 187–92.

9. Usinger, *Deutsch-dänische Geschichte* (pp. 195–208) does not believe that Waldemar had ambitions upon Livonia earlier. The crusades of Borewin of Mecklenburg and Albert of Orlamünde were not connected with the sudden interest that Waldemar showed after Bishop Albert asked for help in 1218. That may be so, but we need not abandon the thesis that the Danish kingdom was very interested in dominating all the shores of the Baltic. Certainly in 1220 Waldemar pressed Bishop Albert hard, and Albert had to submit.

10. Benninghoven, *Schwertbrüder*, pp. 29–36; see also Bippen, *Aus Bremens Vorzeit*, pp. 122ff., and *Urkundenbuch*, 1: no. XLIV.

11. The most cited history of this eastward movement is Karl Hampe, *Der Zug nach dem Osten* (Leipzig: B. G. Teubner, 1921); see also Usinger, *Deutsch-dänische Geschichte*, pp. 253–83, and Thompson, *Feudal Germany*, 2: 501–28.

12. *Henry of Livonia*, p. 192.

13. Ibid., pp. 196–204.

14. Bippen, *Aus Bremens Vorzeit*, pp. 128ff.

15. *Henry of Livonia*, pp. 205–6.

16. Ibid., p. 210; Benninghoven, *Schwertbrüder*, pp. 179–82.

17. *Henry of Livonia*, pp. 211–12.

18. Ibid., p. 215.

19. *Chronicle of Novgorod*, p. 64.

20. Usinger, *Deutsch-dänische Geschichte*, p. 222.

21. The most complete account of the kidnapping and the subsequent negotiations is found in Usinger, *Deutsch-dänische Geschichte*, pp. 287–399; also L. Fromm, *Chronik der Haupt-und Residenzstadt Schwerin* (Schwerin: Oertzen, 1862), pp. 28ff., and Witte, *Mecklenburgische Geschichte*, pp. 149–50.

22. *Annales Danici Medii aevi.*, ed. Ellen Jørgensen (Copenhagen: G. E. C. Gad, 1920), p. 107.

23. Usinger, *Deutsch-dänische Geschichte*, pp. 300–322; *Mecklenburgisches Urkundenbuch*, ed. G. Lisch (Schwerin: Verein für Mecklenburgische Geschichte, 1863), 1: 290–93.

24. *Henry of Livonia*, pp. 220–28.

25. Gustav Adolf Donner's *Kardinal Wilhelm von Sabina, Bischof von Modena, 1222–1234* (Helsingfors: H. Crohns and C. von Bonsdorff, 1929), is the definitive work on William of Modena.

26. Usinger, *Deutsch-dänische Geschichte*, pp. 333–55.

7

The Intervention of the Papacy

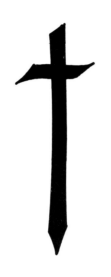

WHEN BISHOP ALBERT WROTE TO THE POPE LATE IN 1224 TO ASK THAT A papal legate be sent to Livonia, he had no reason to fear that he was inviting new troubles. Several years earlier, when he faced native rebellion, Russian invasions, Danish ambitions, and competition from the zu Lippe family and the Swordbrothers, he had had grounds for despair. Now with several bishops under his authority, he exercised the powers of an archbishop; and his enemies were weak and divided. Those who still resisted would be forced to humble themselves before the papal legate, and Bishop Albert would consolidate his empire. Little did he think that the papacy might be more dangerous than any of his previous opponents.

It was not that the papacy had any deliberate designs upon Livonia. The Pope had too much to do in Italy to concern himself much with distant provinces, and William of Modena, the papal vice-chancellor who was sent to Livonia, was a dedicated and honest cleric. But the men who governed the Church believed that the strife that gutted society and the miscarriage of justice that characterized it could be cured if secular governments would follow the directions of the Church and if the Church would follow the directions of the papacy. Therefore, in their belief that a strong papacy could suppress warfare and impose peace and justice upon a divided Christendom, these churchmen often acted in a way that increased papal authority at the expense of local churchmen and secular rulers. It was such a worthy ideal that brought unintended grief to Livonia. Because William of Modena had a reputation for fairness and honesty, as did most papal legates, no one spoke openly against inviting him to Livonia. Bishop Albert saw his mission as the means of eliminating the last of his opposition. His opponents saw the legate as their last hope to regain equality with the Bishop of Riga.

William of Modena arrived in Riga with his retinue in the summer of 1225 and immediately set to work on the various issues affecting the Bishops, the crusading order, the citizens of Riga, the international merchant community, the corporation of pilgrims (representing the crusaders), and the native tribes. He traveled about the countryside, and even to Estonia, receiving embassies and conducting interviews tirelessly. The result was a complicated series of agreements, treaties, and promises that covered practically every aspect of life and government in Livonia.[1]

Although the legate negotiated agreements on many issues, two were paramount in importance: the relationship of the Bishops and the crusading order, and the disposition of Estonia. The first issue was partly a quarrel over the division of land and partly a basic difference in the means of converting and governing the natives. William of Modena wished to enforce the so-called Baltic Manifestos issued by Emperor Frederick II in 1224 and by Pope Honorius III in 1225, which guaranteed the rights of the new converts. Just as the Bishops and Swordbrothers had duties toward their subjects, so, he emphasized, they had duties toward one another. Nevertheless, the results were more favorable to the crusading order than to the Bishops. As a result, encouraged by the legate and reinforced by recruits and donations from abroad, the Swordbrothers began to recover from the disasters they had suffered in the Estonian uprising.

The disposition of Estonia was a more difficult matter, and shortly after William's departure the old crusader, John of Dolen, rebelled. William, in Gothland, reacted with an ecclesiastical censure that restored order and then formally took over administration of all of Estonia, German and Danish regions alike. These legatine decisions weakened the position of the Riga Bishop and prepared the ground for direct papal control of the region. William of Modena, though he brought temporary peace, opened the way for renewed conflict.[2]

It is interesting and informative to investigate the details of many of these arrangements, for they offer valuable insight into the society and government of the era. How, for example, were crusaders brought to Livonia? First, there was the recruitment by absentee Bishops, by specially appointed monks and knights, and by a corporation or guild of pilgrims that may have been organized by Rigan merchants. Money was a problem, for many crusaders were poor and could not afford the ten marks needed for the passage and expenses for a year. This was only half the cost of crusading in the Holy Land, but without the free gifts of numerous merchants and other friends of the Church, many crusaders would have been forced to remain at home. Next was the assembly of the volunteers and mercenaries in Lübeck for the voyage across the sea, which was probably arranged by the shipping interests of the two cities, Lübeck and Riga. Finally, it was necessary to divide the crusaders among the Bishops, the Swordbrothers, and the city of Riga, so that each would have garrison troops for its castles but still leave sufficient numbers for service in the field army. The main body of crusaders served under their own advocate, who was usually chosen from among the leading nobles on crusade. When they arrived in Riga, each crusader did homage to Bishop Albert and then attended church services, where the "pilgrims" made donations of considerable value. The gifts to Saint George's went to the Swordbrothers, while Bishop Albert shared in the gifts to Saint Jacob's and Saint Mary's. Afterward, Bishop Albert had ten days to seek volunteers to garrison his castles, after which the prior of Saint Mary's, the Swordbrothers, and the citizens of Riga could recruit for their castles without hindrance.[3] The mercenaries, of course, served their employers.

Such arrangements, elaborate though they were, were necessary to avoid conflict over the limited number of fighting men available. Many similar examples could be cited, thanks to the rich fund of material from this era that has survived in the various document collections. These documents were issued by the legate and signed by the principal parties, as our best chronicler described.

> The legate of the apostolic see returned to Riga and the bishops, priests, clerics, Brothers of the Militia, vassals of the church, and citizens of Riga came to him. In the presence of all these people he celebrated a solemn council during Lent, according to the provisions of Innocent, to refresh their memories and institute certain new measures that seemed necessary for the newly-planted church. After everything was done and finished that could be done by him and after indulgences had been given, the legate said farewell to everyone, blessed them, and returned to the ships, commending Livonia to Mary, the Blessed Mother of God, and to Her beloved Son, our Lord Jesus Christ, to Whom is honor and glory, world without end. Amen.[4]

William of Modena had not solved all the problems of the region, a fact that was brought home to him when he sighted Oeselian pirates returning home from a raid on Sweden. The impassioned speech for a crusade that he delivered on Gothland impressed few of the Scandinavian merchants, which was perhaps an indication of the unpopularity of his Estonian program. And shortly thereafter he learned of new fighting between the Danes and Germans in Estonia. Although his chaplain suppressed this outbreak and brought each party to agree to cooperate in an attack on Oesel, William thought it wise to send him a number of Saxon nobles to serve as landed vassals. This was the first step toward the settlement of a secular German nobility on the land, something very rare in Livonia, where episcopal vassals supported themselves on tax fiefs as *ministeriales*. Thus it came about that during the first legation to Livonia, in 1225 and 1226, Estonia was placed outside the jurisdiction of the Bishop of Riga, and the Pope became the ultimate overlord of this distant corner of the Baltic. It was also during this period that the first step was taken toward the feudalization of Estonia and the creation of the German Baltic nobility. None of this would have occurred at this time had it not been for the kidnapping of Waldemar of Denmark.[5]

The kidnapping of King Waldemar had upset the stability of German and Baltic politics, and his liberation did little to restore it. His subjects had delivered an initial payment of 18,000 marks and his three younger sons—Eric, Christopher, and Abel—had surrendered themselves as hostages in keeping with the terms of the ransom agreement. Waldemar knew that the Pope was very interested in a strong Denmark, as was evidenced by repeated intervention on his behalf. It was the Pope who had forced the royal uncle, Waldemar of Schleswig, to return to his monastery and abandon his attempt to foment civil war; and it was also the Pope who absolved King Waldemar from his oaths, on the grounds that they had been extorted. Released from his sworn obligations, Waldemar was free to recoup his losses by force of arms.[6]

The chances of Danish victory seemed very good. Only three Princes—Archbishop Gerhard of Bremen and Counts Adolf of Holstein and Henry of Schwerin—were willing to declare their hostility. Others hung back for one reason or another: the Princes of Mecklenburg had passed away, leaving minors in their place; the Duke of Brandenburg, young and inexperienced, remained neutral out of loyalty to his Welf brother-in-law, Otto of Lüneburg; the Duke of Saxony (the crusader Albrecht) was quarreling with the Archbishop of Bremen over the ownership of Stade and Dithmarschen; and the citizens of Lübeck, who had risked Danish displeasure by their daring expulsion of Waldemar's garrison, sought the safest and most advantageous course of action. Thus the Danish King expected to recover all his losses, and to revenge himself on his enemies as well. Taking to the field in the fall of 1226 and invading Holstein from the north while Otto of Lüneburg attacked from the south, Waldemar occupied Hamburg and Dithmarschen after a series of sharply contested battles, and his fleet blockaded Lübeck so as to sever the communications route to Livonia. By the time winter brought the campaign to a close, the Danish Monarch was well on his way to recovering his former hegemony in Northern Germany and the Baltic.

In anticipation of a Danish recovery, the Germans in Livonia had taken steps to secure their position. Bishop Herman had visited the imperial court in Nuremberg in December 1225, where he and Bishop Albert were recognized as Princes of the Holy Roman Empire, a valuable status, which could assist them in opposing Danish or papal claims. The Swordbrothers, on the other hand, went directly to Frederick II in Italy for confirmation of their rights and holdings. Nor was the papacy overlooked, for the citizens of Riga and Lübeck appealed to it for help against the naval blockade in the Baltic. In response, the Pope asked the Danish monarch to lift the blockade, but his requests were at best only partially effective. Certainly the Pope was well informed of events in Livonia. He confirmed William of Modena's actions and adopted his recommendations, but it also appears that, like everyone else, the Pope was making sure of his future position in Livonia.[7]

Not satisfied with their foreign alliances and guarantees, the Bishops, the crusading order, and the citizens of Riga and Lübeck bound themselves in formal alliances against the Danish King. Although significant in itself, some historians have found this to be a true merging of interests between the Swordbrothers and the city of Riga. The knights became citizens and the citizens became associate members of the order; the knights paid taxes and the citizens raised contributions for the order; and each defended the rights and privileges of the other. But if this seems without precedent, it must be remembered that the life of medieval merchants had military and monastic aspects: they were well trained in the use of arms to defend themselves and their goods against pirates and highwaymen; they lived a communal, celibate existence in the various factories where they dwelt with their goods while abroad; they were deeply religious and civic-minded, often contributing huge sums to the churches and public charities of their home towns; they served willingly in the crusades—so that perhaps the majority of the Livonian crusaders were of middle-class origin. Naturally inclined to religious fraternities, the Rigans already had a guild, the Blackheads of Saint Mauritius, that gave its members many of the privileges now offered by the Swordbrothers. Furthermore, the Swordbrothers may have been thinking of these merchants when they petitioned the papacy for permission to take crusaders directly into their service, bypassing the rights of the Bishop of Riga, for later on we find brothers of middle-class origin in the crusading order. Probably the minor nobles and *ministeriales*, who composed the membership of the Swordbrothers, found these warriors of merchant stock to be socially acceptable. Or perhaps the supply of recruits was drying up. Whatever the reason, the Swordbrothers developed a close relationship with the members of the merchant community.[8]

This particular era in Livonian and North German history is difficult for the historian because of the nature of the sources. Documentary evidence, as illustrated above, tells much, but one must still rely heavily upon narrative accounts, and these are very poor. For example, the important battle that drove the Danes from the North of Germany is described as follows:

> In this same year the king of Denmark was freed for 50,000 marks, of which half was paid, and his nobles renounced the land of Holstein and all the lands lying around it that he had taken by force, and he gave as hostages three of his sons and many nobles. . . . Afterwards he broke his oath and promises and came to Rendsburg. Count Adolf and Count Henry of Schwerin opposed him. Count Adolf and his men sought to cross over a stream to the king and many of the king's men were slain, but the king held the field. Then the king went to Rendsburg and took it. . . . The King of Denmark went into Dithmarschen and conquered it and to Itzehoe and subjected it to himself, and led his people on with all the natives to the castle and then to Segeberg and built there a castle. Count Adolf recovered the castle at Itzehoe and of the people who were there many were captured, slain, or drowned. Then Duke Otto came to help his cousin the king. Then the Archbishop of Bremen and Duke Albrecht of Saxony and Count Adolf and Count Henry of Schwerin met in Lübeck and went against the king. They met at Bornhoeved on Mary Magdalen's day. There was a great battle. The king lost, and Duke Otto of Lüneburg was captured, and most of the king's people were slain or captured.[9]

The Battle of Bornhoeved freed Germany south of the Eider and ended a quarter century of Danish hegemony over Northern Germany and the Baltic. It also ended the political stability that had marked that era. Under the protection of the Danes, commerce had bloomed and emigration eastward had become a powerful movement. The crusaders in Livonia were united in their fear of King Waldemar and his Bishops. Now that the firm hand was removed, anarchy was loose in the Baltic. Not even Northern Germany was better off "free," though politically the country remained remarkably stable. It seems that the nobles (whose activities we can follow better than those of the other classes) became less active, less forceful. Certainly we can say that the victors at Bornhoeved waged peace less successfully than they waged war.

Archbishop Gerhard won recognition of his rights in Hamburg, Stade, and Dithmarschen but soon was embroiled in a long dispute with rebellious Frisian peasants north of Bremen. To help him collect taxes from these Stedingeners, he called on the crusaders. The Count of Schwerin died soon after the battle, and his widow squandered the political advantages won by her husband's daring and skill. Having missed every opportunity to profit from the situation, Schwerin was condemned to remain a minor power, even among the weak states of Northern Germany. Duke Albrecht, on the other hand, strengthened his position as Duke of Saxony. Luckiest of the allies, because of his rewards, Count Adolf of Holstein quickly secured his position in Holstein against the rival claims of Albert of Orlamünde and, thanks to his wife's relationship to Archbishop Gerhard, was assured of nearby political and military aid if such were needed. He could not recover the allegiance of Lübeck or tax her citizens, and without money he remained weak; but he had regained possession of Holstein. Lübeck, of course, became independent and, once the Baltic was reopened, entered upon the path to wealth and greatness. Because the unity that had provided successful resistance to the Danes lasted but a short time, weakness and lack of direction were to characterize North German politics for the remainder of the century. This weakness was reflected in the crusade to Livonia: each of the victors had important connections with the crusade, but after the battle of Bornhoeved, their contributions were never as great.

In January 1227 the crusaders in Livonia had their last great success for many years to come—the subjugation of the last independent Estonian tribe. Under the aegis of the vice-legate and Master Volquin, 13,000 crusaders pacified Oesel, from which the stubborn and warlike natives had raided the shores of the Baltic for decades. The huge army marched across frozen ice and crushed that proud and fiercely independent people. Our chronicler chose this campaign to close his work:

So the priests, with great joy, baptized all the people of both sexes in all the forts of Oesel. The priests wept for joy because, by the bath of regeneration, they were producing so many thousands of spiritual children for the Lord and a beloved new spouse for God from among the heathen. They watered the nation by the font, and the faces by tears. Thus does Riga always water the nations. Thus did she now water Oesel in the middle of the sea. By washing she purges sin and grants the kingdom of the skies. She furnishes both the higher and the lower irrigation. These gifts of God are our delight. The glory of God, of our Lord Jesus Christ, and of the Blessed Virgin Mary gives such joy to His Rigan servants on Oesel! To vanquish rebels, to baptize those who come voluntarily and humbly, to receive hostages and tribute, to free all the Christian captives, to return with victory—what kings have hitherto been unable to do, the Blessed Virgin quickly and easily accomplishes through Her Rigan servants to the honor of Her name. When this is finished, when it is all done, when all the people are baptized, when Tharapita is thrown out, when Pharaoh is drowned, when the captives are freed, return with joy, O Rigans! Brilliantly triumphal victory always follows you. Glory be to the Lord, praise to God beyond the stars.[10]

In a sense, that campaign ended the original crusade to Livonia and Estonia, but the crusaders were too disturbed by other events to rejoice long. Dissensions at home, long festering but now reacerbated by the Danish collapse, soon reached crisis proportions. Thus the Danish eclipse produced new and unexpected problems for the Baltic Crusade.

Foremost among the new developments affecting the crusade to Livonia was a crusade in Prussia, which originated with Bishop Christian and the Polish Duke of Masovia, who since 1220 had sought military aid against the pagan Prussians. For many years the Danes had been interested in the region, and Danish arms may have been important in the success achieved in 1221–1223, after which a setback similar to that in Estonia occurred. Bishop Christian then founded a military order, the Dobriners, modeled after the Swordbrothers and perhaps even staffed with volunteers or malcontents from that order. When this failed, he turned to the Teutonic Knights, a powerful and wealthy order with vast possessions in the Holy Land and the Holy Roman Empire, who by 1211 had already shown enough interest in eastern Europe to send a large force to Transylvania, where they established a strong position. Bringing German immigrants to work the land, they grew in power and wealth. At last they began to expand south and east, with the intent of founding a state for themselves, independent of the Hungarian King, who finally put an end to their hopes by expelling them from the country in 1224. Thus a certain danger was implicit when Bishop Christian and the Duke of Masovia invited the Teutonic Knights into Prussia.

Although Herman of Salza, the grandmaster of the Teutonic Knights, was busy collecting knights for the imperial crusade to the Holy Land, he accepted this invitation, sending only a few knights in 1228, but a larger number after Frederick II's return from Palestine. Within a few years the crusade organized by the Teutonic Knights in Prussia was to be serious

134

competition for the Livonian crusade because Prussia was closer to Germany, required less travel and expense, and the recruiting system of the Teutonic Knights, based on their extensive system of churches and hospitals, was superior. Furthermore, the overland route was preferred by the crusaders from interior Germany, who were terrified by the thought of crossing the seas in small vessels. The Teutonic Knights also had close friendships with many important nobles, particularly the rulers of Brandenburg and Bohemia, who provided constant support and sent a steady stream of crusaders overland to Prussia. Because its supply of crusaders was limited, the Livonian crusade suffered from this competition.[11]

Another crusade, which occupied many North German nobles, was mounted against rebellious peasants in the diocese of Bremen. Like his predecessors, Archbishop Gerhard had longed to collect tithes and taxes from the peasantry in Stedingen, but these peasants, who had been attracted to the swamp settlements by generous tax remissions, defended their tax immunity. They expelled the revenue collectors, mocked the Archbishop for his efforts, and indicated their willingness to use their well-trained peasant army if provoked further. Archbishop Gerhard had been selling Stedingen lands to the Cistercians on the condition that they subdue the peasants, but after the Stedingeners destroyed the fortified monastery at Herde, he realized that he had to use his own forces. He should have been warned by the fate of his brother, the Bishop of Utrecht, who perished at the hands of Frisian peasants in 1228, but the zu Lippe clan was as resolute and courageous as it was ambitious. When he was at last free from Danish interference, Gerhard raised a large army and entrusted it to the command of his brother Herman, Count of Lippe. The invasion force entered the reclaimed bottomlands, never to reemerge; on Christmas Eve of 1229 it was destroyed by the Stedingen army, and Count Herman was among the fallen.

Shaken and angered, Archbishop Gerhard convoked a provincial synod and formally convicted the rebels of heretical acts. Appeals to the Pope eventually produced several crusading bulls, and for the next few years many of the leading nobles and clerics of Saxony, Westphalia, and the Rhineland participated in this miniature crusade.[12] Gerhard also continued to harass the crusade to Livonia in hope of recovering control over its bishoprics,[13] and when the King of Denmark and the Count of Holstein attacked Lübeck and severed the sea communications, the crusading movement to Livonia was further weakened.[14] Already contending with compe-

tition from crusades in Prussia, Bremen, and the Holy Land, harassed by
the Archbishop and his friends, and embarrassed by reports of dissension in
Livonia, the recruiters were unable to convince large numbers of volunteers
to take the cross in defense of the Land of the Virgin Mary.

Crusader traffic to Livonia never ceased, but because reinforcements
became fewer and fewer, there were grave difficulties in Livonia, especially
for the Bishops and the papal legate, who were more dependent on the
volunteers than were the Swordbrothers. When the Danes rebelled in the
summer of 1227, Master John, the papal vice-legate, called upon the Swordbrothers to assist him and, unable to govern without their protections,
probably relinquished several provinces, including Reval, to their administration.[15] There is little concrete information on this period, however, as
Henry of Livonia had set aside his chronicle, and therefore our understanding of events in the ensuing decade is very poor. Modern historians, particularly Donner, Johansen, and Benninghoven, have written creditable accounts of the complex events that occurred between the time of the first
legation of William of Modena and the arrival of the Teutonic Knights in
Livonia, but, of necessity, their scholarly arguments rest on careful deduc-
tions from a limited number of facts and much speculation on the interests
of the individuals and groups involved.[16] Because motivation is so important
in assessing the politics of this era, let us look briefly at the position of each
group in Livonia.

The Swordbrothers had recovered from the losses suffered in the Estonian uprising. According to the estimates of Friedrich Benninghoven,
they taxed and governed about 130,000 natives; nevertheless, their own
numbers were amazingly small: there probably were not many more than
110 knights to garrison the six castles and numerous smaller outposts that
defended the inlands and protected the advocates. These knights, all recruited from Low German areas (Westphalia, Hesse, Bremen, and Holstein), were of *ministeriale* or mercantile origin, except for a very small
number of officers who may have been of truly noble birth. They were supported by a larger number of sergeants, who had entered the order voluntarily but were restricted to the rank of serving brothers because of their
common origin; they may have numbered 400 or 500 mounted warriors.
There were also about 700 mercenary troops, and perhaps 400 Germans
from Estonia (the Swordbrothers acquired vassals in Estonia when they
received its government from the papal representative, and in 1230 they

invited forty merchants from Gothland to settle in Estonia). All of these fighting men were probably of German origin, and in addition there were large contingents of native troops, about 5,000, which were now an integral part of the Swordbrothers' army.

The greatest problem was money. As a practical measure, the order interfered little with the natives' life and limited its activity to the supervision of justice, collecting taxes, and defending the lands. (It was safer to allow the elders to govern their own people according to traditional practices than risk another rebellion.) The order turned to improvements on the land: building mills, introducing the three-field system, and so forth; but these were not widespread enough to have significant impact—to raise productivity so as to support the men, castles, priests, and hospitals in the countryside. The order therefore turned to the merchants, giving them trading privileges in the land and enfeoffing some; but even this was insufficient. Then, when support from abroad began to fall off (and the order had only a few possessions in Germany), its financial position became acute. Moreover, the knights needed mercenaries to replace the annual outflux of crusaders, and this required money. Because additional land seemed to offer the only solution, the Swordbrothers began to look upon military expansion as necessary for survival.

The merchants, and particularly the merchants of Riga, grew wealthy on trade with the new converts. The population of Riga approached 3,000, and merchants and artisans began to settle in the interior, usually within the walls of the larger castles. They sought to live on good terms with bishops and Swordbrothers alike, their principal interest being trading privileges, not only with the natives but with Russians as well, as many traveled to Russian cities by water in the summer and overland by sled in the winter. The Rigans were now practically independent, being governed by an advocate of their choice, and they asked that a portion of the newly conquered lands be set aside for them. The merchants therefore looked forward to the future, expecting the opening of new lands to bring new opportunities for acquiring fortunes.

The bishops felt the decline in crusader numbers most keenly. Because they had modeled their churches after the practice in the homeland, they did not command such large military forces as did the crusading order. There were too many churchmen and too few resources: an area roughly equal to that of the Swordbrothers had to support the Bishop of Riga, the

Bishop of Leal-Dorpat, the Bishop of Oesel, and the Bishop of Semgallia.

If Bishop Albert's plans had matured, he would have been archbishop and exercised increased authority over the entire region; also, he would have profited from the expansion in Estonia and on the frontiers. As it was, however, he had not prospered; moreover, he had been deathly ill for many months. His death in January 1229 changed the picture greatly, because he had been a strong leader who could not be replaced. Although his successor could count on the military support of a few vassals, *ministeriales*, and mercenary troops, their numbers were scarcely adequate to garrison the castles. There were, of course, the native militias, some of which were organized and led by German advocates. But, all in all, too much had depended on Bishop Albert personally. Now the position of the bishops was weak—they depended upon an influx of crusaders and gifts to the Church, none of which was available in adequate amounts because of the situation in North Germany and Denmark.[17]

The canons of Saint Mary's elected Nicholas, a cleric from Magdeburg, as Bishop Albert's successor; but because this tended to recognize Riga's submission to the Archbishop of Magdeburg, the Archbishop of Bremen objected and—as his predecessors had appointed the three previous Bishops of the Rigan post—he named a candidate from his own chapter, Albert Suerbeer. Thus there was a contested election. Each candidate sent to Rome for confirmation, but Pope Gregory IX, too deeply involved in his dispute with Frederick II to look into the controversy, ordered William of Modena to investigate and settle the matter.

William of Modena was in Poland or Silesia, en route to Italy from Denmark and Prussia, when the papal message reached him. Had he still been in Scandinavia, or even Prussia, he could have taken the time to investigate the matter, but it was important that he return to the Pope and report on the situation in the north. William therefore forwarded the papal instructions to another legate, Cardinal Otto, who was on business in Germany; but, as it happened, Otto also was too busy to travel to Livonia. Because he could not settle the question without a hearing, Otto decided to send a vice-legate to investigate the situation in Riga, and as he was near Tournai when the papal messenger reached him (in May 1230), he sought a capable assistant from the nearby Cistercian monastery at Alna. The abbot, apparently, recommended a monk named Baldwin, whom Otto empowered to act as vice-legate and recommend one of the two candidates. Meanwhile Otto would hold hearings in Denmark. Because Germany was not safe for papal legates at that time, Baldwin set out by ship for Denmark, visited Lund, and then sailed to Riga via Gothland.[18]

So it was that Baldwin of Alna came to Livonia as papal legate, to find a land beset with dissension. The Swordbrothers, bishops, citizens of Riga, and members of the other estates were suspicious of one another and quarreling; and Baldwin was to leave Livonia in worse condition than he found it. Because papal policies are questionable at this juncture, this is a most interesting chapter in Church history as well as Livonian history.

What were Baldwin's goals? How far did the papacy support him? Why did all the parties later consider this episode so unworthy of themselves that they suppressed it from their histories? It may be that these questions cannot be answered because the nature of the problem, the necessary judgment about papal ambitions, and limited information thrust one back upon his own prejudices to a dangerous degree. Simply stated, the basic question is whether the papacy attempted to create a subject state in Livonia. Apologists for the Church argue that the papacy was only attempting to restore peace and order, protect the natives, and coordinate the crusading movements; other historians have been far less charitable—and it is obvious that the line between "coordinating" and "dominating" is a fine one. It is certain that the Pope recognized the need for intervening in Livonian affairs, but it is even more certain that the interpretations of papal instructions were not consistent. William of Modena and Baldwin of Alna were very different personalities with very different backgrounds. Also, the situation of the Church had changed; the papacy was fighting the Emperor Frederick, whereas a few years earlier (and a few years later) its relations with the Emperor were relatively good. In the end, personality, not policy, may well have been the determining factor in the ensuing difficulties between papacy and crusaders.[19]

In spite of the dearth of narrative sources, we can study Baldwin of Alna by deduction, by interpolating these documents. Thus it becomes clear that he was an unusually forceful person. A traveling legate was willing to trust him with a difficult mission in a distant part of Europe; he was capable of formulating daring plans and persuading powerful men to support them; he intimidated brave warriors, inspired his subordinates, and defied his opponents; he antagonized every estate in Livonia and appealed to the Pope for support against them. He was, in short, forceful and ambitious but also hasty and intemperate. As vice-legate, he had considerable authority and acted as if he possessed even more. Although it was certainly unwise for him to have acted as he did, it is difficult not to admire the courage with which he pushed his unpopular programs in the face of mounting opposition.

The projects of Baldwin of Alna conflicted with the interests of the Rigans at several points, but most importantly in Semgallia, that region southwest of the Dvina which had been occupied only briefly, before a revolt had driven the crusaders back to the Dvina, and in Kurland, the next province to the west of Semgallia. The natives of Semgallia, which had been subdued between 1228 and 1230 by dint of hard fighting, struck at the crusader strongholds along the frontier, sacking and burning Dünamünde; but later the Christians held the upper hand. The Bishop of Semgallia then lost control of operations because of his lack of troops, so that the Sword-brothers became predominant in the campaigns and, of course, expected rewards commensurate with their sacrifices. When they demanded much of Semgallia for their support, the Bishop was displeased, but there was little he could do, and he left the country for Germany, ostensibly to re-cruit more crusaders (but with little likelihood of success), after which the Bishop-elect of Riga and the citizens claimed his lands. After the successful conclusion of the war, the Swordbrothers, and the other estates as well, began to look upon nearby Kurland as an easy conquest, but Baldwin of Alna intervened by accepting the Kurs as converts to Christianity and sub-jects of the Pope. The period of 1230–1231 was a famine year along the en-tire Baltic, and the Kurs needed imported grain, which Baldwin promised in return for their conversion. The Livonian estates were furious. If they had been suspicious of papal motives before (imperial propaganda gave them reason to be), their suspicions were now multiplied. Undoubtedly, rumors of papal plots abounded, especially among the Swordbrothers, whose plans had been frustrated by the new legate. They accused him of being a false legate, a disrupter of the Church, an interloper who had been sent to stir up trouble.[20]

Baldwin sensed the rising resentment and fought back, relying on his wit and authority to see him through the crisis. He had won the loyalty of the Cistercians at Dünamünde and recognition from the corporation of pilgrims in charge of the crusaders, but he could not reconcile the mer-chants and the Swordbrothers. He had already removed the merchants' officials from Kurland, and even used his power of excommunication to recover the hostages they had taken, so that now they were completely ex-posed to the natives' hostility. The merchants turned to their friends, the

Swordbrothers, and together they searched for allies against Baldwin, finding one in the city of Lübeck and another in Duke Albrecht of Saxony. Attempting to frustrate the opposition by drawing one of the Bishops-elect to his support, Baldwin sent Cardinal Otto a recommendation that Nicholas be confirmed as the rightfully elected Bishop of Riga.

It was too late, however, for Baldwin to prevail against the general hostility. In January 1231, three days after his second treaty with the Kurs, a public meeting of the various estates confronted him with the oath he had taken on Gothland not to injure the rights of Riga and demanded the return of the hostages. Apparently Baldwin made a public apology and promised to return the hostages, but the next morning he fled with them to the new stone castle at Dünamünde. Meanwhile Cardinal Otto had made his decision and forwarded Baldwin's recommendation to the Pope. Several months later, however, when the new Bishop was formally recognized, Nicholas reversed the many actions taken by the vice-legate, nullified the treaties with the Kurs, and sent an army into Kurland to force the natives into full submission. Baldwin, unable to resist the Bishop, set sail for Germany and Rome, determined to explain his plans to the Holy Father in person. [21]

After sailing across the Baltic and traveling over Germany, Baldwin crossed the Alps in January 1232, met Pope Gregory IX in Rieti, and apparently found him an eager listener. The vice-legate told Gregory how an armed body of outlawed knights and merchants was disturbing the crusade and obstructing the conversion of peaceful natives; how these knights followed the Templar rule (and were therefore subject directly to the Pope) but were not within the Templar organization (and therefore escaped papal supervision), and how necessary it was, and how easy it would be, to impose direct papal rule upon the entire region. The aged Pope was bellicose even in his better moods, and when aroused could be angry indeed. Incensed by Baldwin's reports, he dismissed the Swordbrothers who had come to plead their case. Then, acting upon Baldwin's recommendations, he ordered Baldwin to return to Livonia and finish the work he had begun. To make this possible, he named him papal legate with extraordinary powers.

Pope Gregory did not underestimate the difficulty of the task in Livonia. Church history and his own long experience had taught him much about the ability of the laity to resist the authority of the clergy; so he invested his legate with extensive authority over all the lands and estates in Livonia.

He named him not only papal legate but Bishop of Semgallia and Kurland; he gave him full disposition of all disputed lands in Livonia and Estonia, as well as all vacant bishoprics, and the administration of the provinces of Wierland, Jerwan, and Wiek (which the Swordbrothers held); and he empowered him in all questions pertaining to war and peace, levies of troops, and ecclesiastical penalties. Finally, he confirmed all of Baldwin's previous dispositions. In short, he armed his legate with every legal weapon known to the Church.[22]

The delegation of Swordbrothers and citizens of Riga withdrew from the papal audience in consternation. If Baldwin were allowed to return to Livonia and put his program into effect, they would be undone; therefore he had to be delayed and hindered so that they could plan some means of reversing or defying the papal decision. Their return journey north took them to the court of Duke Albrecht of Saxony, where they found a sympathetic hearing. Perhaps they did homage to the Duke at that time, after which, as overlord of the crusaders' lands, he could defend their cause before the Emperor. Evidence points to such a tactic, as not long afterward the Emperor took their lands into his protection and forbade outside interference in their affairs. Again, a papal-imperial quarrel loomed over the fate of the Livonian crusade.

When Baldwin came north he understood that his opposition was desperate enough to commit any act. True, he had papal authority to act as he wished, but so did Conrad of Marburg, the notorious inquisitor who had recently been murdered on a German highway. Not desiring martyrdom, Baldwin decided to raise an army to accompany him and therefore began to preach a crusade to defend the interests of the papacy in Livonia. He was occupied a full year in recruiting and organizing this army. He had many difficulties (only his Cistercian brethren gave him unstinting support), but by the summer of 1233 he was under sail for Livonia.

Landing in Riga and exhibiting his letters of authority to the people, Baldwin quickly won the submission of several estates. The Cistercians recognized his authority, as did the bishops, canons, and their vassals, and even the Swordbrothers and citizens of Riga did not dispute his jurisdiction. Then, step by step, Baldwin moved against his opponents, so as to subject them to his will. He recovered the lands, castles, and hostages he had held previously. Soon his garrisons held the castles of Wierland, Wiek, Reval (with the exception of a small castle), and Semgallia. Then he pressed for more territory, forcing the Swordbrothers back at every point. His goal was the submission or destruction of the Swordbrothers—and everyone knew it. Some may have joined him for this very reason; certainly the relatives of the late Bishop Albert had no love for the crusading order; nor had they given up all ambition for wealth and power.

The Swordbrothers were well aware of Baldwin's ambitions. They had heard his accusations to the Pope; they had read his letters of authority; they had known other presumptuous clerics and thus recognized Baldwin as cunning and resolute; and they hated him for what he was and what he represented. They had fought for their lands for three decades, and the list of their knights who had been slain in the enterprise was long indeed. Now an upstart monk, a low-born rascal, threatened to take away everything from them and appropriate it for himself. Already in financial trouble, they would be ruined if they lost more territory. And perhaps Baldwin would not be satisfied with such concessions (the fate of the Teutonic Knights in Transylvania could not be ignored). One faction among the knights clamored for immediate action—to fight while they still were able—but Master Volquin quieted them; he saw that the legate's strength was almost equal to theirs and that behind the legate stood the power and prestige of the Pope. Volquin insisted that they rely upon the good faith of Mother Church; surely God and the Pope would see that right triumphed.

Baldwin was firmly in control. If he had brought in vassals, the mere passage of time would have given him overlordship in Livonia. His military forces, estimated at 1,100 men, were very nearly equal to the total number of Swordbrothers, and though many of the former might leave his service, others would come as vassals or crusaders. Most important, the lands held by himself and his friends were double the area of the lands held by the Swordbrothers, and he would profit most by expansion. In the future, whether he settled vassals on these lands or raised mercenary soldiers from the revenues, the balance would swing in his favor. Sensing total victory in the offing, Baldwin pressed on. Inside the city of Reval was a small castle that had been built and garrisoned by the Swordbrothers after the region was given to them in 1227 by the papal administrator to govern in his behalf. No one had ever questioned their right to maintain a convent of knights in this castle, until Baldwin ordered them to surrender it to him. Master Volquin refused, because the loss of this castle and the lands that supported it would be a fatal blow to the order, but he was compromised by his unwillingness to oppose the legate with force. When Baldwin brought 400 men and their supporting troops into the larger castle in Reval and demanded that the question be arbitrated by the estates of Livonia, Volquin was faced with a difficult choice. He rejected war, but in choosing arbitration he fell into a trap: Baldwin was well within his authority in demanding the return of territory that was under theoretical papal administration. Moreover, Baldwin had packed the court, and most of the estates were favorable to his cause. The decision, of course, favored the legate, and Volquin was ruined. Cunning and ambition had triumphed over simple honesty. But Baldwin's victory was short-lived.

Many of the Swordbrothers had disagreed with Master Volquin's policy of appeasement: they believed in meeting force with force and cunning with cunning. Until the moment the unfavorable decision was announced, Volquin had held these knights in check; when his policy collapsed, they seized the reins of power. Still unable to persuade Volquin to make war upon the legate, they arrested him and chose one of their own number, John Selich, to act in his place. The ensuing battle in Reval was fought in August or September 1233.

The Swordbrothers attacked and captured the large castle in the citadel area, slew several hundred papal warriors in battle, and then pursued the survivors into the nearby church and put most of them to the sword, in violation of the right of sanctuary. They stripped the dead of their armor, piled the bodies in a heap, and brought in the natives to convince them that they reigned supreme. They extracted oaths of obedience from the prisoners and allowed some of them to return to their lands in Estonia. The Swordbrother armies then swept through Estonia and Livonia, occupying legatine lands and punishing legatine supporters, including members of the Buxhoevden family, who were heavily fined. Baldwin escaped to Dünamünde, where he was besieged by the Swordbrothers and their allies from Riga. The Swordbrothers released Master Volquin after three months' captivity and restored him to office, for he would be needed when the Pope heard the many appeals that were being directed to him. Also, the knights respected and loved their commander. Volquin resumed his duties and directed the operations against the legatine supporters, refusing, however, to attack Dünamünde.

Baldwin fought back as best he could. Because his former allies were cowed or out of the fight (Dorpat was under Russian attack), he sought out new ones. He offered concessions to the merchants, invited new vassals from Germany, and was making considerable headway when a letter arrived announcing the termination of his mission.[23]

144

Pope Gregory had learned, at last, that he had been deceived. Petitions from Livonia and information supplied by William of Modena had convinced him that Baldwin's ambitions were immoral and impractical, and he granted William's request to be sent back to Livonia as papal legate. The papal announcement dismayed Baldwin, but he did not despair: again, he hurried to Rome to explain the situation to the Pope. It was too late, however, because Pope Gregory had already decided the matter, and although he was angry at the crusading order, he would not reverse his decision. Instead, he ordered Bishops Nicholas and Herman, Master Volquin, and representatives of Riga to come to him to personally explain their conduct. The Pope would not be deceived again; he would decide everything personally, if necessary.

Delay would be fatal to Baldwin's ambitions, and William of Modena's depositions would have the same effect. Baldwin was never again to enter Livonian politics. He charged his many enemies with heresy, impiety, and disobedience, but the Inquisition, not yet strongly organized, was particularly weak in Germany. Unable to destroy his enemies, he passed from the scene, and with his passing went the privileged position of the Cistercians in Livonia. Because the Cistercians had supported their ambitious fellow monk, the crusading order and the citizens of Riga turned to the Dominicans, who had first come to Livonia with William of Modena. The Cistercian influence, dating from the earliest days of the crusade, declined everywhere except in the diocese of Dorpat.

William of Modena was slightly delayed on his journey to Livonia by the Danish blockade of Lübeck and by requests that he mediate the dispute between the Archbishop of Bremen and the Stedingen peasants; therefore he did not sail from Germany before the summer of 1234. Once he arrived in Livonia, he acted with great swiftness to restore peace and order. He annulled all of Baldwin's acts and then he redivided the lands, giving the larger share to the crusading order. He installed a bishop on Oesel, moved Bishop Herman permanently from Leal to Dorpat, and established a bishopric in Kurland in addition to the one in Semgallia. It should be noted, however, that William did not surrender any of the theoretical rights of the papacy; he merely acted in the most practical manner to end the civil dispute.[24]

Papal involvement in the Livonian crusade had brought the Swordbrothers to power; but Bishop Albert could not have expected this outcome when he had sent for a papal legate a decade earlier. Whereas in 1224 the

Bishop of Riga had triumphed because of unexpected events in Germany and Livonia, the Swordbrothers now came to the fore as a result of equally unexpected developments. The Swordbrothers now faced the task of consolidating their position. However, by assuming the leadership of the crusade they were also assuming new risks, which would soon bring about their downfall.

NOTES TO CHAPTER SEVEN

1. It is at this point that documents become the basic source for the history of the crusade. Fortunately, at the very moment that the narrative sources begin to fail, the documentary evidence becomes more extensive and detailed. See *Urkundenbuch*, 1: document no. LXXVf.

2. *Henry of Livonia*, p. 239; Benninghoven, *Schwertbrüder*, pp. 194–206.

3. *Urkundenbuch*, 1: nos. LXXV–LXXXIX; 3: nos. LXXXII and LXXXIIa.

4. *Henry of Livonia*, pp. 236–37.

5. Ibid., p. 239; Hellmann, *Das Lettenland im Mittelalter*, p. 223.

6. Usinger, *Deutsch-dänische Geschichte*, pp. 347f.

7. Benninghoven, *Schwertbrüder*, pp. 194–222.

8. Benninghoven, *Schwertbrüder*, pp. 206–17. "Man muss daher vermuten, dass ein unwesentlichen Teil der Schwertbrüder selbst dem Kaufmannstande entsprossen war." Paul Johansen, "Die Bedeutung der Hanse für Livland," *Hansische Geschichtsblätter*, 55–56 (1940–1941): 25.

9. *Sächsische Weltchronik*, pp. 246–47. Also see the *Holsteinische Reimchronik*, in *Monumenta Germaniae Historica, Deutsche Chronicon*, ed. Ludwig Weiland (Berlin: Weidmann, 1877), pp. 620–24.

10. *Henry of Livonia*, pp. 245–46.

11. Christian Krollmann, *Politische Geschichte des Deutschen Ordens in Preussens* (Konigsberg: Grafe und Unzer, 1932). As early as 1230, Pope Gregory warned the Teutonic Knights not to interfere in lands occupied by the Livonian crusaders (*Urkundenbuch*, 3: no. CXLIVb).

12. Bippen, *Aus Bremens Vorzeit*, pp. 132–33; King, *Chronicles of Three Free Cities*, pp. 51–53; the Count of Arnstein was in Livonia despite this distraction (*Reimchronik*, l. 1647).

13. The Archbishop made it difficult for crusaders to embark from Lübeck, as they first had to cross his territories. Complaints were to go all the way to Rome for years to come, but the Archbishops maintained their pretensions to the patriarchate of the North just as they had in the past. *Hamburgisches Urkundenbuch*, 1: 422.

14. Riga was bound to Lübeck by treaty in opposition to the Danes. *Urkundenbuch*, 1: no. XCVIII.

15. Johansen, *Estlandliste*, pp. 707–10.

16. Hausmann commented: "Was uns hier für Geschichte überliefert wird, ist fast nur ein Gebilde der Phantasie, bei welchem wir nur mitunter im Stande sind, den Wegweiser zu ahnen, der die einzelne Richtung bestimmt hat, bei dem es aber unmöglich is, jeden einzelnen Schritt zu erklaren." *Das Ringen der Deutschen und Dänen um den Besitz Estland*, p. 106.

17. The sudden decline in Bishop Albert's status is striking, in spite of the lands and position he and family members held. He was Bishop of Riga, Herman was Bishop of Dorpat, Rothmar was prior in Dorpat, his brother-in-law Engelbert of Thisenhusen was in Dorpat, and Theodoric had lands around Riga. Furthermore, John of Apeldorn, a half-brother, had been to Livonia on crusade, and several cousins held lands in the countryside. See Gnegel-Waitschies's *Bischof Albert*, and Benninghoven's *Schwertbrüder*, pp. 223–53, 380–412.

18. Benninghoven, *Schwertbrüder*, pp. 269–70; Donner, *Kardinal Wilhelm von Modena*, pp. 112–59; Johansen, *Estlandliste*, p. 717.

19. Johansen (*Estlandliste*, p. 717) suggests that Cardinal Otto may have instructed Baldwin to injure Emperor Frederick II in every way possible. Since the Swordbrothers were closely connected with him, he may have seen an attack upon them as a means of assisting the Pope in Italy. Donner (*Kardinal Wilhelm von Sabina*, p. 112) suggests that he was continuing William of Modena's policy in separating Estonia from Livonia for the protection of the natives.

20. Hermanni de Wartberge, "Chronicon Livonia," in *Scriptores rerum Prussicarum*, ed. Theodore Hirsch, Max Toppen, Ernst Strehlke (Leipzig: S. Hirzel, 1863), 2: 32 (hereafter cited as *Herman de Wartberge*); *Albert von Stade*, p. 360; "Auszug aus der Chronik des Ordens vom deutschen Hause," in *Scriptores Rerum Livonicarum*, ed. A. Hansen (Riga and Leipzig: E. Franzen, 1853), 2: 848.

21. In a long series of documents in the collection *Liv-, Est-, und Kurländisches Urkundenbuch* are treaties, letters, and occasional lengthy complaints. These documents, which need not be cited here, are the basis of the reconstructions made by twentieth-century historians.

22. *Urkundenbuch*, 1: nos. CXV–CXXIV.

23. Johansen, *Estlandliste*, pp. 717–28; Benninghoven, *Schwertbrüder*, pp. 269–301; Peter von Goetze, *Albert Suerbeer, Erzbischof von Preussen, Livland und Ehstland* (St. Petersburg: W. Gräff, 1854), pp. 123–27; Donner, *Kardinal Wilhelm von Sabina*, pp. 166–67; Paul Johansen, "Eine Riga-Wisby Urkunde des. 13. Jahrhunderts, "*Zeitschrift des Vereins für luebeckische Geschichte*, 38 (1958): 43.

24. Donner, *Kardinal Wilhelm von Sabina*, pp. 169–78; Johansen, *Estlandliste*, pp. 111, 730–32.

8

The Teutonic Knights Take Charge

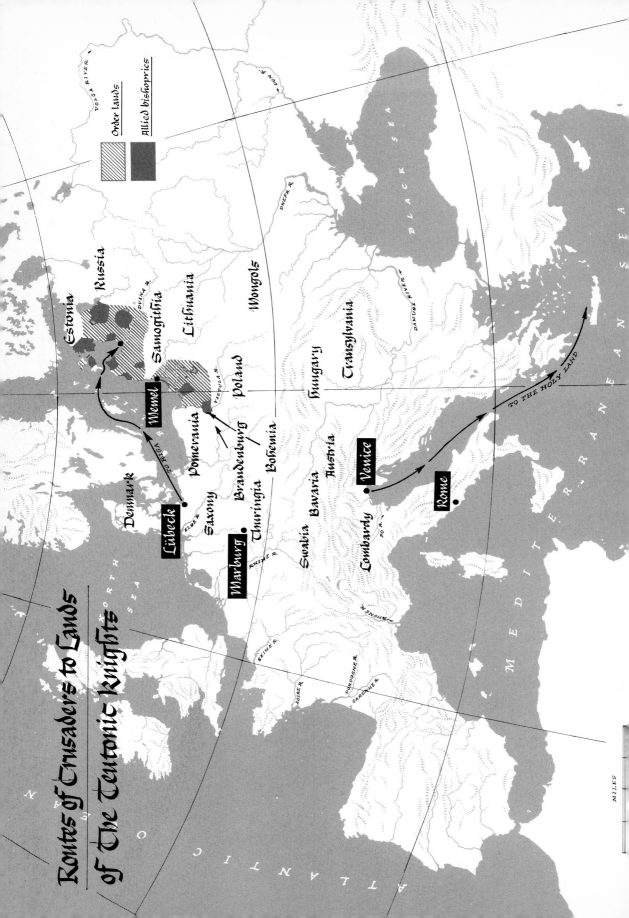

Routes of Crusaders to Lands
of The Teutonic Knights

Order lands

Allied bishoprics

VOLGA RIVER

DON R.

DVINA R.

DNEPR. R.

BLACK SEA

Estonia

Russia

Samogithia

Lithuania

Mongols

Transylvania

Hungary

Denmark

Pomerania

Poland

VISTULA R.

TO RIGA

Memel

Brandenburg

Bohemia

Austria

DANUBE RIVER

TO THE HOLY LAND

Saxony

Thuringia

Swabia

Bavaria

Venice

Lübeck

ELBE R.

Marburg

RHINE R.

Lombardy

PO R.

Rome

SEINE R.

LOIRE R.

DORDOGNE R.

GARONNE R.

RHONE R.

NORTH SEA

ATLANTIC OCEAN

MEDITERRANEAN SEA

MILES

THE DISPUTE BEGUN BY BALDWIN OF ALNA HAD SAPPED THE STRENGTH OF the crusader states in Livonia and had discouraged armed pilgrims from traveling there, but it would be an error to attribute the decline in crusaders solely to that dispute. The political situation in Germany and Denmark was very much responsible for the problems faced by the crusaders in the fourth decade of the thirteenth century, and these problems eventually became too great for the slender resources of the crusading order and its allies.

The foremost political problem concerned leadership in the Holy Roman Empire. The German princes had begun to understand, at last, that Frederick II had no interest in German problems, that he saw the Empire only as a reservoir of men and money to be used for his Italian ventures, and that he would surrender royal prerogatives if he were pressed to do so. Once they understood the implications of his attitude, they extorted concessions from their distant Emperor, so that eventually the only real authority from above was derived from a weak feudal oath of loyalty to his person. The magnificence of the imperial Court and the exotic personality of Frederick II dazzled the more uncouth German nobility, but in fact those nobles were learning to rule their lands without royal direction, so that when Frederick passed from the stage, no successor was necessary. The princes later maintained relative peace and security because Frederick II had so neglected German affairs that they had learned to do without his aid or intervention. As early as 1227, northern princes had defeated the Danes without imperial help; now they were seeking a new equilibrium, and the process tended to hurt the crusade to Livonia.

The Danes, expelled from Northern Germany by the battle of Bornhoeved, made no effort to recover their losses but instead sought a position of influence within the new system. King Waldemar gave up his control of Mecklenburg and Holstein, retaining only his claims to Lübeck. This city was important not just because of its wealth but because it was the key to the Baltic trade. If Waldemar could reestablish his authority there, he could also force his enemies in the east to submit. In light of this, the marriage of a Danish Prince to the daughter of Adolf IV of Holstein has great significance because Adolf was also interested in dominating Lübeck and taxing its wealth. United by marriage and common interests, the rulers of Denmark and Holstein blockaded Lübeck by land and by sea, which threatened to sever communications with Livonia.

The city fathers complained to the Pope that their enemies were hindering the crusade, and the Pope asked his legate, William of Modena, to see that the sea lanes were reopened to crusaders; but the papal action was too slow. The citizens were unwilling to sit idly by while their commerce was ruined, and the councilmen hired Duke Albrecht of Saxony as their advocate, who forced the Count of Holstein to cease his interference with road traffic. The blockade on the Trave River was more serious, however, and Albrecht was not powerful enough to overawe the King of Denmark. The merchants, looking downriver to the two castles and the heavy chain attached to sunken hulks, must have realized that their independence was contingent upon capturing the castles and removing the chain. Detmar's account of the Lübeckers' victory is probably distorted, but somehow the citizens forced the Danish monarch to lift his blockade or perhaps the current simply washed the hulks away, so that the barrier was useless. Once the merchant captains could enter the Baltic Sea, they routed the Danish fleet and liberated a number of Wendish cities (which became the nucleus of the Hanseatic League). Soon aware of their newly found power, the citizens began to sign treaties, coin money, hold tournaments, and make war and peace—like any other sovereign state. A new era and a new power were born.[1]

Count Adolf ceased to strive for worldly glory and turned increasingly to things spiritual. He built and endowed churches and cloisters throughout Holstein. He was so occupied in these works that he did not take part in the great troubles disturbing the diocese of Bremen.[2]

Even if the blockade of Lübeck had been lifted before 1234 there would have been few crusaders to Livonia because of the crusade against the peasants north of Bremen. This crusade had come about because Archbishop Gerhard, after failing to raise taxes from the citizens of Bremen, had tried to impose illegal taxes upon the peasants of Stedingen, who also had resisted and had killed Gerhard's brother in a pitched battle. Thus in addition to Gerhard's belief that only by collecting such taxes could he rebuild his war-shattered fortune and achieve his political ambitions, revenge became a motive for war on the peasants. Consequently, he was determined to crush all resistance, whatever the cost. With that in mind, he unleashed one of the cruelest crusades ever recorded.

When the battle on Christmas Day 1229 had demonstrated that the

Archbishop could not suppress the peasantry without outside aid, he used the papal call in 1230 for crusaders to Prussia to assemble a provincial synod, which formally condemned the peasants as rebels and heretics. Then he asked his neighbors and the Pope for assistance against them. The Albigensian crusade provided a model for his action, and there were grounds for his accusations: superstition was rife throughout medieval Europe, especially in rural areas; moreover, plays and buffoonery were common on holidays and apparently the Stedingeners mocked the churchmen and their tax-collectors on these occasions. Probably every community was guilty of similar "heresies," but the others paid their tithes, and the Stedingeners would not. The Pope cooperated by issuing crusading bulls in 1231, 1232, 1233, and 1234 against the peasants of Stedingen. The Counts of Oldenburg struck immediately. The Archbishop, however, was unable to attack before 1233, because he needed the naval support provided by the merchants of Bremen. He won their help by promising them permanent remission of taxes and tolls, good coinage, proper justice, relief from military service, and one-third of all the booty won in the campaign. Thus Bremen won her civic liberties by helping to enserf her neighbors. This was not unusual, however, as the cities and the countryside had never worked together.[3] A local chronicler described the confused struggle in these terms:

> Just before Pentecost of 1233 Duke Otto of [Bräunschweig] sent his men and ravaged around Bremen, because he wanted to help the Stedingeners. He wanted the lands back that his cousin, Duke Henry, had given to Bremen. So he went to Stade and ravaged the land. Meanwhile the crusaders came to Bremen and went out in a great army, both in ships and over land, and captured the eastern part in mid-summer on Saint John and Paul's Days and ravaged and burned all the land, and slew everyone they found, men, women, and children, more than four hundred of them, and the men they captured, they burned alive. Meanwhile the Stedingeners killed Count Burchard of Oldenburg and two hundred of his men.[4]

The peasants thus beat back the main threat. And Count Burchard of Oldenburg-Wildeshausen, crusader to Livonia in 1215 and 1225, was dead. Because the zu Lippe and Oldenburg families competed for possession of the bishoprics of Utrecht, Paderborn, Osnabrüch, Münster, and the Archbishopric of Hamburg-Bremen, Archbishop Gerhard was probably not unhappy that a hereditary enemy of his family suffered such disaster, but he needed all the help he could get against the peasants and requested the support of Burchard's brother, Henry.

Although the Stedingeners suffered terrible losses on the right bank of the Weser, their position was still strong on the left bank. Protected on the north by the Weser, on the west by the small rivers, and on the south by drainage canals, they had only one land route to defend—to the east, where the canals fell just short of connecting with another small river. They built a wall and dike there but relied more on the forest in that area. It was difficult for cavalry to penetrate their lands because of the canals although now that Bremen had joined their enemies, the merchants' navy could carry hostile forces to any frontier. Even so, the Archbishop and the Count had no convenient place from which to begin an attack—all the castles in the neighborhood had been destroyed by the Stedingeners and tent camps were not safe from surprise attack. The peasants could raise perhaps 6,000 men for their phalanx, and that many men, in a mass bristling with spears and axes, could repel even mailed knights; and so the Stedingeners fought with a confidence born of experience and proven courage.[5]

The Archbishop had sought, and obtained, additional papal support. Papal letters urged the Bishops of Lübeck, Ratzeburg, Minden, Paderborn, Hildesheim, Verden, Münster, and Osnabrück to send men and money. Dominicans, Cistercians, Franciscans, Praemonstratensians, and Benedictines preached the crusade. And nobles urged their friends and relatives to defend their class interests. Thousands took the cross and came to the aid of the Archbishop, including Count Henry of Oldenburg-Wildeshausen and the unwilling Otto of Lüneburg, who feared to defy the Pope further. The Archbishop evaded William of Modena, who might have ended the dispute peacefully, and launched his attack. A chronicler summarized this complicated campaign in these words:

> The duke of Brabant took the cross, as did the count of Holland, the count of Cleves, and many other noble men, against the Stedingers, and led the great force overland. The count of Holland went with many ships on the Weser. In all one estimated forty thousand crusaders who went into the land on Saint Urban's Day. The Stedingers came out to meet them and there was a great battle.[6]

Apparently the Stedingeners chose a battlefield at Aldenesch, a field lying behind the dikes and only barely above the water, so that ditches and the high water table turned the meadow into a bog. The battlefield was to be a muddy trap in which they might ensnare and massacre the crusaders. In any case, the mud would so impede their cavalry that it would be a close fight. The armies were probably of equal size, with perhaps 4,000 or 5,000 men on each side, and the battle was hotly contested. After arranging their lines, the knights charged into the peasant formation, and then, after desperate fighting, they retreated and regrouped. We are told that "the priests, who stood in the distance and awaited the outcome of the affair, sang 'media in vita in morte sumus,' and other sorrowful tunes sadly and prayed for the victory of the cross."[7]

A second charge also failed to break the peasants' lines, and Count Henry of Oldenburg fell in the melee. The knights reformed and attacked a third time, and again the peasants held their ground. Bodies covered the field, and horses and broken and discarded weapons were piled into heaps or mired in the mud. At that moment the Count of Cleves succeeded in flanking the Stedingeners and charged into their rear. The crusaders offered no terms and took no prisoners, as the peasants died where they stood, resisting to the last.

The following day the victors gave up the attempt to separate the dead on either side, dug that great pit whose mound still stands above the level field of Aldenesch, and buried crusader and heretic alike. After receiving the submission of those Stedingeners who survived, the crusaders returned to Bremen for a festival (which became an annual event down to the nineteenth century, when more liberal minds saw to its abolishment). The Archbishop had his victory, but it was a hollow one. The area, ravaged and depopulated, produced few taxes for many years.[8]

This crusade undoubtedly diverted crusaders from Livonia, as Bremen and the Rhineland had been prime recruiting grounds. Saxony also was distracted by the quarrel between the Welf Duke, Otto of Lüneburg, and the Archbishop of Bremen. Only after 1234 were significant numbers of crusaders again sailing to Livonia from Northern Germany.[9]

The Germans changed somewhat as a result of their experiences during these few years. The princes were not particularly active, having acquired many imperial prerogatives from Frederick II, who ignored their problems and concentrated on Italy; and no one family was strong enough to overawe or threaten its neighbors. Even the Welfs were content to live in peace. Consequently, the civilizing and christianizing (and self-aggrandizing) impulse that had spread western culture to the east was weaker. The crusade to the Holy Land lost popularity, as well as the crusade to Livonia. The only Germans who retained an interest in foreign affairs were the merchants, who began to organize and advance their special interests in

155

the Baltic and the North Sea. And because the merchants' military assistance was less important than their economic assistance, the crusade in Livonia also suffered for lack of money. There was no sudden and drastic decline in the activity of German princes, though crusading became steadily less important each decade. Furthermore, because the enemy was more formidable than before, even larger crusading armies were needed.

The Pope continued to encourage the nobles to sail across the Baltic to the aid of the Rigans, and in 1235 the Count of Haseldorf (from Holstein) and the Count of Dannenberg took the cross to Livonia, where the Swordbrothers, who exercised hegemony in Livonia, had faced serious difficulties since the time of their quarrel with Baldwin of Alna. Although William of Modena had restored peace and stability, he had not been able to restore the brothers' respectability. Nor had he been able to reconcile them with the powerful families, particularly the Buxhoevdens, the kin of the late Bishop Albert. Nor had King Waldemar given up his claims to Estonia—a particularly troublesome quarrel. The Swordbrothers regarded their income from Estonia as absolutely vital, and its uninhabited areas could be exploited in the future. For these reasons they kept a firm grip on the land and refused to return it to the Danish monarch.[10]

Money was at the heart of the problem, as the Swordbrothers needed a large army and many castles to defend their lands. Natives made up the bulk of the infantry, but westerners were needed as officers for native units and as garrison commanders, public officials, and trained knights. The Swordbrothers, unable to recruit enough brothers and desperate for enlistments, admitted the sons of burghers. Still, the number of brothers was not adequate. Nor were there sufficient crusaders. Thus it was necessary to hire mercenaries to fill the ranks, and therefore money was needed.[11]

Because Livonia and Estonia did not provide adequate revenues, the Swordbrothers were forced to adopt a policy of expansion southward. Semgallia and Kurland had been occupied earlier, and now the Swordbrothers pushed farther south and attacked the Lithuanians. In 1235 Master Volquin led successful attacks on the settlements around Nalsen, perhaps from a new castle that had been built near Lake Rasno.[12] A chronicler described the campaign:

> The Master's mind was on Lithuania. He had to see that region. So he rode to Nalsen and found a powerful army of heathens from everywhere. They came toward him in uncounted numbers with pride and shouting to their doom.

156

The Master addressed his men, "Mighty heroes, think about what we have come through to get here, and let that be a warning. If you want to return home safely, don't let them frighten you. With God's help and with arms we should be able to cut our way through." Then the entire army cried, "Let the speeches end, and let's get on with the exchange of spears and swords." And they all went into the fight like a hungry falcon. Many pagans were slain by the Estonians. The Letts were willing to suffer because they fought for glory, and the Livs were good heroes who knew how to fight. Two thousand Lithuanians were cut to pieces, and fell on the battlefield. The rest tired of the fight and fled in various ways.[13]

No people had yet been conquered in a single campaign, nor were the Lithuanians expected to capitulate at once. Despite their signal victory, therefore, the Swordbrothers knew that they would not be able to conquer, occupy, and then raise revenue from the Lithuanians in time to stave off financial disaster. The Danish monarch, meanwhile, would have recovered his strength, and Baldwin of Alna might be able to induce the Pope to attack them again. Also, a new crusade in Prussia was drawing potential crusaders away from Livonia. Master Volquin, nevertheless, saw hope and opportunity: if he could amalgamate his order into the Teutonic Knights, he would be able to resolve the problems of money, recruitment, and papal authority.

Founded in the Holy Land in 1198 as a medical unit by crusaders from Bremen, the Teutonic Knights had experienced spectacular growth in recent years. Patronage from both the Emperor and the Pope, together with skilled leadership, had made the order wealthy and influential. Herman von Salza, the grandmaster for many years, had been asked to take up many duties, such as the arbitration that followed the kidnapping of King Waldemar of Denmark. He had sent his knights into Hungary in 1211 and had practically established an independent state there before, thirteen years later, the king realized their menace and expelled them from his country. In 1228 and again in 1230 a Polish Prince had invited him to assist in a crusade against the pagan Prussians, but after the other German and Polish crusaders had returned home he established his Teutonic Knights in a castle at Thorn, from which they continued to attack the pagans. As they advanced down the Vistula, they built new castles and used them as bases for new attacks—the same strategy that had been followed in Livonia. By 1236 the Teutonic Knights had eliminated the competing orders and the Poles and had begun to appropriate Prussia for themselves.

Unlike the Swordbrothers in Livonia, the Teutonic Knights did not depend upon their conquests for income. Their vast estates in Germany and Italy supplied them with men and money for the wars in the Holy Land and the Baltic, but, unfortunately for the Swordbrothers, the Teutonic Knights were not willing to share their fortune. Perhaps they would have been willing to absorb a minor order, but they were not disposed to grant concessions. It may have been that a member of the Teutonic Knights, later a grandmaster, negotiated with his order on behalf of the Swordbrothers, and that this man, Louis of Naumburg, was Master Volquin's son, born before his father entered the Swordbrothers. (He is so identified by Friedrich Benninghoven.[14]) Nevertheless, the attempt was not successful. Two knights had been sent to Livonia to investigate the brothers, and their report to the annual assembly at Marburg had not been favorable. Their report, combined with the Swordbrothers' demand for autonomy within the order, doomed the discussions.

These tidings were followed by worse news from Rome. Acting on a list of charges prepared by Baldwin of Alna, the Pope ordered the Swordbrothers to appear before him and answer charges of disobedience, rebellion, and heresy. The hearings took place in the winter of 1235–1236 at Viterbo. William of Modena defended the order so forcefully that Baldwin of Alna retired in disgrace to the Latin Kingdom of Constantinople, where he died a minor bishop. But the Swordbrothers' enemies were too numerous even for William. Perhaps inspired by the Danes, the Pope dispatched William as legate to preach the crusade to Livonia and to resolve numerous quarrels in the Scandinavian kingdoms, and then he rebuked the order. His verdict was its death blow: he decreed the return of Estonia to the Danish King and the Archbishop of Lund; compensation to its enemies for their losses in battle, ransom, and incomes; and all future disputes be appealed to the papal curia.[15]

No one can say how the Swordbrothers would have reacted to the papal decision—whether they would have resisted to the last or bowed to the inevitable—because the order did not survive long enough to face its dire predicament. In 1236 an army of crusaders, led by the Counts of Haseldorf and Dannenberg, arrived in Riga and demanded to do battle against the Lithuanians. Master Volquin raised a force equal to that of the crusaders, perhaps 100 knights and 1,200 men, and called up 1,500 natives and 200 Russians from Pskov. Then he marched them through Semgallia

and into Samogithia to attack a Lithuanian settlement south of the Saule
River. Emerging from the wooded wilderness, they fell upon the Lithuanians without warning.

> They robbed and burned wonderfully in many bands, and ravaged up and
> down the land freely. Then they returned by way of Saule through the woods
> and heath. Alas, it was a great misfortune that this campaign had ever been
> conceived. As they came to a stream, they saw the enemy. Few of those who
> had been so bold in Riga now rushed into battle. The Master said to the best
> of them, "Fight now, it is the time. All our honor rests on it, because if we can
> slay those leaders over there, then we can proceed freely home." But the heroes
> said, "We don't want to fight here. If we lose our horses we will have to stand
> on foot." The Master answered, "So you prefer to lose your heads here as well
> as your horses?" It happened as he said. Many more heathens arrived. The
> next day the Christians decided to ride away, but they had to fight the pagans.
> Their arms were weak in the swamp, and they were cut down like women.[16]

It was a total disaster. The foot soldiers panicked and dispersed in the
woods. Those who escaped were able to do so only because the master and
some of his men sacrificed themselves to slow down the pursuit. Forty-
eight Swordbrothers perished, as well as Master Volquin and 2,000 crusaders and native allies. Lithuania was saved, and Semgallia and Kurland
reverted temporarily to paganism, but it was the end for the Swordbrothers. It was as if God's judgment had confirmed the papal condemnation.
The survivors—perhaps fifty or sixty knights and 600 troops in garrison
duty—appealed again to the Teutonic Knights.

The negotiations for the union of the two orders had continued at the
papal Court without making much progress. The Swordbrothers would
not give up their demand for autonomy or surrender Estonia to the Danes,
and the Teutonic Knights would not concede these vital points. However,
when news of the disaster at Saule arrived, the Swordbrothers could hardly
delay the union in hope of better terms. Apparently Herman of Salza,
who was acting as mediator at Viterbo in the dispute between the Pope
and the Emperor, arranged an interview between the Pope and the Swordbrothers' emissaries—a carefully staged ceremony whose intent was not
imparted to the Swordbrothers. One of the eyewitnesses later wrote a
memoir about the ceremony of 14 May 1237:

> The Grandmaster summoned us to the pope, and asked "Are the mantles
> here?" I said, "Yes." Then he told us to come quickly and said, "The pope will

do as we wish." Then the brothers from Livonia came and kneeled before him. Then the pope forgave them all their sins, both those before entering the order and those after, and admonished them to honor the order, and gave them the white mantle with the black cross. When he gave them the mantles, I seized the old mantles; the chamberlain grabbed also, and I pulled against him. Then our brother spoke, "Let it be! They are his, and belong to him." When he returned to our convent the master asked, "Now tell me, brothers, what we have in castles and lands?" I wanted to say then, but the others spoke, how rich the lands were. The master said that the pope would not have allowed [the union], except that the king would be returned his lands. Then brother Gerlach spoke to me, "Brother Hartman! If it had not already taken place, then it would not ever take place."[17]

It was the formal end of the Swordbrothers, absorbed completely into the Teutonic Knights. One might say that bankruptcy proceedings had been concluded, and all that remained was the final disposition of the remaining assets among the creditors, but of the assets only Estonia was strongly contested. The commander of Prussia, Herman Balke, arrived in Riga with reinforcements in the summer of 1237 and took over the castles and advocacies from the unhappy Swordbrothers, who were quickly enrolled into the order of the Teutonic Knights.

Thus the question of Estonia loomed over all the parties, threatening civil and even international war. The question had arisen even before the Swordbrothers' emissaries left the palace at Viterbo, and they pressed the new master to retain all the disputed lands. Master Balke was in a difficult position, on one hand wanting to satisfy the new members of his order and, on the other, forced to obey the papal instruction to return the lands to King Waldemar. In an attempt to bring about a solution, William of Modena returned to the Baltic to negotiate with the contending parties. He had visited Denmark in 1236; he went to Estonia in 1237, and after a visit to Prussia, was back again in Denmark in 1238. The careful investigations of several eminent historians reveal how very difficult these negotiations were and how the conflicting claims and political relationships boded ill for the crusade to Livonia.[18]

The Teutonic Knights wanted to end the dispute. It was too dangerous to have a discontented and powerful monarch such as King Waldemar in their rear—a warlike neighbor who might fall upon them when they were deeply committed elsewhere. It seemed particularly foolish, moreover, to postpone a settlement if this same monarch might be converted into a firm ally. Their interests lay to the south, in Prussia, where they faced dangerous competition from Svantopulk of Pomerania and Bishop Christian of Prussia, each of whom wanted to evict the order from their valuable territory. The international situation was bleak, unless a settlement with Denmark was forthcoming.

Fortunately for the Teutonic Knights, the Danish Monarch was embarrassed by unrest in his own lands. Ever since his eldest son had died in a hunting accident the King had been plagued by jealousies among his other children. Abel, in particular, was an obstinate and headstrong Prince. Duke of Schleswig and regent of Holstein for his nephews, he had considerable autonomy and authority, but he desired more. King Waldemar therefore sought to bring his sons together, fearing his death would doom his kingdom to another era of civil war such as had beset Denmark in past generations.

The secular knights in Estonia were unruly and thus were another potential difficulty for the Teutonic Knights. The Swordbrothers had enfeoffed numerous vassals with lands in Estonia, but after the battle of the Saule they could not control them. The Teutonic Knights preferred to surrender Estonia to the Danes rather than become involved in the endemic civil conflict between the great lords and the newer arrivals. However, these German nobles did not want the Danes to return and vowed to fight for their independence and lands if necessary.

The papacy, viewing all this dissension with distaste, concluded that Baldwin of Alna may have been right after all. The crusade was stagnating and threatened to become a disaster. Was there an alternative to papal leadership? Pope Gregory wrote angry letters to William of Modena, urging him to bring the controversies to a quick and decisive end, and he did so. By his ceaseless travel and negotiation, William brought the parties to a compromise after convincing them they should look beyond the comparatively small territories of Estonia to the vast stretches of Russia that lay east of them. He urged them to settle their grievances and join in a vast crusade against Novgorod.

William, Herman Balke, and King Waldemar met at Stenby on Zeeland, and after long negotiations the latter two signed a treaty, 7 June 1238, that ended all disagreements between them. The Teutonic Knights returned Reval, Harrien, and Wierland to the King, and Herman Balke retained Jerwan for his order, which should have mollified the former Swordbrothers and their friends but probably did not. They agreed that,

pending the arrival of Danish officials, the Teutonic Knights would continue to supervise the government of Estonia; but the order governed
Estonia in a very unsatisfactory manner, so that the great lords subjected
the lesser nobles or expelled them from the region. Afterward those nobles
preferred to look out for themselves.

That they hesitated to offer fealty to an unfriendly monarch and refused
to obey the Bishop of Reval, the royal governor, is understandable. Only
by the promise of rewards in Russia and, later, by a guarantee of their
rights in Estonia could they be won over to support the treaty.[19] Thus the
crusade against the Russians in Novgorod was essential to the maintenance
of peace among the crusading states, for it united the Danes and their
erstwhile vassals in Estonia, as well as the Swedes, the Buxhoevden supporters in Livonia, the Bishop and merchants in Riga, and the Teutonic
Knights. William of Modena lost little time in publicizing the new venture.
The first to take the cross was the Count of Holstein:

> In 1239 God's Word came to him as I shall describe. The honorable count
> decided upon a great venture. He wanted to do it for his soul's sake. He had
> to sail. Therefore he called on his son-in-law, Abel, to rule Holstein and all its
> people. . . . His countess went with him to that pious land. Her name was
> Helvegia. They went to Livonia for the first time, where they suffered much,
> just as they would have in the Holy Land. When their sins were absolved . . .
> he decided to dedicate himself to Mary and Saint Francis. He wanted to enter
> into the order of Saint Francis.[20]

Doubtless many others sought salvation through pious deeds on the
crusades—many who left no chroniclers to record their intentions—but we
know only that William and his contemporaries counted on such men as
the Count of Holstein to achieve the goals of the Church and bring about
peace on earth.

Unfortunately, because few men are visionary idealists like William
of Modena, historians see the motivation for the crusade against Novgorod
differently. Donner, who wrote the biography of William of Modena, sees
his hero as the faithful churchman who united the Christians against an
external foe, thus carrying forward the program of the Church Universal.
Johansen, who worked with Estonian documents, sees the ambitions of
the Danish King and his troublesome vassals as important motives. Benninghoven, who has investigated the Order of Swordbrothers, sees the

survivors of that organization as the instigators of the push eastward. Others, finally, tend to see either imperialist aggression or defensive precaution in the attack on Novgorod. And certainly the allied crusaders themselves saw numerous reasons for the advance eastward: it would relieve domestic pressures; it would give credence to their professed raison d'être, the protection of the Church. Furthermore, they could christianize the remaining pagans and force the Russians to recognize the supremacy of the Roman Church, thus repeating the success of the Fourth Crusade over Byzantium in 1204, ending the desultory warfare on the Russian frontier, and allowing them to turn again against the Lithuanians.

There was considerable hope that pro-western Russians would make the campaign short and easy. Pskov, in particular, had been ruled alternately by pro- and anti-western princes. Many years before, Bishop Albert's brother, Theodoric, had married into the royal family; thereafter, in periodic exile, his relatives had taken refuge in Livonia and had often held important offices in Livonia while awaiting recall to their homeland. At this time, 1238, Prince Jaroslav Vladimirovitch was in Dorpat, asking for help against his domestic enemies. German garrisons had been in Pskov before, and now they could be reestablished, perhaps permanently.[21]

The crusaders could count on Swedish cooperation as well. For many years the Swedes had maintained a hold on the Finnish coast and had expanded toward the Novgorodian frontiers from time to time, only to be thrust back. The Swedish force in the north and the German force in the south would make a two-prong assault against a weakened Russian state.

It is important to remember that the Novgorodians were particularly vulnerable to attack at this moment. After the Lithuanians had granted a truce to the crusaders, after the battle of the Saule, they had turned to Pskov and Novgorod, defeated the Russians in battle, and plundered their lands. But the greatest danger, in the Russian mind, was neither the crusader nor the Lithuanian—it was the Mongol horde. A Russian chronicler bewailed the Mongol presence:

That same year foreigners called Tartars came in countless numbers, like locusts. . . . And who, brothers, fathers, and children, seeing this, God's infliction on the whole Russian land, does not lament? God let the pagans on us for our sins. God brings foreigners on to the land in his wrath, and thus crushed by them they will be reminded of God.[22]

The Russians, who had lived with the memory of the earlier Mongol invasion, feared the return of the fierce steppe warriors of Genghis Khan, but they were unprepared for the sudden assault that overran the eastern Russian states in 1237; and this time the Mongols did not depart. They besieged and captured city after city, and by the end of 1241 only Novgorod was unconquered, temporarily protected by its distant location. But even Novgorod doubted its ability to withstand the Mongol onslaught.

The sudden appearance of the Mongol army on the frontiers of the European world and its unexpected successes against the Russians surprised those western Europeans who heard of its exploits. Stories of Mongol hordes were circulated, reporting that hundreds of thousands of savage riders—the vanguard of the anti-Christ—were whipping their shaggy ponies westward to overrun all Europe. On the other hand, the crusaders in the Holy Land, who welcomed their attacks on the Moslem states, identified them with the forces of Prester John, the mythical Christian king in the heart of Asia. But most of the stories were dismissed by the proud nobility and clergy of the west, who remained confident of the ability of their superior civilization to defend itself. Soon enough, however, those same skeptics were to wonder if the stories had not been prophetic.[23]

The ferocity and skill of the Mongol warriors gave them a reputation that magnified their number into a "horde," but their organization and tactics were much more important than their number. Their discipline and mobility were unequaled by any of their opponents; they seemed to be everywhere and nowhere at once. Their scouts kept their commanders informed of all enemy movements, so that they were rarely taken by surprise themselves but could always seize upon an opponent's temporary disadvantage. They also kept a force in reserve, which was considered unchivalrous in western Europe; and their light, speedy ponies were perfectly adapted to the hit-and-run tactics their warlords preferred. Every battle was marked by a rain of arrows on their enemy's troops and by a series of feints and stratagems designed to confuse or entrap them. When their opponents retreated into fortified places, the Mongols collected local manpower for use as storm troops, drove them forward by fear, and used skilled engineers to direct the assaults. Efficient though these tactics were, the consistent use of terror gave them an even greater advantage, because the enemy population would either surrender quickly or flee in wild panic. Well led, well armed, and well disciplined, the Mongol forces had several major advantages over the foot soldiers of Russia, the light cavalry of Poland and Hungary, and the mailed knights of Germany.

It is small wonder that the Prince of Novgorod found little time to prepare the defense of his western frontier. It was not until the summer of 1241 that the Mongols decided against an attack on Novgorod to destroy this last independent Russian state, and instead turned west. Only then was the Prince free to deal with the crusaders' threat, and by then they had made great advances.

The subsequent movement of the Mongol army affected the Baltic Crusade greatly, though in an indirect manner. The Mongol commander had decided to punish King Bela of Hungary for giving refuge to the Cuman tribe, a hereditary enemy of the Mongols. One Mongol army therefore made for the Carpathian passes leading into eastern Hungary while another swung across southern Poland, through Silesia, Bohemia, and Moravia, and into Hungary from the northwest. A few Polish Princes tried to stop this second force, but when the Mongols cut down their light cavalry with a hail of arrows, the remaining Princes fled north and west, abandoning their towns and countryside to Mongol destruction. Fortunately for the peasantry, and the refugees, the Mongols lacked the time for a thorough massacre and pressed into Silesia. The Duke of Silesia, a thoroughly germanized noble, was too attached to the code of chivalry to flee or to await reinforcements from his cousin, the King of Bohemia—his mailed knights were overwhelmed after one valiant charge. Some Teutonic Knights, who had fought with him, also died in the battle. The King of Bohemia then withdrew into his fortresses and allowed the invaders to pass through his lands. Once inside Hungary, the Mongols outmaneuvered and then outfought the small Hungarian army. A squad of Mongols pursued the King to the Adriatic islands while the main army occupied the Hungarian plain, attempted to depopulate the country, and departed only when the Great Khan died, as they were needed for the election of his successor. Behind their withdrawal eastward was a vast and desolated region.

The effect of this Mongol invasion has lasted to the present day. Eastern Europe was politically disorganized, so that the great states of Russia, Poland, and Hungary recovered only slowly and in a power vacuum that could be exploited by the Lithuanians and the Teutonic Knights. The success of the Teutonic Order in Prussia and the Lithuanians in Russia was due in large part to the fact that they escaped the Mongol attacks that laid competitors low. The alarm, meanwhile, had spread to Northern Germany:

> In this time the Tartars came with a powerful army into Poland, having already conquered the Russians and many other lands. Henry of Poland fought with them and was slain, and more than thirty thousand men with him, not counting the women and children slain in the land. They ravaged the land and overran cathedrals, cloisters, and churches. When the news came to Germany, many princes and lords gathered at Magdeburg and counseled that because of the great danger they give the cross to all the people, women, and children along the way. It was decided that all who were there should go, all those who had life and goods; and those who had goods but lacked strength should help those who had the strength but not the money, and of five, four should help the one so that he would be useful to the expedition. . . . King Conrad, the emperor's son, took the cross, and princes and lords, knights, men, women, and children, just about everyone in Germany.[24]

But this enthusiasm did not last. The army did not march; the Hungarians were left to suffer their fate alone; and the imperial power and authority were shown to be hollow. Frederick II did nothing, nor did the Pope; each concentrated on his own private duel to the death. Thus the German Princes realized that they were truly on their own.

Moreover, the Mongol threat passed quickly and the Germans reverted to their normal habits. Those who were interested in the Livonian crusade saw the Mongol invasions not as a danger to themselves but as an opportunity to force the Russian Church to submit and to gain new lands for themselves. Novgorod was isolated; the crusaders were prepared; and the attack was launched without further consideration, the first stroke being delivered by the Swedes. The Russian chronicler recounted the proud episode in these terms:

> The [Swedes] came with their [ruler] and with their bishops, and halted in the Neva at the mouth of the Izhera, wishing to take possession of Ladoga, or in one word, of Novgorod, and of the whole Novgorod province. But again the most kind and merciful God, lover of men, preserved and protected us from the foreigners since they laboured in vain without the command of God. For the news came to Novgorod that the [Swedes] were going toward Ladoga, and [Prince Alexander] with the men of Novgorod and of Ladoga did not delay at all; he went against them and defeated them by the power of

Saint Sophia and the prayers of our Sovereign Lady the Holy Mother of God and eternally Virgin Mary on the 15th day of July [1240]. . . . And there was a great slaughter of [Swedes].[25]

The danger to the Russians was that the Swedes would seize and blockade the great rivers leading from Novgorod to the Baltic so that the Russian merchants could not sail out to purchase grain, for Novgorod was dependent on grain supplies from the west as long as southern Russia was in Mongol hands. A blockade could not be imposed by other means. The merchant cities of the west, such as Lübeck and Visby, would not agree to sacrifice their commerce for royal benefit and therefore the blockade could not be imposed except by capturing the trade routes. Consequently, Novgorod was saved by the battle on the Neva, and the Russian commander's name was thereafter associated with his victory: Alexander Nevsky.

The next threat to Russia was more dangerous. A combined force of Teutonic Knights, Danes under Princes Canute and Abel, Germans under Bishop Herman of Dorpat, and Russians under Prince Jaroslav (then in exile from Pskov) pushed into Novgorodian territory from the west. In the fall of 1240 this army captured Isborg, smashed a relief force from Pskov, and then marched upon Pskov and obtained its surrender, fully expecting to win complete victory the following year.[26] But the succeeding year, 1241, turned out to be much better for the Novgorodians, as the Mongol storm had passed to the west and freed the Russians for an all-out effort against the crusaders. Also, King Waldemar of Denmark had died, so that his sons remained home in expectation of imminent civil war, and the Teutonic Knights were no longer fully committed to the venture.[27]

Alexander Nevsky struck first at the German-Danish garrisons east of Narva. Significantly, he spared the westerners for ransom but hanged the Estonians as rebels and traitors.[28] Thus he demonstrated his limited aim: to retain control of the vital border territories. He had no intention of driving the crusaders into the sea; his attention was directed more to the south—where the Mongols held sway—than to the west. His next move was against the western garrison Pskov, and was described by the German chronicler in these terms:

He came with a mighty force of many Russians to free the Pskovians. And these latter rejoiced in their hearts. When he saw the Germans he did not delay. He drove the two Germans out of their advocacy and routed their troops.

167

Not a German remained. Then he returned the land to the native Russians.
Thus it went for the Teutonic Knights. If Pskov had been held, it would have
benefited Christianity to the end of the world. It was a mistake to have taken
the land and not have occupied it properly. He cries most about the pain who
could have avoided it easily.[29]

The Russian force then marched into the diocese of Dorpat in a short-
lived invasion. Indeed, Alexander retreated when Bishop Herman called
up every fighting man he could muster. The Teutonic Knights sent a small
force to join the Buxhoevden prelate (the master and most of his knights
remained in Riga); the western army set out in pursuit of the Novgorodians; and the two Christian forces met on the ice of Lake Peipus on 5
April 1242. Neither army was large. The westerners had perhaps 2,000
men, the Russians perhaps 6,000, but these numbers were in effect balanced
by the superior armament of the crusader knights.[30]

The battle has become undeservedly famous, having been endowed—
for twentieth-century political considerations—with much more significance than it merited in itself. Indeed, although Eisenstein's film *Alexander
Nevsky* is a reasonably accurate portrayal of the battle, some of its scenes
tell us more about the Soviet Union just before Hitler's invasion than about
medieval history. But be that as it may, the crusader army proceeded across
or along the lake and met the Russian forces that were massed in a solid
body. The heavily armed western knights formed the spearhead of a
column, made up largely of light cavalry and foot soldiers, and charged
into the Russian infantry.

> The battle began. The Russians had many archers, and they began the game
> manfully against the king's men [Danes]. The brothers' banners then over-
> threw the archers and swords were heard clashing and the helmets cut apart.
> And there were many from both sides who fell dead on the grass. Then the
> brothers' army was completely surrounded. The Russians had such an army
> that there were easily sixty men for every German knight. The brothers fought
> well enough, till they were cut down. Some of those from Dorpat escaped from
> the battle, and it was their salvation that they fled. Twenty brothers lay dead
> and six were captured.[31]

The battle, of course, had repercussions beyond the Livonian-Russian
border region: revolts broke out in Kurland and Prussia that threatened to
involve the Teutonic Knights on so many fronts that they could not cope
with their enemies. Alexander Nevsky, however, had no interest in destroy-

ing the crusader states. Because he considered the Mongol threat so immediate, he offered generous terms to his fellow Christians, which the crusaders immediately accepted.[32]

It had been a dangerous moment for Novgorod, but perhaps less dangerous than is sometimes thought. If Novgorod had been occupied by the westerners, the Russian state might indeed have shared the fate of Byzantium after the Fourth Crusade. However, it is hard to imagine the crusaders permanently suppressing Russian culture, the Russian Church, and Russian political goals. If the Mongols could not do this, was it possible for the westerners, whose capacity vis-à-vis the Mongols' pales into insignificance? The "Battle on the Ice," therefore, was more important for the crusaders than for the Russians.

Victory, if the outcome were reversed, would have given new life to the tensions in Livonia and Estonia. That fraction of the Teutonic Knights that had wholeheartedly supported the attack would have incurred new obligations that the Teutonic Knights as a whole would have had to meet. The Danish vassals in Estonia would have acquired great estates and would have become even more rebellious. And Bishop Herman of Dorpat would have become as powerful as the Bishop of Riga. Defeat, however, precluded all these possibilities. The master of the Teutonic Knights re-established his authority over the rebellious faction of his order composed of former Swordbrothers, many of whom presumably fell in battle; the King of Denmark forced the Estonian vassals to trade their estates for lands on the Russian frontier, where a new government was built around the "headman," who was chosen from among the vassals; and the Buxhoevden family failed to recover the power it had held during the lifetime of Bishop Albert of Riga.

The Teutonic Knights again turned their attention to the south, where the master planned to link Prussia and Livonia across Samogithia, a forest region inhabited by pagan Lithuanians. The citizens of Riga founded a permanent trading station in Novgorod, and thereafter peace with Novgorod was their principal interest. The other Germans—the advocates, the canons, the vassals, the priests, the merchants—concentrated on improving their own position and making it superior to that of the natives.

In this era, then, the Swordbrothers passed from the scene and were absorbed by a wealthier and more disciplined crusading order. The Teutonic Knights could renounce those goals of the Swordbrothers that had brought conflict with the Bishops, the Danes, and the Russians. Instead, they could turn to a new field of conquest with less complicated forms of competition, Samogithia, a resolutely pagan country peopled by excellent warriors. The future would bring a new type of crusade—less international and less concerned with the spiritual salvation of the enemy, but militarily more difficult and dangerous. Armies of crusaders large enough to have won easy victories in the past were now barely sufficient to garrison the frontier castles. The Teutonic Knights backed by their resources in the Holy Roman Empire—churches, monasteries, manors, and wealthy friends —instituted a more professional crusade and directed it at the weakest of their pagan neighbors, the Samogithians, who lived in the wilderness separating Livonia from Prussia.

NOTES TO CHAPTER EIGHT

1. Paul Hasse, "Der Kampf zwischen Lübeck und Dänemark vom Jahre 1234 in Sage und Geschichte," in *Hansische Geschichtsblätter* (1874), 20: 118–48.

2. *Holsteinische Reimchronik*, p. 625.

3. Henry Charles Lea, *A History of the Inquisition of the Middle Ages* (New York: Harper Brothers, 1888), 3: 182ff.

4. *Sächische Weltchronik*, p. 249.

5. King, *Chronicles of Three Free Cities*, pp. 56–57.

6. *Sächsische Weltchronik*, p. 250.

7. *Albert of Stade*, p. 362.

8. Ibid.; *Sächsische Weltchronik*, p. 250. Even Roger of Wendover, the English chronicler, noted this great battle.

9. The Welf claims were settled by granting Otto the title Duke of Braunschweig. Thus the title of Duke, lost by Henry the Lion, was returned to his family. Its importance was mainly symbolic, however.

10. For the economic resources of the Swordbrothers, see Benninghoven, *Schwertbrüder*, pp. 388–412. See also Johansen, *Estlandliste*, pp. 730ff.

11. Benninghoven, *Schwertbrüder*, pp. 215–16.

12. Hellmann, *Das Lettenland im Mittelalter*, p. 191.

13. *Reimchronik*, ll. 1802–1837.

14. Benninghoven, *Schwertbrüder*, pp. 424–28.

15. Ibid., pp. 321–27; *Urkundenbuch*, 1: no. CXLV.

16. *Reimchronik*, ll. 1902–1933.

17. Hartmann von Heldrungen, "Bericht über die Vereinigung des Schwertordens mit dem deutschen Orden und über die Erwerbung Livlands durch den letzteren," *Mitteilungen aus dem Gebiet der livländischen Geschichte*, 11 (1868): 89.

18. Benninghoven, *Schwertbrüder*, pp. 362–69; Donner, *Kardinal Wilhelm von Sabina*, pp. 199–211; Johansen, *Estlandliste*, pp. 699–700.

19. Johansen, *Estlandliste*, pp. 694–700, 730ff; Donner, *Kardinal Wilhelm von Sabina*, pp. 199–211; *Urkundenbuch*, 1: no. CLX.

20. *Holsteinische Reimchronik*, p. 625.

21. Goetze, *Albert Suerbeer*, pp. 24–25, 137–42.

22. *Chronicle of Novgorod*, pp. 81–84.

23. See George Vernadsky, *The Mongols and Russia*, vol. 3 of *A History of Russia* (New Haven: Yale University Press, 1953); Michael Prawdin, *The Mongol Empire: Its Rise and Legacy* (Toronto: Allen and Unwin, 1952); Aleksander E. Presniakov, *The Formation of the Great Russian State* (Chicago: University of Chicago Press, 1970).

24. *Sächsische Weltchronik*, pp. 254–55.

25. *Chronicle of Novgorod*, pp. 84–85.

26. *Reimchronik*, ll. 2099–2173.

27. Benninghoven (*Schwertbrüder*, pp. 369–82) suggests that the former members of the Swordbrothers refused to follow the more cautious policies of the master of the Teutonic Knights. Consequently, when they set out against Novgorod it was against his wishes and without his support. Therefore the attack on Novgorod did not have the official sanction of the order, and once the rebellious faction was decimated in battle, there was no one to revive an interest in war with Russia.

28. *Chronicle of Novgorod*, p. 86.

29. *Reimchronik*, ll. 2183–2202.

30. Paul von Osten-Sacken, "Der ersten Kampf der Deutschen gegen die Russen," *Mitteilungen aus dem Gebiet der livländischen Geschichte*, 20 (1910): 87–124.

31. *Reimchronik*, ll. 2240–2261.

32. *Chronicle of Novgorod*, pp. 86–87.

9

Reorientation of the Crusade

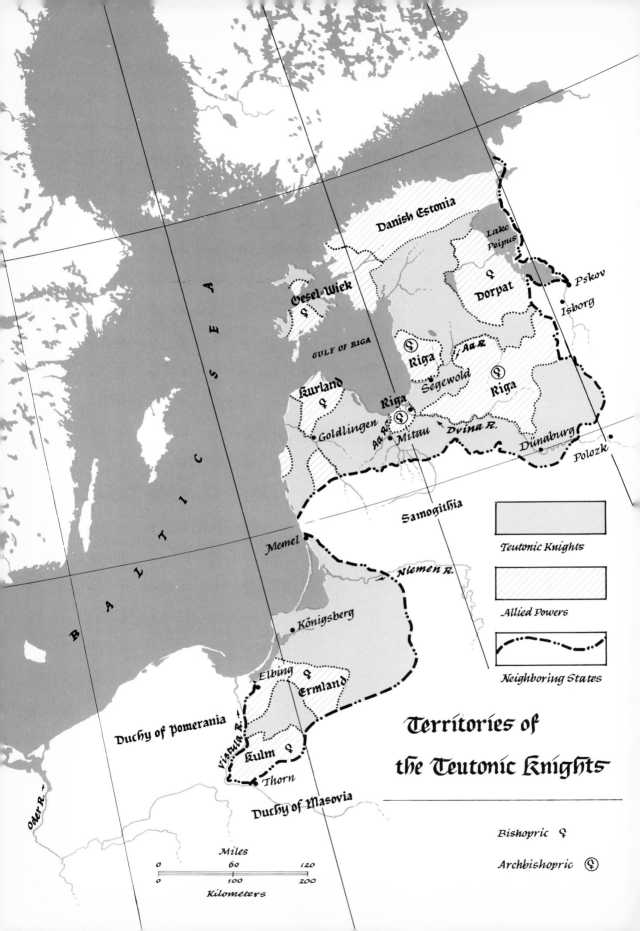

BALTIC SEA

Danish Estonia

Lake Peipus

Oesel-Wiek ♀

Pskov

Dorpat ♀

Isborg

GULF OF RIGA

Riga ⊕

Aa R.

Kurland ♀

Segewold

Riga ⊕

Goldlingen

Riga

Riga ⊕

Aa R.

Mitau

Dvina R.

Dünaburg

Polozk

Samogithia

Memel

Niemen R.

Königsberg

Teutonic Knights

Allied Powers

Elbing

Ermland ♀

Neighboring States

Duchy of Pomerania

Vistula R.

Kulm ♀

Thorn

Territories of
the Teutonic Knights

Duchy of Masovia

Oder R.

Miles

0   60   120

0   100   200

Kilometers

Bishopric ♀

Archbishopric ⊕

IN THE DECADE FOLLOWING THE DISASTER AT LAKE PEIPUS THE LIVONIAN crusading effort turned again to the south, with the intent of reconquering the native tribes of Semgallia and Kurland, and even of subjecting the warlike Samogithians. This plan met with considerable initial success, as even their most dangerous enemy, the Lithuanians, reacted to the crusaders' advance by combining into larger political units and accepting the Christian religion. The formation of a Christian Kingdom of Lithuania was the most important development of the decade, but we have only meager information concerning it; and the kingdom did not last. Significant changes also were taking place in Germany and Denmark. The deadly duel between Pope and Emperor could no longer be confined to Italy, and the papacy, determined to remove the imperial threat to the Church once and for all, carried the war into Germany. Denmark entered a period of internal conflict in which murderous wars of succession destroyed the cohesiveness of the kingdom and brought a serious quarrel with the Church. Danish civil war, papal and imperial ambition, and Lithuanian unification continued to affect the crusade in mid-century.

The origin of the Danish conflict was the jealousy between the princely brothers—Eric, the heir to the throne, and Abel, Duke of Schleswig. Eric, who believed in a strong monarchy, dreamed of rebuilding the empire his father had lost at the battle of Bornhoeved. This dream lay behind his crusading ambitions in Estonia and his desire to obtain the royal appanages assigned to his brothers. In particular, he was interested in Holstein, which was governed by Duke Abel on behalf of his nephews, who were studying in Paris. He saw Abel's marriage to Matilda of Holstein as a danger to the kingdom—and indeed it marked the beginning of that union of Schleswig and Holstein that lasted until the era of Bismarck.

When Eric came to the throne in 1241, he began to press this matter with his brother, but without success. Abel, who refused to surrender any of his prerogatives, began to look for allies to help him if he should have to fight against royal encroachment—efforts that soon met with resounding success. In 1242 he signed a marriage contract with Duke Albrecht of Saxony on behalf of the young Countess of Holstein, which won him both the Duke's friendship and that of the Archbishop of Bremen, the young girl's relative. These nobles brought Mecklenburg and Schwerin into the alliance. And Abel, as regent of Holstein, was able to bargain successfully for the Lübeckers help when they asked the young Counts to serve as advocates. Backed by such friends and allies, Duke Abel felt safe in defying his royal brother.[1]

If King Eric had been satisfied to deal with only this problem, he might have had more success, formidable though the coalition was; but he impetuously overreached himself, and his folly soon brought him into great danger. Several years earlier, when he was studying at the University of Paris, he had struck up a friendship with the churchman who had become Pope Innocent IV. He now used the friendship to obtain papal favors, particularly favors concerning money, and although Eric received papal permission to levy special taxes, his attempt to collect them from Church lands provoked the usually compliant Danish clergy to loud protests. Needing the money badly and seeing this issue as part of a wide range of Church-state relationships, Eric refused to back down. He decided to fight the churchmen, but in a clever manner. Without breaking with the Church and the Pope, he negotiated with Emperor Frederick II for the latter's cession of the lands north of the Elbe. The Emperor granted him the lands in hope of winning an ally, but Eric did not move so far toward the Hohenstaufen cause as to antagonize the papacy. The common interests of the two monarchs were nevertheless sufficiently obvious to frighten the Church and to spur the churchmen into conciliatory gestures.

If the Church in Rome responded to these tactics, the Church in Denmark did not. Some prelates fled the country. Others, more willing to resist secular authority, assembled at Odense in February 1245 and threatened King Eric with excommunication and the interdict unless he relented. They were joined by two of the King's brothers, Christopher and Canute, and by the petty nobility and much of the peasantry. Thus a formidable coalition was opposed to the King.[2]

Although faced by enemies everywhere, Eric commanded sufficient resources to defeat them in the initial clashes. Then new foes appeared.

In this time there was a quarrel between King Eric and his brother Duke Abel. The duke was aided by Count John of Holstein, the Archbishop of Bremen and their vassals and also those from Lübeck. Duke Abel took the town of Ripon from the king and ravaged around and captured his people. The king took it again and defended it in a manly fashion. Duke Abel and the Archbishop Gerhard of Bremen, Count John and other lords came with a great army into Denmark to win Ripon back. The king defended it manfully. They besieged it so long that they had to leave for hunger. The king and the duke were reconciled, and the other lords witnessed their pact. Those from Lübeck fought with the ships of the king and ravaged from the sea and killed many innocent men.[3]

King Eric had maintained himself against his brother and the Church through 1246, but the day of reckoning had not yet arrived; the struggle between secular and ecclesiastical authority was being fought too hotly in Italy for anyone to engage in it with safety. Although Eric extorted concessions from both the Emperor and the Pope, the time was coming when militant churchmen would turn their attention to Denmark. As early as 1245, in fact, Pope Innocent IV had decided upon a program that would make such secular threats less effective. Calling the churchmen together for a general council in Lyons, ostensibly to discuss a new crusade, the Pope obtained the formal deposition of Frederick II, his archenemy in Italy, and then arranged the election of an anti-King in Germany. Once this had been done, the Pope struck at those German princes and prelates who were pro-Hohenstaufen or neutral. Because the Archbishop of Bremen had not shown sufficient enthusiasm for the papal cause, the Pope listened sympathetically to the complaints of malcontent canons from Hamburg and disgruntled citizens of Bremen; and fearful of unfavorable papal decisions, the Archbishop abandoned his monarch's cause. The citizens of Lübeck were more stubborn, however, and refused to give up their traditional Hohenstaufen allegiance, and upon hearing this, the Pope ordered King Eric to reprove them.[4] By such means the Pope succeeded in harassing the imperial party in Northern Germany—to the delight of the Danish Monarch, who found himself still a favorite of the papacy despite his many hostile actions against the Danish Church.

As the papal policies met with increasing success in Germany, King Eric decided to resume the offensive and humble his own churchmen before the situation changed. The hostile prelates fled the country but could not obtain a sympathetic hearing from the Pope. Toward the end of 1248 the royal forces overran Schleswig and reached Segeberg in Holstein, advancing so swiftly that Abel's two daughters had to flee in disguise, slipping away barefoot through the snow in peasant clothing. There were other such successes, but there were also some indications of trouble. Mecklenburg had come over to Eric, and his ally, Duke Otto of Braunschweig, had occupied Schwerin; but the Archbishop of Bremen was again giving aid to Holstein, and the King of Norway was preparing to enter the war. The last royal success had been matched by a setback, in that the capture of Christopher was preceded by Canute's regaining his freedom. The Pope had already sent William of Modena on a mission to Norway and Sweden to restore peace to their restless people, and now he was offering to send him to Denmark to mediate its civic dispute. Thus, it was obvious that Eric's campaign was not a success and that each side was exhausted and needed a truce. Late in 1248, Archbishop Gerhard of Bremen mediated an agreement for the cessation of hostilities, part of which required everyone to cooperate in the crusade to Livonia.[5]

King Eric was willing to sail to the east on crusade. His neighbor, King Eric III of Sweden, was already in Finland, fulfilling his promise to William of Modena. The Danish Monarch therefore took the cross, lifted his blockade of Lübeck, which had hindered crusaders seeking to pass through Mecklenburg, and began to collect a crusading army. Because he lacked money, he ordered another special tax of one penny on every plow in the kingdom, an unpopular tax that applied to Church and secular lands alike and provoked great dissatisfaction among the free peasantry. Derisively, the petty nobles and peasants nicknamed him Eric Plowpenny, shouted down his proposal at the assembly in Schonen, and rioted and attacked his guard, so that he had to flee for his life. Eric, nevertheless, returned with his troops to collect the taxes; and in May 1249 he fulfilled his crusading obligation by sailing east, but he returned before the end of July, having accomplished nothing. Thus it appeared to contemporaries that his crusade had been only a pretext for the new tax.[6]

The crusades had not been forgotten by either the North Germans and the Danes or by Europeans as a whole. Just as Saint Louis of France raised a large army and sailed to Egypt during the great struggle between the Pope and the Emperor, the Lübeckers (and others) continued their support of the Livonian crusade. In 1246 a large fleet had sailed to Samland, established a foothold there, and returned with many hostages for a great baptismal service in Saint Mary's Church in Lübeck.[7] Nor had the papacy forgotten the Baltic mission. Because he believed he was fighting for the very survival of papal authority, Pope Innocent IV tended to view every act as either helping or hurting his cause, and because the Teutonic Knights seemed to be rendering insufficient aid to him against the Emperor, the Pope named a new Archbishop in Prussia who would force them into line.

The Teutonic Knights had been very satisfied with the services performed by their friend, William of Modena. They had defeated Swantopulk of Pomerania militarily, but it was William who had brought about the favorable peace treaty; they had beaten the Lithuanians in battle, but it was William who had confirmed them in their possession of Kurland. They could always rely on this papal legate to understand their difficulties and defend their interests. His knowledge of politics, his skill in negotiation, and his vast experience marked him as a man with a great future in the Church, and they were not surprised when Pope Innocent named him Cardinal Bishop of Sabina in 1244. Because his next assignment was to prepare for the Council of Lyons in 1245, his regular duties as legate were assigned to his chaplain, which opened the way for a shift in papal policy— from concilation to intimidation, from cooperation to domination. Unfortunately for the next legate, the Teutonic Knights did not submit to such roughhanded tactics any more readily than had the Swordbrothers before them.

The Council of Lyons had been called so that the Church could act decisively against the Emperor, striking at his government and his supporters in every manner possible. Although they took no action against the crusading order, the churchmen did not overlook the close connection between the Emperor and the Teutonic Knights, and although the crusading order made every effort to avoid being involved in the controversy, it could not avoid the suspicion that it was pro-Hohenstaufen. The Pope did not want to attack the order, but he hoped to subordinate it. Since William of Modena was too friendly toward the order, Innocent looked for a man who would be willing to use harsh measures if necessary, and at the council he found a prelate from Ireland, Albert Suerbeer, who seemed perfectly qualified to carry out his plans.

Albert Suerbeer was no stranger to Baltic politics, having been nominated in 1229 as Bishop of Riga by the Archbishop of Bremen. The report by Baldwin of Alna had been unfavorable, however, and another man, Albert's opponent, had received the disputed office. But Albert's apprenticeship had not been wasted, as it acquainted him with the problems of Northern Germany and the Baltic. A few years later, Cardinal Otto appointed him Archbishop of Armagh, over the objections of the English King, and once installed as Archbishop, Albert ruled his Irish subjects in a despotic manner. But his success in taxing his poverty-stricken people was not discountenanced by a papacy that was hard pressed for funds. Coming to France in 1245, he performed such valuable service at the Council of Lyons that many considered him suitable for higher promotion;

not only was he a German and a strong supporter of papal pretensions, but it would be unsafe for him to return to Ireland. Thus it was quite logical that Innocent IV saw him as the proper man to deal with the Teutonic Knights, and early in 1246 the Pope named him Archbishop of Prussia and papal legate.

The Teutonic Knights realized that the new Archbishop was dangerous. Not only could he revive the claims of the first Bishop of Prussia against their lands but he could revise William's settlement of the dispute between the Teutonic Knights and Swantopulk of Pomerania. Rightfully fearing his presence in Prussia, the Teutonic Knights said it was unsafe for him to reside there (because of the pagans), and consequently he took up residence in Lübeck. However, his subsequent actions affected the course of the crusade to Livonia more than the crusade to Prussia.[8]

The Teutonic Knights had made considerable progress in Livonia after the disaster at Lake Peipus in 1242. Their new master, Dietrich of Gruningen, had come to Livonia with Herman Balke as the latter's second-in-command and had ruled during Balke's absence. Although he had been passed over in favor of Andreas of Velven (who may have been a former Swordbrother), in 1242 he exchanged office with Andreas and became the third master to govern in Livonia. The rhymed chronicle dwells upon the enthusiastic support he found among his knights—a sharp contrast to the earlier situation.[9] Dietrich reorganized the convents, appointed new commanders, won over the Bishops of Riga, Oesel, and Dorpat to an alliance, and then advanced into Kurland.

A day was set when everyone was to be ready, and messengers were sent to the Letts and the Livonians. The Christians came gladly, as was the established custom. The bishops and the king's men were informed of the expedition, and they came willingly in several stately detachments. The assembly was in Riga. And many glass-bright helmets were seen in the midst of the army. Guides were chosen who knew Kurland well. On the beach by the sea, the army was divided among the various banners for the journey. The army that rode in such good order into Kurland was long and wide, and everything was well under control. Many large detachments were sent out here and there and brought in large amounts of booty, but I will condense my account. They distressed many, and whoever did not escape died. The Kurs groaned, and they understood that if they wished to live peacefully, they would have to surrender to the Master. Their elders took counsel, came to agreement on that, and sent messengers to the army.[10]

He did not burden the natives with extraordinary taxes, but before 1245 he built a great fortress at Goldingen to assure their loyalty. This castle, built on a high hill overlooking the Windau River, was the key to the entire region and was sheltered from direct attack by smaller forts to the east and south. Its large garrison provided cavalry that protected the outlying settlements from the Semgallians and Samogithians. Although it was a conquest by terror, the crusaders did not deplore the fact. The chronicler remarked that "one has to show them both mildness and sternness before they will make the decision to accept baptism, which they will make only under duress."[11]

Not all the Kurs submitted; some appealed to their Samogithian neighbors for help, who, though eager to send assistance, doubted their ability to harm the Germans without even more help. Prior to this there had been no one they could call upon, but recently an eastern chief, Mindaugas, had been uniting tribes under his leadership, and the Samogithian elders, led by their foremost warrior, Lengewin, asked him to direct the attacks against the Germans. They did this only because they understood that small forces could not capture the Christian castles, and the castles were fundamental to control of the land. It was only because they had no hope of achieving success on their own that they submitted to Mindaugas, whom they did not trust.

In the opening campaign of the war, to which only the approximate date 1244 can be assigned, Mindaugas led a large army to Amboten, the southernmost castle in Kurland, and began siege operations against it. Perhaps unknown to him, an enemy watchman had seen his approach and had hurried to Goldingen, so that very soon a relief column of thirty knights, accompanied by a Kurish force of 500 warriors, was hurrying south. Their arrival at Amboten was not noted by Mindaugas, who was busy assaulting the castle.

The Lithuanians came out proudly and in great force. The shouts of their army rang out and many bold pagans advanced. . . . Mindaugas had ordered his men to build siege machines with which he could threaten those in the castle. Those there knew how to deport themselves in war, and had prepared a stubborn defense. Mindaugas ordered an attack, and many a pagan fell from his horse onto the grass. The brothers rejoiced. For the first time they had a true estimate of their power. It was a huge band of pagans, thirty thousand men. Mindaugas began to storm the castle in a frenzied attack. The brothers said: "Let us not rush out too soon [from their hiding place in the woods].

It is to our advantage to let them go so near the castle that they will notice nothing behind them. Great glory shall be rendered unto God here before this very castle." They rode out of the woods a little way so that the horses could make a better charge. "Now you heroes fight!" cried brother Bernec. "This is the way it should be. Whether things go for good or ill, stay by the flag and have the courage of lions."[12]

Leaving 500 dead warriors behind, Mindaugas fled into the woods, but his army was not pursued by the Christians. He had lost the battle because he had been caught in the open. Nevertheless, he had inflicted heavy casualties on his opponents, and he would be back. And next time he would be less reckless.

The border war that ensued was very bloody. The Lithuanians raided Kurland and Livonia, and the Christians responded in kind, so that many lives were lost in the mutual massacres.

Since God had given honor to them, they praised his mercy which is ever present for the down-trodden. The Kurs also rejoiced and remained loyal. But the brothers had great travail, of which, however, they complained little, for they labored in God's name. They steadfastly propagated the True Faith. Often they suffered. Whenever they were near a castle, each one had to do everything just right or he died because of his negligence. They suffered many hardships: they kept watch, fasted, and seldom rested. Their misery was great.[13]

At last the fighting diminished, due to developments in Semgallia and Lithuania rather than the prowess of the crusaders.

The Semgallian tribes that were independent at this time apparently were still at peace with the Christians. The leading Semgallians, three brothers named Tusche, Milgerin, and Gingeike, had feuded with the Samogithians' Lengewin long before Mindaugas had come west with his army and announced his hostility to any enemy of the Samogithians, meaning the Semgallians as well as the Christians. About the year 1245–1246, realizing that they could not resist the Samogithians by themselves, the three brothers decided to ask the Christians for aid. Then, after they approached the master of the order and made certain of his good will, they set out for Samogithia, determined to strike such a blow that the Lithuanians would not recover for many months. They entered Samogithia without being detected, captured Lengewin, and brought him to Semgallia; then they gathered their families and possessions, marched to a wood just outside the Christian frontier at Ascheraden, and informed the master that

Lengewin was their prisoner. Dietrich, greatly pleased, offered the Semgallians lands and protection in exchange for Lengewin. Thus these Semgallians became Christian and, because of the capture of Lengewin, the Lithuanian attacks on Kurland and Livonia diminished.

With the famous war chief of the Samogithians in their hands and the fierce Semgallians by their side, the crusaders from Livonia and Estonia fell upon the Samogithian settlements and burned and plundered wide areas. On their return, the Christians defeated a Samogithian force and killed Lengewin's brother, a deed Lengewin had foreseen in oracular bones while at table with his knightly captors. (Superstition was already strong among the knights, and this raised Lengewin's formidable reputation even higher.) The war was not at an end, however, for the Teutonic Knights ransomed their captive for 500 coins, and Lengewin soon resumed his attacks.

Penetrating deep into Livonia, Lengewin defeated the commander of Wenden and his 500 men, killing nine knights and forcing another to carry his commander's decapitated head back to Lithuania, where it was sacrificed in pagan ceremonies in memory of Lengewin's brother. The courage and ability of the native warriors rose, in the estimation of the crusaders, with each exploit. The Christian attitude changed slowly—if it had ever been otherwise—to recognize the chivalry of their unbelieving enemies.[14]

It was at this time, 1245–1247, that Master Dietrich left Livonia to accept new duties in Germany and Prussia and was replaced by Henry of Heimburg, and later by Andreas of Steierland. Dietrich stopped in Lübeck to confer with Albert Suerbeer, but the responsibility for dealing with this prelate fell to Master Andreas, who, before assuming his duties in Livonia, spoke to the Pope about the Archbishop. Archbishop Albert Suerbeer, unable to establish himself in Prussia, had resided in Lübeck, where he could keep watch on events in the eastern Baltic and from time to time cause difficulty for the Teutonic Knights.

Because the order could bring its men and supplies overland into Prussia, Albert concerned himself more with the Livonian crusade, which was dependent upon Lübeck as its base in the west. In 1247, when the bishopric of Lübeck became vacant, it was occupied by Albert, who confiscated the donations that assisted poor crusaders in meeting the heavy costs of equipment and transportation. He also used his position to interefere in the Danish civil war and in German politics. As papal legate, he raised a crusading army against the imperial city of Aachen, which had refused to admit the anti-King for his coronation. Similarly, he used every available means to embarrass the Teutonic Knights. It was not papal directives alone that drove him forward, for he was possessed of considerable personal ambition; unlimited possibilities lay open to him, and perhaps even the papacy. No wonder, then, that he felt frustrated by his inability to strike at the Teutonic Knights. Even though his plans eventually fell through (including his attempt to make Lübeck a great Baltic archbishopric, in anticipation of which he had made arrangements for submitting to the Archbishop of Bremen), he continued to ignore the officials of the Teutonic Knights who sought to confer with him. He wanted submission, not negotiation.[15]

Time was running out on Archbishop Albert. As the imperial position collapsed, strong action against imperial supporters was less necessary, and when the great Emperor died, it was no longer justified. In 1249 the papacy began seeking a reconciliation with the Teutonic Knights—a change of policy that was marked by the sending of a new papal legate to Prussia. Archbishop Albert viewed the new legate as a grave danger because he might settle the dispute between the order and Swantopulk of Pomerania, which was the only issue Albert could use against the order. In vain he threatened to excommunicate anyone who dealt with the new legate. The Archbishop had also proposed a new Russian policy, one that would bring the Russians into the Roman orbit, but the Teutonic Knights were suggesting that the conversion of the Lithuanians would be much easier. And of course the two policies were mutually exclusive, as the Russians and the Lithuanians were traditional enemies.

Master Andreas undermined Archbishop Albert's proposal by waging successful warfare against Lithuania. Raising great armies, he burned and plundered in Nalsen, Samogithia, and the pagan areas of Semgallia. The Semgallians bought peace by promising to pay taxes, and in 1250 Mindaugas finally asked for an interview. The master agreed to talk to the Samogithian chieftain, and with a large retinue rode across the wide heaths and deep into Lithuania to the royal hall of Mindaugas.

> He was received by him as one should a lord. The queen also came and received the master and all the brothers who had come with him politely. Afterward, when the time came that they should eat, I have heard that nothing was forgotten that one should have to honor them. They treated their guests well. When the meal was eaten and they had not sat there long, the king thanked the master of Livonia for coming to him. Then the master listened to the king

till that point where he could say a good word, when he spoke to Mindaugas, the king of Lithuania, "If you were a Christian, I could give you great honor, and I could win a crown for you, unless I died first." The king was pleased by that statement. He promised the master part of his land and had good will toward him. When all this had happened, the master and the king immediately swore oaths on it, which pleased the Christians.[16]

The master returned to Riga with Lithuanian representatives, and a message was dispatched to the Pope. Although the only conditions for peace were the acceptance of Christianity and the opening of the country to Christian merchants, Mindaugas turned Samogithia over to the Teutonic Knights—but at little loss to himself. As the Samogithians had not agreed to terminate the war, they would not recognize Mindaugas's authority now that the war had ended, and thus he could ask the Teutonic Knights to punish certain "rebels."[17] What happened to Lengewin is unclear—the chronicles never mention him again—but his people continued their fierce resistance to the Christians, both German and Lithuanian.

The Teutonic Knights finally forced the papacy to recall Albert Suerbeer, who had fought a desperate rearguard action, making and repudiating agreements, scattering excommunications, and interfering with the crusade. In the end, the Pope ordered both parties to appear at the papal court and submit their quarrel to arbitration. Hearings began in the spring of 1250, but after the passage of half a year nothing had been accomplished, and in September, when papal patience was exhausted, the Pope stripped Albert Suerbeer of his legation. Unable to hear the case personally, he empaneled a special court in Lyons, whose members included Cardinal William, the former Bishop of Modena and longtime papal legate to the Baltic region. William dominated the hearings that winter, asking questions that penetrated to the heart of the controversies and destroying the subterfuges that had so long delayed a settlement. He was working against time, hurrying to finish the hearings while his strength lasted, and he succeeded: the court's report was approved by the Pope only shortly before William died, late in March 1251. This faithful servant of the Church had completed all his work in the Baltic; the Pope's decision was acceptable, if not pleasing, to all; and the crusading order preserved the lands and rights necessary to continue its role as the dominant crusading power in the northeast. The decision guaranteed the Teutonic Knights supremacy in Prussia and Kurland, where they received two-thirds of the land, with the remainder divided among small and powerless Bishops, and it ordered

Albert Suerbeer to return all confiscated funds. In turn, the order was to do homage to the Archbishop and allow him to settle in Prussia. Finally, each party was to forgive and forget the wrongs of the past. The decision was final. The Teutonic Knights in Prussia rejoiced; but those in Livonia, and Albert Suerbeer, had other problems.

The Pope listened to further requests sympathetically. He gave the Teutonic Knights permission to crown Mindaugas King of Lithuania, which heartened the Livonian branch of the order because it accepted Lithuania in the ranks of Christian nations under the protection and domination of the Teutonic Knights. On the other hand, the Pope removed Albert Suerbeer from his perfunctory post in Prussia and gave him the expectancy of Riga. He had already promised that Riga would be raised to an archbishopric, and had added Semgallian lands to that see. Albert Suerbeer would inherit the title and lands that Albert I had so desired. Bishop Nicholas was still alive, but he was not expected to live much longer; and therefore Albert Suerbeer traveled north to close out his affairs as Bishop of Lübeck and make preparations for assuming his duties in Riga.[18]

Master Andreas ordered extensive preparations for the coronation of the Lithuanian King so as to make it a memorable moment in the history of that nation, a moment that would wed it firmly to the Christian world and the Teutonic Knights. Bringing a Bishop from Prussia, he crowned Mindaugas with all the pomp and formality for which his order was famous. Priests and monks were left behind in the land, and the Queen was converted wholeheartedly to the new faith, although the bishopric was slowly established and proved to be short-lived. Mindaugas, apparently, was more interested in politics than in religion and would be Christian or pagan depending on which aided him most in his political ambitions. At the moment, Christianity helped him most.[19]

Not everyone was pleased by his conversion. The Bishops of Livonia were jealous that the Lithuanian kingdom was exempt from their authority yet still under the influence of the Teutonic Knights. But they could do little about the situation, and Master Andreas, in any case, was engaged in other matters. After suffering several attacks of illness, he had written the grandmaster to ask for a replacement. The master in Germany, Eberhard of Seine, came to Livonia in 1252, which allowed Andreas to make a last visit to Mindaugas and then to travel to Germany, where he hoped to recover his health.

Albert Suerbeer remained in Lübeck, where he could deal with the problems arising from the Danish civil war and also could make arrangements for assuming office as Archbishop of Riga. He understood how important Lübeck's good will would be in the future and therefore sought to please the city fathers in every way. This was difficult, however, because of the war in Denmark, which had flared up again in the summer of 1250, when the zu Lippe family came to the aid of their relatives in Holstein and Schleswig. (Archbishop Gerhard of Bremen and Bishop Simon of Paderborn were blood relatives to the Counts of Holstein, who desired the return of Rendsburg, and all were related by marriage to Duke Abel of Schleswig.)

When King Eric heard that the German army was moving north, he hurried to Schleswig and sought a reconciliation with his brother, Duke Abel. The brothers had taken the initial steps toward mutual forgiveness when an untoward incident brought forth all the old hatred and upset the stability of the kingdom. The King had retired to a corner of the great hall of the ducal castle for a game of chess and was deeply engrossed in the game when Abel approached and asked him if he remembered how Abel's daughters had been forced to flee through the snow barefoot and in disguise. Abel must have been angry already, but when the King continued to study the board and said, "Don't worry, I'll buy them each a new pair of shoes," he could no longer contain himself. He called the guards and threw the King and his party into chains. Later that evening he ordered the King removed to a dungeon that could be reached only by boat, at the same time making secret arrangements for assassins to intercept the boat and dispose of the King, thus averting the charge of fratricide. Abel then swore his innocence of any conspiracy against the late monarch, which was compurgated by twenty-four knights, so that Abel was eligible to succeed to the throne, and did so in November 1250.[20]

There was popular suspicion that Abel was in fact "Cain"—a notion which became even more widespread after the mutilated body of the King was recovered by fishermen—but nobody dared accuse Abel of the deed. The new King did not change the unpopular policies pursued by his late brother; he continued the heavy and illegal taxes and persecuted those who opposed him in any way. Almost everywhere the Church and the peasantry submitted, but not North Frisia, whose swamps promised security against royal invasion—except in 1252, when a freeze allowed Abel to cross the swamps, enter the country and ravage the land. When a sudden thaw trapped the royal forces, the King attempted to flee, but a wheelwright felled him with an ax. The canons at Schleswig thereupon recovered their courage, refused his corpse burial, and sank the fratricide in a swamp.[21]

Circumstances prevented Abel's son, Waldemar, from assuming power, for he was kidnapped in Cologne, while en route from his studies in Paris, and was held for ransom. By the time his Holstein relatives could free him, Christopher, the fourth son of Waldemar the Victorious, had seized the crown. All that Holstein could do was declare a feud, in alliance with the Danish Church and rebellious peasants. As the war showed signs of success, Lübeck declared its hostility to the King and began to harass the Danish shores.[22]

Because he was acting Bishop of Lübeck, this conflict occupied Albert Suerbeer's attention for many months. He was also involved in warding off more dangerous attacks upon the Lübeckers. The city fathers had not looked upon William of Holland, the would-be Emperor, as a danger and consequently had refused to pay taxes to him. But when William married a Welf Duchess (a daughter of Otto of Braunschweig) in 1251, sold his tax rights to the Duke of Brandenburg, and gave the bishoprics of Schwerin and Ratzeburg to the Duke of Saxony, he acquired powerful allies against those recalcitrant taxpayers. It was Albert Suerbeer who assisted the citizens by hiring the Counts of Holstein as advocates of the city, thus guaranteeing military protection. He also sought to abolish the salvage practice by which all shipwrecked goods (and sometimes the mariners themselves) became the property of the lord who owned the coast; by 1253 he had persuaded a number of princes to renounce this practice, and he himself promised to abolish it in Livonia. By assisting Lübeck in furthering its civic interests, Albert Suerbeer pointed the way to the formation of city leagues. By encouraging cooperation between Lübeck, Hamburg, and Riga in removing tolls and taxes, in policing the highways and sea, and in fighting common enemies, he encouraged the growth of a Hanseatic League that would one day dominate the north of Europe. Meanwhile he was assuring mercantile support for himself, in case it would be needed in a struggle against the Teutonic Knights in Livonia.[23]

The Teutonic Knights also were working closely with the Lübeckers. They realized that naval power was necessary if they were to conquer and hold areas along the coast and then develop the regions commercially. The occupation of Memel, which occurred at this time, shows how well the Teutonic Knights understood the vital role of sea power in the Livonian crusade. Winter weather isolated Livonia half of each year by making the

sea unsafe, and although Prussia was but a comparatively short distance
overland, a traveler or messenger had to pass through hostile Samogithia to
reach Riga. There were ports in Prussia and Kurland, but they were too far
apart for safe sailing in wintertime. Disliking these long periods of isolation,
Master Eberhard decided to establish a base halfway between Prussia and
Livonia, a base that would be safe for ships and would also serve as a rest-
ing place for parties traveling overland. He decided upon a site where the
Courland lagoon meets the Baltic Sea—the site of present-day Memel. From
that point, a one-day ride up the coast or along the Dange River would
bring mounted force to the southernmost castles in Kurland. Toward the
south, it was no farther to the mouth of the Memel River and Samland,
areas that already were under attack by the Teutonic Knights. After obtaining the cooperation of Lübeck and the Bishop of Kurland, Eberhard
built a castle at Memel in 1252, which became a very important base in the
war against the Samogithians.[24]

Shortly after this, Master Eberhard pleaded illness and his temporary
appointment in asking for a replacement, and Anno of Sangerhausen succeeded him in office in 1253. Master Anno continued the push to the south
to link Livonia and Prussia by land, so that the northern province would
not be isolated by contrary wind and weather for half of each year.

The Samogithians did not appreciate the danger of a castle at Memel
to the same extent as the Samlanders. The Samlanders, who lived on the
peninsula between Memel and Prussia, were already under attack and thus
had a better understanding of the use of sea power than their landlocked
neighbors. Sparing no effort, they gathered all their men and ships and
proceeded to the Dange River to besiege the new castle.

Part of their force traveled by ship around that land called the Frische. Then
they turned into the Memel and rejoiced. As they came in from the sea in
ships, the brothers recognized the Samite intentions and their morale sank.
The time had come for both storm and battle. One could see so many Samites
that they could not be counted. They filled the Memel with ships so that one
could cross it on them. That never happened again. The Memel is a great
river, but the ships were drawn together so that it was covered just as if a
bridge went all the way across the river. That discouraged the brothers, who
were preparing their defenses. Meanwhile the heathen army from Samland
arrived. They all assembled and took up spear and shield, and stood anxiously
ready to attack. They pressed against and onto the castle. But some had gotten
up too early that morning, and those had to pay for it with the lives they

brought there. None had expected that, but it happened to many, and there-after they did not come so near. After they had lost those people, they were angry that they had ever considered the attack, because that had happened to their people and they now lay dead. Immediately the elders ordered them to burn the dead and send them hence with all their weapons so that they could make expeditions and attacks in the hereafter also.[25]

Master Anno was eager to follow up the victory and encompass the sub-jugation of Samland. Summoning a vast army from Livonia to join the many crusaders who had crossed the sea that year, he led his army across the Memel River and into the great wilderness.

The land is almost surrounded, being on a peninsula, by the wild sea, which had been a protection for it. No army had ever invaded there, and on the other sides no one can fight against it because a wild stream, wild and deep, flows along it. . . . A narrow peninsula extends toward the Memel, and there the Christians came with their stately army. The Christians rejoiced. They found the great forest of the Samites there. It was wide and thick, not of puny sap-lings, but trees so large that they were heavy to move. And they had been felled and so placed that they served as a bulwark. . . . The Christians came upon it and vowed not to rest till it had been cut in two. . . . Then, when they had cut and slashed through the forest, the army advanced directly into the land. The Samites learned that they were visited by guests who wished to do them harm.[26]

Thus far the raid was a great success. But, as they had learned on pre-vious expeditions, getting into a country may be much easier than getting out. As the crusaders passed deeper into the forest, they were ambushed and all but annihilated. However, the crusaders were not deterred. New attacks were launched against the Samlanders, but from Prussia instead of Livonia. Assisted by great armies from Brandenburg and Bohemia, the Teutonic Knights conquered the region and advanced their frontiers from Prussia to the south bank of the Memel River. The great city they founded in Samland in 1256 was named Königsberg in honor of King Ottokar of Bohemia, who had brought large armies on crusade to Prussia. The next step was obvious: the occupation of the territories between Memel and Kurland, which would open the land route to Livonia. The Livonian branch of the Teutonic Knights was assigned the difficult task of clearing this narrow strip of land.

The conquest of Samland again demonstrated the advantage of launch-ing attacks from Prussian rather than Livonian bases. Prussia was more accessible to crusaders from central Germany, the home of the most power-ful princes—both then and in the future. Nor was Livonia, isolated by the sea, as attractive to crusaders as a goal of pilgrimage. Therefore, as a prac-tical measure, most future operations on the Livonian border were relatively minor, designed to harass the Samogithian flank, while the main attack came from Prussia.

It was at this time that Albert Suerbeer returned to Riga. When the news arrived, early in 1254, that Bishop Nicholas had died, Albert sailed for his new see without waiting for "congratulations" from the aged Arch-bishop of Bremen, Gerhard II (who probably still desired to reimpose his authority over Albert's bishopric). He visited the Bishops of Oesel and Kur-land, inspected his own dioceses, and was dismayed by what he found. The Bishops were weak and listened to the counsel of the Teutonic Knights; his lands around Riga were defended by only a handful of landed vassals and mercenary troops; and Bishop Nicholas had allowed many of his resources to slip away over the years. Albert had considerable ability to act, because he again had legatine powers, but he decided not to take immediate action. Instead, he announced that he would return to Germany, settle his affairs in Lübeck, and then speak to the Pope.

Knowing the pugnacious nature of their old opponent, the Teutonic Knights were reluctant to enter into a legal controversy with him, especially if they could settle their differences through diplomacy. Master Dietrich, who was then grandmaster in Germany, met the Archbishop in France in December 1254. Their compromise (at Sens) provided that the order would honor its obligations to the Livonian prelates, so long as this did not injure the vital interests of the crusading order. It also arranged satisfaction for many minor complaints. It was well that Albert signed the agreement, be-cause Pope Innocent IV died at that very moment and was succeeded by a Pope who was friendly to the crusading orders, Alexander IV.[27]

As Albert Suerbeer returned to Riga to direct the affairs of his dioceses and as Master Anno renewed his attacks on the Samogithians, it was clear that another era in the Baltic Crusade had ended. The reorientation of the crusade, begun in 1242, was complete. The Danes were in Estonia, but weak and quiet; the Bishops were unsatisfied, but powerless; the merchants were growing wealthier, but presented no threat; and the Teutonic Knights, seeking little more than to distract the Lithuanians from Prussia, were dom-inant in the northeastern Baltic.

The era ended as it had begun, with civil war in Denmark. The strong-minded Archbishop of Lund, striving for greater autonomy under royal control, provoked the King to exclaim that Lund was acting like a German. Each antagonized the other. The Archbishop appointed his subordinates without royal permission, and the King collected all the taxes instituted by his predecessors, including those repugnant to the Church. As compromise was impossible, civil war began again in 1256. The King reacted vigorously to the rebellion, razing illegal castles recently erected by the churchmen, and throwing the Archbishop and other prelates in prison. Excommunication caused the King to release the Archbishop, but the King sent the prelate into exile, so that the war continued until 1259, when King Christopher died suddenly (poison in a communion chalice was suspected). The new King, the ten-year-old Eric, was no match for his opponents, and thus the power of the Danish monarch continued to decline.[28]

The Empire suffered a similar setback. The Emperor, William of Holland, had been a weak prince, but at least he had understood German problems and had tried to deal with them. If he could have built a base in the northwest, perhaps he could have acted effectively at least in Northern Germany; but all his plans came to naught when he was killed by Frisian rebels in the winter of 1255–1256. The Holy Roman Empire was leaderless thereafter.[29]

Other princes, long associated with the Livonian crusade, also passed away in this period. Archbishop Gerhard of Bremen, whose career had stretched over several decades, was so aged that he could no longer direct his affairs. When he died (in the summer of 1258), his nephew, the Bishop of Paderborn, tried to seize his seat, but the zu Lippe family was beaten in battle by a candidate from Oldenburg. The archbishopric thereafter tended to reflect the interests of that noble house. The heritage of Bishop Bernard lapsed and interest in Livonia waned.[30]

The Teutonic Knights could look back on the era with satisfaction. They had made themselves supreme in Livonia; had conquered Kurland, Semgallia, and Samland; and had converted a major part of the Lithuanians to the faith. They looked to the future confidently, expecting eventual victory over the Samogithians, the last major pagan group in the Baltic region. Little did they know that the Samogithians and Albert Suerbeer, acting separately, would undo much of their work, so that three decades of bitter war would be necessary to regain the positions they held in 1254.

N O T E S   T O   C H A P T E R   N I N E

1. John Birch, *Denmark in History* (London: John Murray, 1938), pp. 76–78.

2. Münter, *Kirchengeschichte*, pp. 172–74; Dahlmann, *Geschichte von Dännemark*, 1: 399ff; King, *Chronicles of Three Free Cities*, p. 176ff.

3. *Sächsische Weltchronik*, p. 257.

4. Barraclough, *Origins of Modern Germany*, p. 232; *Hamburgisches Urkundenbuch*, 1: 451; *Lübeckisches Urkundenbuch* (Lübeck: Asschenfeldt, 1843), 1: nos. 110–116.

5. Dahlmann, *Geschichte von Dännemark*, 1: 400–401.

6. Ibid., pp. 402–3.

7. *Urkundenbuch*, 1: no. CXCIV; Krollmann, *Politische Geschichte des Deutschen Ordens*, pp. 22.

8. Goetze, *Albert Suerbeer*, pp. 1–14; Schönebolm, "Besetzung der livländischen Bistümer bis zum Anfang des 14. Jahrhunderts," in *Mitteilungen aus dem Gebiet der livländishen Geschichte*, (1910), pp. 321ff; Donner, *Kardinal Wilhelm von Sabina* pp. 293–94; Krollmann, *Deutschen Orden*, pp. 19–20.

9. *Reimchronik*, ll. 2332–2346.

10. Ibid., ll. 2363–2397.

11. Ibid., ll. 2444–2448.

12. Ibid., ll. 2498–2535.

13. Ibid., ll. 2589–2603.

14. Ibid., ll. 2705–3120.

15. Goetze, *Albert Suerbeer*, pp. 15ff.

16. *Reimchronik*, ll. 3471–3504.

17. *Urkundenbuch*, 1: nos. CCXLIII, CCLII.

18. Goetze, *Albert Suerbeer*, pp. 30–37; Krollmann, *Deutschen Orden*, pp. 19–20; Donner, *Kardinal Wilhelm von Sabina*, pp. 401–6.

19. *Reimchronik*, ll. 3497–3575; Goetze, *Albert Suerbeer*, pp. 56–58.

20. Dahlmann, *Geschichte von Dännemark*, 1: 402–5.

21. Ibid., pp. 405–8; *Annales Danici*, pp. 112–13, 158.

22. Dahlmann, *Geschichte von Dännemark*, 1: 408–10; *Sächsische Weltchronik*, p. 257; *Annales Danici*, pp. 114–15.

23. Goetze, *Albert Suerbeer*, pp. 47–49; Schönebolm, "Besetzung der livländischen Bistümer," pp. 321–24.

24. *Urkundenbuch*, 1: no. CCXXXXI.

25. *Reimchronik*, ll. 3830–3877.

26. Ibid., ll. 3955–3996.

27. Goetze, *Albert Suerbeer*, pp. 51–67; *Urkundenbuch*, 1: no. CCLXXVIII.

28. Dahlmann, *Geschichte von Dännemark*, pp. 410ff.

29. Barraclough, *Origins of Modern Germany*, p. 244.

30. Bippen, *Aus Bremens Vorzeit*, p. 150; King, *Chronicles of Three Free Cities*, pp. 63ff.

10

Albert Suerbeer and the Teutonic Knights

THE SETTLEMENT AT SENS DID NOT END THE JEALOUSY AND SUSPICION THAT separated Archbishop Albert and the crusading order, for, as we shall see, the ensuing era was marked by recurring quarrels and, finally, a showdown between them. But the difficulties caused by the Archbishop were merely bothersome at first, and became dangerous only later, when the Teutonic Knights were preoccupied with bitter wars against Lithuanians and rebellious subjects. It was then that the fortunes of war finally turned against the crusaders from the west, and thereafter it was long in doubt whether they could defend their possessions in Kurland and Livonia against their numerous enemies.

The Samogithians had never ceased their wars against the Christians but had shaken off their defeats in battle, and even the defection of Mindaugas, to continue their raids against Kurland and Memel. Because the frontiers were too long, the Christians could not stop these attacks. Although they built castles and outposts and stationed watchmen along the borders, parties of guerrillas, and occasionally a large army, slipped through to burn villages and fields, carry off men and women as slaves, and massacre those who resisted or were economically useless. The Kurs complained bitterly to their advocates, observing that orphans could not defend the frontier and demanding revenge on the Samogithians. The officials promised action, understanding that they could maintain their authority only if they protected their subjects and assisted them in wars against their traditional enemies. They also believed that the Samogithians looked upon Kurland as the first stage in a conflict that would end only with the liberation of all the subject peoples from western domination. This meant that the Samogithian war was much more than mere banditry in the backwoods—it was a war of survival.

Master Anno had been committed to the conquest of Samogithia in any case, but the situation in Kurland gave special urgency to his proposed attacks. He could rely on the Livonians who hated the Lithuanians, and in 1255 he summoned them. The description of the raid is well worth reading, as it is typical of many campaigns that follow in later years:

The expedition was very large, which pleased the Christians. The assembly was at Riga, and Master Anno summoned all the noble crusaders to him from

197

Riga and said, "Now, show that you have taken the cross for the sake of Christianity and give proof that you will be joyful to the end." No one had to invite the Estonians, Livs and Letts, for they were all ready for the journey and without fear. Soon afterward the well-ordered army moved off toward Semgallia. When the Master came to that land, he made it known that they should come along, and that he would not leave anyone behind. Whether they like it or not, they had to join him. The Kurs, I have heard, showed their trustworthiness: they joined the expedition manfully and with wrath. Then the army went toward Samogithia successfully. After these people had joined the army, coming in from both directions, the Master and his advocates and the crusaders deemed it time to group the people under the various banners, as is the custom in war. That was done straight away. Now they arrived at the borders of that land, and the advocates grouped their forces better and drew them up for combat. The banners were assigned to those who were anxious for battle and who knew how to conduct themselves in such affairs. There were many peoples there. One saw formations which no foe could ever break. There were many banners, the natives were so well trained that they would not stray; they constantly kept their lords in sight. The army arrayed itself in many proud formations as should be done in a battle. Guides were assigned to the leaders, and that benefited the entire expedition. Those were the proper sort of Lithuanians, and good heroes. They protected the army well. . . . Then the army rushed into Samogithia and did tremendous damage. At that time the Samogithians were fully overmatched and the Kurs did not mind that at all. Friars and priests were in this same army. The first burning was set by a priest's hand, and the next by a friar's. As I have heard, everyone who had come on the expedition was eager to burn. The army was well-protected, and well-ordered at all points. Meanwhile one group rode here and there plundering, and another group did the same. The third group did not neglect that, but devastated even more. When evening came, the great army of the Christians took up camp. In the night some heroes continued the attacks. Much booty was brought in: men, women, and children, and all kinds of cattle. Whatever one did not wish to drive or carry away was slain.[1]

Anno's army remained in the land nine days, and the troops amassed enough wealth to enrich many of their number. Master Anno had tried to end the war with this one bold stroke, and had almost succeeded. But the Samogithians rallied from the blow and continued the war so aggressively that Anno was forced to remain in the field at a time when he should have been responding to the problems created by Archbishop Suerbeer.

The Archbishop, determined to resurrect the rights and privileges of his office, was maneuvering to align and subordinate the other estates in

Livonia. In his visits to Lübeck he had assured himself of the good will of the merchant communities, and by legislation at home he was reorganizing his dioceses so as to enlarge his authority. An unscrupulous and ambitious man, his plans are revealed in the various transactions that ultimately led to an attack on the Teutonic Order. He was not completely at fault for the quarrels, because more than once the Teutonic Knights provoked such trouble, but his bellicose attitude won him few friends and supporters in his contest with the wealthy and influential crusading organization. The Archbishop did not always act selfishly, but most of his actions as papal legate strengthened his position as Archbishop.

The ecclesiastical institutions in Riga, having become wealthy and independent, were in need of reform—a typical medieval problem. As he looked about the city, Albert saw that many churches and convents had so benefited from gifts and bequests that they had been able to acquire much property that had formerly yielded tax revenues. To prevent further loss of income, he issued edicts forbidding his subjects to will urban property into mortmain. This bolstered his authority over various institutions because they could not expand or function smoothly, without his cooperation. Of these institutions, the most dangerous to his authority were the canons of Saint Mary's, his own cathedral chapter. Throughout Germany the canons were usurping the prerogatives of their prelates, and the Archbishop recognized this threat. In ordering his canons to adopt the more restrictive Cistercian rule, he reestablished his control over them.

By a series of such acts, Archbishop Albert Suerbeer so strengthened his position that soon he felt ready to confront the Teutonic Knights by demanding special services that they had not performed but that were implied in the relationship of Archbishop and vassal. Despite his lack of written authority, the Archbishop tried to collect tithes and taxes from the order's lands, threatening ecclesiastical censure if its officials refused. He ordered the officers to render personal fealty and present him with gifts of food, clothing, and cattle as tokens of their submission. When they refused, he interfered with the crusaders, levied taxes on the order's property in the city, and—to add insult to injury—asked the Teutonic Knights to pay his expenses when, as papal legate, he attacked their interests. If he had succeeded in making the order submit, he would have become the leading figure in the Baltic region and one of the most important prelates in the Church. Failure, on the other hand, would cost him little.

The Archbishop experienced only a temporary triumph, when in

1255, he signed a treaty with the commander of the convent in Riga, who was governing in the absence of Master Anno. Albert persuaded him to divide the lands around Gerzika in a manner advantageous to the Archbishop, in return for which he surrendered his claims to certain illegal tithes and taxes. The commander signed the treaty without consulting his brothers, which turned their wrath against the commander. Although the treaty may have brought temporary harmony, the fundamental disagreements were so deep that the settlement could not endure, and thus their quarrel persisted. The Archbishop also quarreled with his independent-minded citizens in Riga, but with no more success than he had with the crusading order.

No one expected the Teutonic Knights to comply immediately with Albert's demands, if they complied at all. In fact, one could predict the counter arguments that their spokesmen eventually presented to the Pope in an appeal. They objected to the new taxes on the grounds that a division of incomes had been made in the past, and these divisions had been approved time and again by papal legates, and even by the Popes. In refusing homage, they argued that only the master was required to render it, and therefore the officers were not required to offer fealty or make gifts or payments to the Archbishop. Furthermore, they said that such efforts and allegations were aiding the pagans by disrupting the crusaders. They concluded by asking the papacy to intervene and to order the Archbishop to cease and desist.[2]

Albert Suerbeer may have expected the Teutonic Knights to have a measure of success with the papacy, but he could hardly have anticipated the far-reaching decisions that were handed down in favor of the Teutonic Order. As the years passed, his complaints against his enemies were turned back one by one. Pope Alexander IV granted far-reaching immunities that put the order almost beyond archiepiscopal control: the right to settle all disputes within the order; the right to accept into membership former adherents of Frederick II and nobles who had been accused of robbery, simony, and assaults on clerics; the right to defend themselves against all attacks; freedom from all taxes, tolls, and payments in support of papal legates; and, most important of all, immunity from excommunication without express papal permission. Thus armed, and having been granted many special privileges, the order ignored Albert Suerbeer's complaints; and when he brought economic pressure to bear upon them, the master either procured or falsified a document that gave them permission to engage in commerce.

The Archbishop continued his ineffectual attacks, impugning the integrity and morality of his opponents rather than arguing on legal grounds. It is by drawing on this material that Olins has penned such a frightening portrait of the Teutonic Order in this period, but it is not a completely accurate picture. The Teutonic Knights were neither as moral as they should have been nor as bad as they have been described by their enemies. Drawn to a military order rather than to another religious vocation because of their desire for glory, family honor, and adventure, the knights were not always capable of living up to their professed ideals, but they did not lose sight of their ideals or their duties. Their rules were strict, and usually were enforced, and their courage never faltered. In short, they lived up to their code rather well, and this should be distinguished from standards set by outsiders. They were judged—and should be judged—neither by the standards of the twentieth century nor by those of their more scrupulous contemporaries but by the standards of the political-minded churchmen of their own era. Their spokesmen successfully defended them against repeated charges of falsifying bulls, of incest and adultery, and of interfering with the administration of the sacraments. Eventually, the papacy refused to listen to such accusations.[3]

Master Anno had served his order well in Livonia. He had inflicted great defeats on the pagans and had thwarted Archbishop Albert. Furthermore, by helping them subdue rebels and by securing peace with the Russians, he had won the friendship of the Bishops of Oesel and Dorpat. Nor did his conduct and achievements go unnoticed; officers of the Teutonic Order recommended him for promotion. In 1256, when the grandmaster decided to retire, he called all the commanders together to elect his successor, and their choice was Master Anno, who therefore vacated his post in Livonia. Asked to choose a successor from among their worthiest subordinates, the important knights in Germany debated and finally chose Burckhardt of Hornhusen, commander of the castle at Königsberg in Samland.

Master Burckhardt had a fine reputation in Prussia. Because he was experienced in the customs of the pagan natives and in warfare against them, hopes were high that he could continue the war against the Samogithians successfully. Despising travel by ship as too safe, in the spring of

1257 he took a body of men from Samland to Memel, then on to Kurland, and finally by the direct route across hostile Samogithia and Semgallia to Riga. He was welcomed outside the city by an armed host that presented him with wine and mead and, after proper ceremony and celebration, escorted him into the city. His journey signified that the land route from Prussia to Livonia was feasible and that his term of office would see further efforts to make it safe for all travelers.

His first duties were ceremonial: meeting all the important men in the crusader states, sending gifts to all friends and allies, and swearing loyalty to Archbishop Albert Suerbeer. He renewed the friendship with King Mindaugas, and the two men exchanged mutual promises of aid. Then, later in 1257, he prepared for war in Samogithia.

Hearing that the pagans had besieged Memel, Master Burckhardt marched south with forty knights and 500 Kurs to relieve the castle. He and the Samogithians, understanding how vital the castle on the Dange was to the future of the region, were determined to fight to the end, but the more numerous Samogithians were better acquainted with the area and therefore were able to lay a trap for their Christian opponents. Master Burckhardt and his men fought valiantly, but they were both outnumbered and outfought. Twelve knights were killed and the master was severely wounded. The survivors (who escaped to Memel) counted themselves lucky.

When Master Burckhardt had recovered sufficiently to travel, he rode back to Riga. In the meantime a large crusading force from Holstein had come to Riga under the command of the Count of Buxtehude; so Burckhardt had a numerous force. While his brother knights were thirsting for revenge, the master awaited an opportunity to attack, but just at that moment, a Samogithian embassy arrived in Riga to discuss peace.

The chronicler's description of the negotiations merits quotation:

The Master spoke to the envoys, "Stay a little while and I will send a messenger swiftly and answer the request you have made." The envoys thought that counsel good. So the guests were cared for like envoys should be, and the Master sent messengers summoning the commanders. In a few days' time the Master's people all came willingly to Riga. Why should I make a long speech? The archbishop also came to the brothers' court in Riga, to the good of Christianity, and a large number of citizens were accepted into the council. When they had come together, they prayed to our Lord God that He through his noble death convert the Samogithians and show them the way that Mindaugas had taken, for he was a Christian man converted in a very few days. . . . Those same persons thought that the Samogithians might be brought to Christianity if approached cautiously. But the situation was not yet ready for that, so for the time being they decided to improve relations by giving them peace and a quiet life to last for two years. . . . When they concluded this, they sent for the envoys. They explained the conditions on which they would make peace, and the others rejoiced. They made a peace treaty with the Samogithians which was to last two years, that's true. The treaty was confirmed in the proper manner. The bishops came, as you have heard, from far away. There were many men who rejoiced for peace. They came to the city, but the heathens wanted only to return home again, as strange people generally do even today. They gave their hand to the Master and were satisfied, according to the custom of the land, for whoever gives his hand to another, even if in a third land, has made an honorable peace.[4]

For two years, 1257 to 1259, there was peace. Merchants traveled into and through the pagan lands, and the Samogithians visited the Christian domains without escort. It seemed that Master Burckhardt had achieved his object without incurring the expected losses and expenses. Merchants settled in Memel, so that a town was organized in 1258 and mills were built in the neighborhood. Prosperity increased, and everyone was so pleased with the truce that it was expected to last indefinitely.

The Christians had been in need of peace. The bishops, in particular, were faced by grave financial difficulties; their territories were all too often impoverished or still in the hands of the pagans. No matter how the various bishops and legates moved the prelates about or juggled their lands, their financial problems remained. Sometimes unable to maintain a body of canons, the bishops tended to spend much of their time in Germany, moving from place to place and traveling vast distances every year, everywhere assisting in ceremonial functions, collecting money, and presumably preaching the crusade. Those few who were able to remain in Livonia often went abroad as well, so that absentee government was widespread. And some of the bishops had difficulties with their vassals, so that from time to time they had to call upon the Teutonic Knights for aid. The governor in Estonia was hardly stronger than the average bishop.

Neglected by the Crown, the Danish vassals in Estonia had formed two distinct groups of German-speaking nobles, one in Harrien and the other in Wierland. Though led in war by their headman, the Danish vassals tended to be dominated by the great magnates, many of whom were settled on the eastern frontier. By 1249 these magnates had expanded to the Narva River, and by 1255 they had crossed permanently into Novgorodian territory. When they requested another bishop for this area, the Pope agreed to appoint one, and ordered Archbishop Albert Suerbeer to make a nomination (the Archbishop of Lund, at war with the King, was not in papal favor).[5]

Government in these areas, of course, was similar to that described earlier and in use throughout Europe. Advocates, *ministeriales,* and vassals supervised some minor courts, the collection of tithes and taxes, and provided defense for the lands. While responsible to their superior—bishop, governor, or city—they usually ran things pretty much as they wished. Petty tyranny was universal. In Livonia, of course, excesses were controlled by treaties, appeals to the Archbishop of Riga and the Pope, and fear of the armed natives. Subordinate to these officials were knights, sergeants, priests, and native chiefs, each of whom was responsible for various aspects of local affairs. The natives, lead by their chiefs and councils, had a significant role in their own governance. The native nobility in particular retained high status, and sometimes intermarried with the immigrant knighthood. The cathedral chapters were important too, and the canons visited the parishes to oversee spiritual affairs and collect fees and taxes. Although it appears simple, it was a complicated system with overlapping and conflicting responsibilities that made for many petty disputes. Nevertheless, it provided effective and respected government.

The administration of the lands of the Teutonic Knights differed little from that of the episcopal districts, except that authority was more centralized in the hands of the commanders and the advocates, who were professionals at the height of their careers. Consequently, a more uniform administration, and probably a more rigorous one, was to be found in their lands.

The Teutonic Knights had many difficulties with other branches of the Church, and needing help in preaching the crusade, they asked the Pope to organize a regular mission. Not long afterward, a friar formed a preaching group, but when he demanded financial support of the order, it was necessary to call upon the papacy to stop his harassment. Competition for pilgrims was keen because many clerics were preaching the crusade to the Holy Land, and even against the Mongols. Sometimes, however, the competition helped, because vows to fight the Mongols could be redeemed in the crusade to Prussia or Livonia. On balance, however, the Teutonic Knights found that it was best to do their own recruiting and not to rely on others to do it for them.

In Livonia, no Church-related difficulties were equal to those presented by Archbishop Albert Suerbeer. Although his various schemes went awry, he harassed the order unmercifully, until a papal order put a stop to each scheme. Also, he was resourceful. Forbidden to excommunicate individual knights or place the order under the interdict, he excommunicated its lay brothers and servants, thereby preventing the milling of grain and baking of bread. At the same time, he interfered with the collection of money for the crusade, and even quarreled with his canons who leaned toward the crusading order. Time and time again it was necessary to appeal to the Pope for assistance in individual cases and for reaffirmation of the rights and privileges of the crusading order. If Albert failed to humble the order, he at least made life difficult for its members, and when war in Samogithia resumed, he had an even greater opportunity to bring pressure upon them.[6]

No one knew if the Samogithians would allow the truce to expire in 1259; and although many hoped that an extension would be arranged, it was not to be. The Samogithian elders who longed for war invited their leading men to a carouse, and when they were sufficiently drunk gave them patriotic speeches, urging them to uphold their honor by fighting the enemies of their people and their religion. They promised that proper sacrifices to the ancient gods would restore the warriors to divine favor and bring victory. They spoke of booty—slaves, young maidens, horses, and cattle—that would enrich every warrior and revenge all their losses. Inflamed with desire for battle, the warriors immediately vowed to attack Kurland as soon as the truce expired.[7]

When the news arrived in Goldingen and Memel that a Samogithian raiding party had struck into Kurland, the order's commanders called their men, gathered the native militia, and set out in pursuit with a very large force. When the united Christian forces intercepted the pagans near Schoden, its commander, a famous hero, Bernhard of Haren, called on his men, both German and Kurish, to fight for everything they held dear, and then he led a charge toward the enemy ranks. The Samogithians charged in turn, so that the two cavalry forces clashed and then broke up into scattered melees. As the fight progressed, many Kurs, who were tired from the long march on foot, retired from the battlefield.

> The loyal ones remained there in the disaster and died with the brothers. Some . . . escaped from the battle even after the hardest fighting and managed to live through the battle, while others were destined to die. . . . The cowards fled and left the brave outnumbered so that they had to bathe in blood. Some were capable of fighting their way out and returned home with honor though alone. . . . The commander spoke, "Brothers, be cheerful. That happened which had to happen. We will find help in our distress for all is in God's hands."[8]

Thirty-three knights had perished. It was as great a disaster as the debacle at Saule twenty-three years earlier. Moreover, the ranks of the victors were soon swelled by recruits, so that in the next few months there were more victories over small bodies of Christian troops. When the news arrived that another Samogithian army was about to attack Kurland, the master sent summons to his commanders and advocates, who in turn called up their men and native followers. After gathering in Riga, the army hurried to Goldingen and camped on the field outside the castle. Soon the raid was reported, and this time they were ready. Although Archbishop Albert had prevented his men from joining the expedition, the master had collected a great army that was numerous enough to fight any enemy force. Furthermore, the Christian warriors were well armed and well trained. Learning that the raiders were near Memel, Master Burckhardt ordered his army to march south and cut off their retreat.

Pushing inland and southward, the army passed through a pathless wilderness for an entire day, finally making camp in an open meadow many miles to the south, while the scouts went on ahead. The next morning, Master Burckhardt learned from the scouts that the Samogithians were numerous and well armed. Calling his officers and allies to council, he informed them of the report, asked their advice, and, acting on their counsel, ordered the army to move farther south to a small castle, where they pitched camp and resumed the council, together with the knights of the garrison. Because the master wanted to fight in the morning, they agreed to divide the cavalry into two bodies and send one of them out immediately to locate the enemy. As it happened, however, some Samogithians discovered the tracks left by this force and reported it to their elders. That night the Samogithians met in council and decided to return home as quickly as possible, not making camp until they were far away. The Christian pursuit was not swift enough, so that the expedition came to naught.[9]

The Christians' reverses had an impact on the Semgallian tribes because the elders who had long opposed the Germans became dominant in the councils. Also, it is likely that the Germans had imposed a heavy emergency tax. Meeting in formal session, the elders voted to abandon the Christian alliance and return to paganism, and to adopt a position of neutrality in the Samogithian war. They ordered the advocates to leave the country and take their possessions with them, never to return. The Semgallians escorted them to the frontier in a chivalrous manner, which the knights appreciated and respected. Once they had crossed the Dvina, the advocates hurried to Riga to report the coup d'état to their master.

Master Burckhardt summoned his convent to council and asked its advice. When the reports had been thoroughly discussed, the convent voted for war against the apostates, advising the master to call up a general levy of the troops in Kurland, Livonia, and Estonia, to subjugate the Semgallians, and then to build castles in Semgallia to prevent future risings. Master Burckhardt followed their counsel and raised a great army that very winter. The first attack, at Terwerten, was not a success, however; so he had to proceed with the construction of the castles at Doblen and Karshowen while the land was still in rebellion. This was to lead to further complications with the Samogithians, who came to the aid of the Semgallian rebels.

In spring of 1260 the Samogithians attacked the two new castles, hoping to destroy them and thereby further erode the Christians' position. But their first effort, a direct assault on Doblen, was a failure, and after suffering great losses without causing a single fatality among the garrison, the Samogithians tried another expedient. Crusader tactics were such, they had found, that it was not easy to counteract them; German garrisons were firmly planted in the countryside, and raiding parties from the Dvina basin were ravaging the lands of the apostate Semgallians. Therefore, unless something was done, Semgallia would again be lost to the Christians. But if delay would be fatal, direct assault had proved useless. Driven to devise a new expedient, the pagan commanders decided to imitate the crusader policy and build a castle in enemy territory—directly opposite the castle at Karshowen. Establishing a garrison in their hastily constructed fortification, the Samogithians were able to harass their Christian opponents in daily combat and to neutralize their castle as a base for raiding the countryside.

Master Burckhardt was greatly worried by the reports of the situation at Karshowen, for it appeared that his resources were not adequate to his needs. He could neither protect every castle adequately nor deal a death blow to the Samogithians. However, he may have been waiting for an opportunity to test a new strategy based on the experience in Samland. Having been an officer in Prussia before he became master in Livonia, he had seen that the attack in Samland had been easier to direct from the south than from the north. Were not the two situations similar? Could an attack be launched from Memel directly into Samogithia and in such strength as to overwhelm the pagans? Resolved to test his theory, he set out to win the consent and cooperation of his brothers in Prussia.

The Prussian branch of the Teutonic Knights was pleased to receive a visit from its old comrade and heartily agreed to a joint expedition from Memel to Karshowen through Samogithia. A number of knights from Prussia were assigned to the force, as well as thirty knights recently arrived from Germany, and the natives in Samland were summoned to join them at Memel. The Teutonic Knights in Livonia, with large numbers of native troops, followers of two Counts from Germany, and a levy of Kurish warriors, assembled in Riga, proceeded to Kurland, and then along the coast to Memel. The united army was very large: there were more than 150 Teutonic Knights and thousands of secular knights, crusaders, and natives.

The army was at Memel when word came that a large Samogithian force was raiding southern Kurland, whereupon Master Burckhardt called a council of his brothers, knights, and natives to decide whether they should follow these Samogithians and fight them. With the council's consent, he ordered the march north. The Christian army was very large and well equipped, but so was the Samogithian army it met near Durben, in the hilly region southwest of Goldingen. After hearing the scouts' reports, the master called the council together again and asked its advice. They decided upon battle but they disagreed on the proposed distribution of the booty. Because large numbers of Kurs were held captive by the Samogithian raiders, the Kurish elders asked that these captives be released and not be considered part of the booty. The other natives, however, rejected the request; they were allies rather than subjects and therefore had rights to share in the gains of battle, which they refused to surrender.

The Kurs were angry, and repaid the bad blood on the battlefield. When the two armies began to move toward each other, the Kurs pulled out of the line of battle. When the Estonians saw this, they realized that the day was lost and fled for their lives. Soon the whole formation was broken, as most of the Christian warriors fled for the woods in a mad rout, and the knights and their loyal native allies (including many Kurs) fought to buy time for those who chose to retreat. Honor, of course, kept many on the field. As the Samogithians surrounded and at last overwhelmed the knights, a few broke out and escaped, but 150 Teutonic Knights were killed, together with Master Burckhardt and the marshal of Prussia. It was a total disaster. On that July day in 1260, thousands perished on the battlefield and in the rout that followed.[10]

The defeat nullified the gains of twenty years of warfare. Large parts of Semgallia and Kurland went over to the pagans, and fierce revolts broke out in Prussia and Livonia. It was to take fifteen years for the Teutonic Knights to recover the territories in Prussia, and thirty years in Livonia.

The temporary commander of the Teutonic Order, an officer whose name was George, faced mounting difficulties with the natives, because each defeat inspired further rebellions. His foremost problem was Kurland, where the natives made a desperate effort to free themselves from foreign control. Past loyalty was no longer a guarantee of conduct, as the commander of Goldingen and a small party of knights learned, to their horror. Taken by treachery, they were martyred by brutal means, some being roasted alive and the others slaughtered. The reprisals were equally horrible. A knight who had survived several days of torture returned to a post of command, and afterward became renowned for his cruelty to his captives. Nevertheless, several castles were lost to the insurgents' attacks, and others, such as Karshowen and Doblen, were abandoned as untenable.

Because of the Samogithian attack on the Dvina region, the vice-master was unable to leave Segewold, but he raised an army and sent it into Kurland under a subordinate. From Goldingen, it moved to a nearby rebel stronghold that was garrisoned by Samogithians, and mounted a full-scale attack. The chronicler tells how desperate the fighting was:

They all hurried to the attack, and filled the ditches with wood and set it ablaze. Many Lithuanians garrisoned the castle . . . and would gladly have given gold and silver to be able to escape from the brothers without fighting. When the ditches were ignited, the fire rose on the castle with a great blaze. The fire caught on more and more, and the Lithuanians stood in the middle of the flames fighting against the brothers' army. Their mood was grim, for they were suffering greatly and faced certain death, and could not escape it. They had to lose their lives, and they were slain amidst the flames. The army also took great booty from the fire, that is true. The Kurs over eleven years of age were all killed and thrown back into the fire.[11]

The lesson was clear, and many of the neighboring tribes hurried to Goldingen to renew their ties with the Teutonic Knights. By collecting hostages, the knights resorted to the best precaution known to that or any other age.

If the war in Kurland was proceeding satisfactorily for the crusaders, it was not going well in Livonia. The Samogithians and Semgallians were crossing the Dvina to raid deep into the interior, and Vice-Master George sent his best men to intercept the raiding parties as soon as they were detected.

The brothers' army set out, taking supplies with them, according to the custom of the land. Of those who were mounted, they chose the best and sent them to the routes the heathens would need to use for their return home. They were to guard the roads. The brothers' army marched after them, hurrying in pursuit of the heathens. The scouts observed carefully and came running. They informed the brothers, saying, "Quick, an immediate decision must be made! The heathen army is nearby. Whatever the circumstances, let no courageous man lose heart."[12]

On one raid the raiders proved too strong for the defending force and defeated the Teutonic Knights near Lennewarden, afterward escaping with a great amount of booty.

The news of the pagan victory near Lennewarden encouraged the Oeselians to rebel, so that the vice-master had still another opponent to fight in the winter of 1260–1261. He could not delay, lest the pagans come to the aid of the Oeselians and thereby encourage further defections from the Christian ranks. Calling up the Danish vassals, the episcopal troops, and the native warriors, he led the army across the ice to the islands and wrested more booty from the wealthy rebels than had been acquired in many a year. The Oeselians retreated into the wood at Carmel, where a great battle was fought, first the rebels and then the Christians having the upper hand. The field before the wood was covered with bodies, but the warlike natives showed a vigor worthy of their ancestry. Although no longer able to offer effective resistance, they continued to defy the crusaders, and the next morning the vice-master ordered the archers to advance into the woods. Soon there were loud cries as the crossbowmen began a massacre of young and old alike, the few warriors who were still alive being unable to defend the numerous noncombatants. On the morning of the third day, the Oeselians asked for a truce to discuss peace. When the treaty had been arranged, the army returned to the mainland across the ice, each man greatly enriched by his share of the loot.[13]

The disaster at Durben alarmed the grandmaster of the Teutonic Knights, Anno of Sangerhausen, who recruited reinforcements and forwarded them to Prussia and Livonia. And just as important, he sent a new master, Werner of Breithausen, to Livonia. A new commander usually inspires morale, but when Master Werner arrived in the fall of 1262, his own morale must have been severely shaken, for he found even greater difficulties than had faced Vice-Master George. Archbishop Albert Suerbeer, instead of cooperating, was capitalizing on the difficulties to advance his own ambitions. He made a member of the Buxhoevden family Bishop of Oesel, which displeased the order. Furthermore, he took crusaders for his own service and withheld money from the order—actions that may have been justified by the need to protect his lands but nevertheless interfered with the plans of the Teutonic Knights. But a far graver danger was implied in the apostasy of King Mindaugas of Lithuania.

Mindaugas had observed the Christian defeats with concern and feared that his fate might be linked with the fortunes of the Teutonic Knights. The embassies of the crusading order could not convince him that loyalty to Christianity would serve him well if his subjects should demand to be led against the Germans. Nor did the Samogithians forget the King and his numerous warlike subjects; indeed, they sought his support, and that of other Lithuanian princes, in the war against the Rigans. The elders sent messengers to King Mindaugas and another eastern prince, Traniate, to denounce Christianity and to offer an alliance against the foreigners, but in their promises of great rewards was a scarcely veiled threat to overthrow them if they refused the offer. Threatened also by Mongols and Russians, Mindaugas was not eager to move against another enemy. He investigated the possibility of Russian cooperation against the Teutonic Knights, and when he was certain that he could lead a Lithuanian-Samogithian-Russian attack into Livonia and that he would retain most of the conquests, he agreed to renounce Christianity and put himself at the head of the armies.

In the fall of 1262 he expelled the Christian priests and advisors and began to campaign across the Dvina.[14]

Because of these escalating dangers, the Teutonic Knights made every effort to recruit more aid from the west. In 1261 the vice-master offered land to every knight or citizen of Lübeck who would settle in Livonia,[15] an opportunity for wealth such as had rarely been offered, but few responded. It was not because of the hopelessness of the situation in Livonia that so few crusaders sailed east in these years; in fact, the stream of crusaders was never interrupted. However, many potential crusaders were tied down in Germany and Denmark by local troubles, so that the number of pilgrims did not increase sufficiently to rescue the Teutonic Knights from their plight. When a large army at last came from the west, the greatest danger had passed.

In Denmark, the civil war was still unresolved, despite the death of King Christopher in 1259. His widow, acting on behalf of her ten-year-old son, King Eric, continued the quarrel with the Church and the House of Holstein. "Black Greta," as she was called, was a stubborn and domineering woman. She continued the effort to recover Schleswig for the royal line when the young heir died without issue, but she was opposed by another widow, the duchess Matilda, who had been born a Countess of Holstein and had married Duke Abel of Schleswig, who had been King of Denmark from 1250 to 1252. Matilda fought for the right of her young children to inherit their brother Waldemar's estate, which Christopher had claimed by right of escheat. The events of 1259 had occasioned intervention by the Kings of Norway and Sweden, but the truce they arranged was short-lived, and later, Matilda broadened the feud by marrying her eldest son, Eric, to a daughter of Jaroslaw of Rügen and marrying Earl Birger of Sweden (a frequent "crusader" to Finland) herself. Wars, murders, excommunications, and peasant unrest kept the kingdom in constant turmoil so that no Danish help was available to the hard-pressed crusaders in Livonia.

The prelates of the region could not act effectively because of their involvement in numerous feuds and their heavy taxation by the papacy (there was scarcely a bishop who was not in arrears in his payments). Many were in papal disfavor because of the Church's situation in Denmark, and all were dominated by the papal legates who visited the region periodically, ostensibly to settle local problems but practically to increase papal control over Church affairs.[16]

Lay princes were hardly better than their ecclesiastical colleagues. Otto of Braunschweig, the Welf who exercised great power because of the clever marriages and ecclesiastical appointments he arranged for his children, was feuding with Brandenburg, Thuringia, and Holstein. Holstein was in turmoil following the departure of the heir to the Haseldorf estates, who was on crusade to Livonia. At first it seemed that he was only following the example of his father, who had fallen in 1236 in the battle of Saule, but when he entered the Church (eventually becoming Bishop of Dorpat), it set off a feud between the claimants to his estates. Such a dispute might have been of little import, but, linked to other crises, it was one of many complex, interrelated problems that plagued the society—a picture that undoubtedly seems more chaotic to us than it was to contemporaries.

An excellent example of the political complexity is an incident that occurred in Lübeck in 1261. The city, a great mercantile center, offered numerous attractions to every variety of visitor. There were markets, festivals, religious holidays, and many entertainers and hostelers of all kinds, and bakers, bankers, gamblers, clerics, prostitutes, and the like serviced their clienteles. Legal protection under the market peace, therefore, was vital to such enterprise, and the man who used arms inside the city was liable to severe punishment. But when this peace was broken by the Count of Holstein, a feud involving several great regional powers was set off.

It happened while the citizens were holding their annual tournament (which probably was a good time for recruiting volunteers for the crusade), in which Count John of Holstein planned to participate. As he walked through the streets he met an old enemy with whom he first exchanged words, then blows, and finally killed him. The Lübeckers, horrified by this breach of the peace, rang the alarm and hurried to arms. Count John, meanwhile, swinging his sword, fought his way through the streets to his family church, where the city constables arrested him in violation of the right of sanctuary. As the crowd was dispersing, a number of John's retainers swept into the church courtyard and released him, and together they fled the city. Count John declared a feud against the citizens for entering his church, and the city called upon Albrecht of Braunschweig to perform his services as advocate. In this manner the princes found themselves at war. Then, as now, rather trivial events could have far-reaching consequences, and because they were related to the opposing parties in Denmark, this quarrel became part and parcel of the Danish problem. The example is especially apt because personalities played such a great role in politics, and because the counts of Holstein participated in most of the disputes that plagued the north in this period.

The Holstein Counts were active and warlike, they welcomed conflict and feared no opponent. Their interference in Schleswig provoked a Danish invasion in the summer of 1261, and after winning a great battle against the Danes and capturing the young King and his mother, they were faced with a great temptation: should they put their nephew on the Danish throne? The matter was swiftly decided when Albrecht of Braunschweig, the Welf relative of the King, invaded Holstein and captured strategic castles in the eastern portion of the country, thereby depriving the anti-Danish forces of valuable territories and their most strategically placed base for an attack on Denmark. Only then did the counts understand the need for compromise. In return for releasing the Queen Mother and the King they obtained the return of their lands and castles. The Queen returned to Denmark to supervise the royal government, but the King was sent to Brandenburg, whose Duke had ties to both Denmark and Holstein and therefore was an acceptable mediator. Neither Prince wanted to fight the feud to a finish. (A family feud to the finish would have been considered in bad taste, according to the standards of the age. Chivalry demanded much more gentlemanly solutions, such as the arrangement that ended the feud between Albrecht of Braunschweig and Herman of Hesse in 1263, who met at Lüneburg with all their vassals and allies and fought it out in the form of a tournament, winner take all. The defeated Welf forces lost all their armor and horses, and the dispute as well, but retained their honor and suffered very few casualties.)

Negotiations regarding the future of the Danish monarchy were slow. Meanwhile the counts obstinately continued their feud with Lübeck, but unsuccessfully, because the citizens hired Albrecht of Braunschweig and the Princes of Mecklenburg to destroy the lairs of the robber barons and to police the roads. Thus the feud continued, fired by old and new fuel.[17]

As the princes quarreled and thereby reduced their power to act effectively, the cities, led by Lübeck, waxed ever stronger. Not only do myriad treaties and agreements to expand and protect trade testify to the vitality of the merchant communities in this era, they also prove that the cities knew how to defend their common interests. Their associations for trade and defense later developed into the Hanseatic League. Now it is in the cities that the main crusading impulse is found, and Lübeck was the greatest of these cities, inspiring the Teutonic Knights to write: "It is through the blood of your fathers and brothers, your sons and friends, that the field of believers in these lands has been watered like a marvelous garden." The citizens of Reval, in asking Lübeck for help, wrote: "We must hang together like the arms of a cross." Indeed, the influence on politics of citizen-raised money and arms could be decisive, and princes courted the favor of the wealthy townsmen.[18] Significantly, it was in Lübeck, where a relatively impartial hearing could be held, that Cardinal Guido, the papal legate, called together the disputants in the various regional conflicts in 1265. His choice reflected political realities.

The Pope and his legates had not ignored the Danish problem, but they had not been able to solve it. Pope Urban IV had ordered the Archbishop of Lund to appear before him in Rome to explain his hostile attitude toward the Crown, but the Archbishop had delayed his trip until a new and more friendly Pope came to office. Nevertheless, papal favor could not restore Lund to his dioceses. Cardinal Guido later placed the Kingdom of Denmark under interdict and excommunicated the King, but the Archbishop never returned to Lund. The Danish Church was in woeful condition indeed, its finances ruined and its Bishops in exile.

The Church in Northern Germany was not in much better condition than the Church in Denmark. Everywhere the prelates were feuding like secular princes, often using ecclesiastical censure to obtain advantages over their opponents. When Cardinal Guido visited Bremen, he called a special council and denounced the widespread vices of the area: marriage of the clergy and the keeping of concubines; attacks upon the clergy by the laity; violence in churches, including violation of sanctuary; entering churches under arms; laymen holding Church offices; and simony. One must conclude that the Church was suffering for its involvement in secular affairs.[19]

Preoccupied with their problems, the nobility of the northern regions was unable to participate in the Livonian crusade for almost a decade. Only after 1266 was sufficient order restored to allow large numbers of pilgrims to sail from the Baltic ports to Riga to assist the Teutonic Knights against their enemies.

The failure of western crusaders to sail to Livonia in large numbers was unfortunate for the Teutonic Knights, who were in grave danger in the years following 1262, when King Mindaugas apostatized and enemies fell on them from all sides. They survived only because the King's great invasion across the Dvina had miscarried, his Russian allies failing to help him at the appointed time and the natives ignoring his call for an uprising against the Germans. He withdrew back into Lithuania, and while the Teutonic Knights were guarding the Dvina frontier against his attacks, the Russians stormed into Estonia and burned Dorpat. The chronicler's malicious joy in describing the terror-stricken monks as they fled into the citadel for safety and his contrasting treatment of the courageous knights illustrates the jealousy between the orders.[20]

Once the immediate threat of disaster had passed, the Teutonic Knights were able to resume their offensive, and because the new commander, Master Werner, was too ill to lead his armies in person, he authorized subordinates to attack Kurland and destroy the strongholds of the rebels. The expedition of 1262 met with notable success, and by punishing some rebels the crusaders induced others to return to the Christian fold. In the south, a large garrison at Memel mounted attacks against the Samogithian castles blocking the road to Goldingen, particularly the castle at Kreitingen, north of Memel on the Dange River. The knights were at first defeated at Kreitingen, losing two knights and numerous sergeants (their captured commander was roasted alive), but finally a large force defeated the pagans outside the castle, forced its way inside with the last of the fugitives, and captured the place. After massacring the garrison and enslaving the women and children, the crusaders secured the region and built new castles to protect it. The significance of such efforts in Kurland—when the line of the Dvina could hardly be defended—is that highest priority had been given to the conquest of Samogithia.

While the Samogithians were not the strongest tribe of Lithuanians, neither those followers of King Mindaugas nor the tribes along the Russian frontier threatened the security of Livonia as did the Samogithians. Under Prince Traniate, Samogithian raiders moved through the unpopulated reaches of Livonia and struck across the ice at Wiek in February 1263, while the island's defenders were on the mainland.

> While they were in Kurland . . . an army came into Livonia from Lithuania, led by Traniate. He came with many bands along back roads and narrow passages till he arrived at Wiek. He ravaged that land with fire and sword, and he was able to ravage freely because those who were to defend against his attack had been sent to Kurland with the brothers' army. The Master, who was ill in Riga . . . sent his messengers after help. They were sent to Segewold and the brothers came to him willingly with their force. Meanwhile Traniate was returning from Wiek. When the Master heard that, he sent the army against

them. The citizens came with many brave men to the brothers' army for the benefit of their souls, it is true. The brothers were happy about that. Then they left Riga. When the army reached Dünamünde, it took up camp nearby. A cloister by that name lies there on the coast. Before it was midnight, Traniate came riding with his force toward the brothers' camp. They sprang up in arms against him and organized a defense. Though one could not see well to fight, each had to do as best he could in the fighting by the moon light. Some of the heathens were slain but who can tell the truth, whether friend had not slain friend. The battle took place in the night. The battlefield was red with blood, and nine brothers were killed, and some of the burghers were slain. One could hear the heroes mourning greatly, and the dead lay all around.[21]

Traniate held the field, and the next day crossed the ice toward home. Nevertheless, he did not raid Livonia in such a bold fashion again.

The Lithuanians might have been much more dangerous if King Mindaugas had been able to lead all his people against their enemies, but he was surrounded by jealous nobles and personal enemies who prevented such a great undertaking, and his role in Lithuanian history came to a sudden end in the fall of 1263, when he was murdered by supporters of Traniate. The assassins also attempted to destroy his family, but his son escaped to the Teutonic Knights and became a Christian pawn in the war against the Samogithians. The importance of King Mindaugas's son derives primarily from his role in the disintegration of his kingdom amid the blood feuds of the Lithuanian nobility. Once the kingdom had been reduced to helpless chaos, he and his opponents passed from the scene almost without notice. Traniate lived only till 1265, and Mindaugas's son but little longer.[22]

Master Werner was no longer in Livonia. Ill and disabled after an insane brother had dealt him a severe wound, he traveled to Germany in early 1263 to ask Grandmaster Anno to relieve him of his duties and appoint a successor, and soon afterwards Conrad of Mandern was sent to Riga to take command of the Teutonic Knights in Livonia. It was Master Conrad who had extorted great concessions from the exiled son of Mindaugas in return for assistance against their common enemies, and it was Master Conrad who now tried to make good these renewed claims to Samogithia. Now father and son had each given Samogithia to the Teutonic Order. It was a better claim than the crusaders usually needed.

Having collected a large body of knights for the ceremony ratifying the treaty with the Lithuanian Prince, Conrad decided to strike a strong blow

against the enemy before allowing such an assemblage to disperse. At first
he met with success: the raiding party sent out from Goldingen surprised
and sacked the castle at Gresen, and the raiders from Riga captured a considerable amount of booty and prisoners in Semgallia. But then misfortune
struck: his force from Riga, greatly harassed by the natives, who had cut
down so many trees that the forest roads became impassable, fell into an
ambush and lost 600 troops and twenty knights. Some escaped through the
woods with the master, and some were later ransomed, but it was a great
disaster. It was mitigated only by the booty that had been won at Gresen
and transported to Riga.[23]

The difficulties encountered in Samogithia and Semgallia made it necessary to reduce the burdens and commitments elsewhere. In 1264 Master
Conrad signed a treaty with the Lithuanians in Polozk, ending the war in
that area, and offered to submit to several of Archbishop Albert's demands.
If the order had honored the agreement to recognize the Archbishop's
authority, Albert Suerbeer's ambitions might have been achieved, but
Conrad was only buying time. His order continued to resist archiepiscopal
taxation for the building of bulwarks, churches, and bridges, and complained about the Archbishop's interference in its internal affairs. As a
result, Archbishop Albert began to contemplate drastic means of forcing
the order into submission, as contracts and treaties had proved to be value-
less. Thus the respite gained by the Teutonic Knights in 1264 brought
greater problems, because the Archbishop had learned to distrust the order
even more than before. But Master Conrad could not look past immediate
needs, and the most immediate need was for victory on the battlefield.[24]

It was obvious that if Semgallia was to be occupied permanently, the
Christians had to build more bases in that country. They had constructed
such fortifications before, but every time they had established a foothold in
the interior a military defeat had forced them to abandon bases as untenable. The basic strategy was sound, however, and they continued their efforts.
In 1265 Master Conrad built a new castle, one that could be supplied by
ship, on an island in the Semgallian Aa at Mitau, just below the confluence
of its northernmost tributary. Based in this strong castle, the knights raided
the pagan settlements to the south, inflicting great damage. This could
bring eventual military victory, but a great drawback was that the territory
belonged to Archbishop Albert Suerbeer, who feared that his rights over
the land would be ignored if it was garrisoned by the order. He had reason
for such fear, as the Teutonic Knights had long fostered a rebellious attitude

among his canons and the citizens of Riga. Therefore, the order had appealed to the Pope for permission to build the castle at Mitau, and in 1266 belatedly obtained such permission. Master Conrad believed he could safely ignore the Riga prelate, because Albert lacked the military resources to threaten the order's castles.[25]

The importance of sea transportation became more obvious as the Semgallian wars progressed because it was the only reliable means of supplying Mitau, which was deep in pagan territory. The pagans, as Master Conrad learned to his sorrow, still controlled the land route. The war had not yet been won, and raids, which were the technique of medieval warfare, were exceedingly risky, especially deep into enemy territory. At the end of such a raid, when his army had reassembled and was returning to Mitau, its transport loaded down with booty, Master Conrad went in advance with a small force to repair the road and bridges so as to expedite the journey. He had left orders that the army was to sound the war horns if it was attacked, whereupon he would return, but when he heard the horns and turned back, he discovered that the Semgallians had interposed themselves between the Christian forces. There was nothing he could do except listen to the sound of distant battle as the main body of troops was overwhelmed. The men who were with him, and those who fled the battle and into the forest, returned to Mitau safely, but its land communications remained uncertain thereafter. Water was the safest and most efficient transportation route to the isolated outpost.[26]

By this time Master Conrad had served three years in Livonia and had tired of his responsibilities. With the consent of his brothers, he wrote to Grandmaster Anno asking to be replaced, and Anno, consenting to his resignation, ordered the Livonian general council to elect a successor. Master Otto, who took office in 1267, was a capable warrior, well acquainted with the country and popular with his brethren, but he was to face grave threats from the Archbishop of Riga and the Russians. It had been obvious for several years that war was brewing on the Russian front. The Danish vassals and the Bishop of Dorpat had pushed their frontiers eastward as far as possible; the merchants complained about bandits along the eastern trade routes; and relations in general were tense. Accordingly, Master Conrad had constructed a great castle at Weissenstein in Estonia to anchor the defense of Jerwan and had sent out calls for the crusaders who would be needed in 1267 and 1268. The new master expected war with Russia. What Otto did not anticipate was that Archbishop Albert Suerbeer would plot against the crusading order while the master was preoccupied with the defense of the frontiers.

Among the crusaders who sailed to Livonia in 1267 was Count Gunzelin of Schwerin, a descendant of Count Henry the Black, a man who was resourceful and dangerous, though not a powerful Prince. He had been active, but unsuccessful, in the numerous feuds of his region. For two decades he had quarreled with bishops and princes, and each time emerged weaker than before. His defeats, however, were not necessarily due to lack of courage or ability but probably more to financial and military weakness. He had fought in the Danish wars in the 1250s, joined in a feud over the Mecklenburg inheritance, and served as a Welf partisan in the feuds of the early 1260s—all the while profiting but little for his efforts. Married to a member of the House of Mecklenburg, he stood to profit from the chaotic situation that followed the death of Prince John of Parchim, but he was eventually defeated by his opponent, young Prince Henry. It was at this time that he took the cross for Livonia, perhaps in the lure of adventure and religion, or perhaps in keeping with family tradition. Or perhaps it was demanded by Prince Henry, who was taking his bride on crusade and did not want to leave any potential enemies at home. Or perhaps he planned to resettle in the east. For many years Count Gunzelin had been gathering estates in Livonia by occasionally exchanging properties with the monastic orders, and he was undoubtedly well informed on conditions in the east.

The crusaders must have landed in Livonia in the summer or fall of 1267 in expectation of waging a winter campaign near Novgorod, for Master Otto, although occupied with Lithuanian attacks along the Dvina, had ordered thirty-four knights from Weissenstein, Leal, and Fellin to support the Bishop of Dorpat. Large numbers of native troops were available in the area, and the Danish vassals were ready to defend their own lands. Among the numerous crusaders was Count Henry of Mecklenburg with his German and Slavic troops. But Count Gunzelin apparently spent little time in Estonia.

His ship would have brought him directly to Riga, where he met Archbishop Albert Suerbeer, whom, it can be presumed, he had met previously during the Archbishop's long stay in Northern Germany. But only now did the two men discover that they could be of service to one another. Albert resented the autonomy of the Teutonic Knights and the fact that they confiscated his lands and stirred up trouble even among his canons. Gunzelin was poor, but ambitious and warlike. Because his lands were held by the Duke of Brandenburg and he had several children to provide a heritage for, he had seen little future in Schwerin. It is not clear who made the proposal to attack the Teutonic Knights and divide their territories, but on 21 December 1267, Gunzelin and Albert signed a pact to work to this end. The Archbishop appointed the Count advocate of all his lands, with the duty of reorganizing his holdings and protecting them against all enemies, and he gave him all authority, all incomes, and all responsibilities associated with his holdings. It was understood that the Count would be rewarded by generous grants of land in the captured territories if he suc-ceeded in taking any from the Teutonic Knights or pagan tribes, but if he failed, the Archbishop would not even pay his ransom, implicitly denying all responsibility for his actions. It was a risky venture for the Count, but no more risky than Henry the Black's kidnapping of Waldemar the Great. Counts of Schwerin were not fazed by heavy odds.

Hopeful of becoming a great landowner in Semgallia and Nalsen, Gunzelin prepared the archiepiscopal territories for war. Presumably he visited the vassals, inspected the castles, and estimated the enemy's strength. Then, after ascertaining how many additional troops would be needed to accomplish his mission, he set out for Gothland to recruit soldiers. Mean-while Albert Suerbeer was in contact with Lithuanian princes, whom it would be necessary to bring over to Christianity. If this could be done, the conspirators might stand a good chance of overthrowing the Teutonic Knights in Livonia.[27]

In the meantime a large Russian army, commanded by Prince Dmitri, the son of Alexander Nevsky, had invaded Estonia. The western army, also very large (estimated by the chronicler at 30,000 men), gathered at Dorpat. The two forces collided in pitched battle in February 1268.

When the people who were supposed to be with the brothers had arrived, orders were given to place the natives on the left flank. That was to be held by them in the battle. A larger army of royal vassals of German birth was brought there, and they held the right flank. Then they changed honorably. The broth-ers and their men struck together. Bishop Alexander was killed. Two forma-tions of Russians advanced upon him, but they were forced into a rout. Up and down the field the Russian army had to retreat. . . . The brothers revenged the injuries they had suffered from the Russians over a long period. The field was wide and deep, and the Russian defeat a great one. . . . Each German had to fight sixty Russians. . . . Prince Dmitri was a hero, and with five thousand chosen Russians he entered into battle. The other army had fled. Now hear what happened. The brothers' flagbearers were opposed to him on a very bad stream. He saw the brothers' army there, and the brothers had many men there, as I now tell you. There were one hundred and sixty there and that had to suffice. There were also footsoldiers, who, standing before the bridge, conducted themselves like heroes. They had done very well, and there were about eighty of them. They did their duty by the brothers and thrust back the Russians so that they were dismayed. . . . Many Russian wives mourned over their husband's bodies when the battle was over. The Russians still hold that against the brothers, it is true. The feeling has lasted many years.[28]

The Russian account of the battle is more coherent:

When they reached the Kegolar River they found a force of [Germans] in position, and it was like a forest to look at; for the whole land of the [Germans] had come together. But the men of Novgorod without any delay crossed the river to them, and began to range their forces; and the men of [Pskov] took stand on the right hand, and Dmitri, and Svyatoslav took stand also on the right higher up; and on the left stood Mikhail, and the men of Novgorod stood facing the iron troops opposite to the great wedge; and so they went against each other. And as they came together there was a terrible battle such as neither fathers nor grandfathers had seen. . . . Now that the great encounter [had] taken place, and the laying down of the heads of good men with their heads for Saint Sophia, the merciful Lord speedily sent his mercy, not wishing utter death to the sinner; punishing us and again pardoning. He, turning away his wrath from us, and regarding us with his merciful eye; by the power of the Honourable Cross and through the prayers of the Holy Mother of God our Sovereign Lady, the Immaculate Mary, and those of all the Saints, God helped [Prince] Dmitri and the men of Novgorod. . . . They pursued them fighting, as far as the town, for seven versts along the three roads, so that not even a horse could make its way for the corpses. And so they turned back from the town, and perceived another large force in the shape of a great wedge which had struck into the Novgorod transport; and the men of Novgorod wished to strike them, but others said, "It is already too near night; how if we fall into confusion and get beaten ourselves." And so they stood together opposite each other waiting daylight. And they, accursed transgressors of the Cross, fled, not waiting for the light.[29]

It had been a confused combat between two huge armies. Apparently each had been victorious on different parts of the battlefield, and afterward the Germans withdrew to defend another river crossing. Each side was exhausted, and the Russians soon withdrew to their own country. (As he left the battlefield, Prince Henry of Mecklenburg came upon an orphan girl and adopted her. Neither mercy nor chivalry was dead.)

The Teutonic Knights knew that the war with Novgorod would continue; so the master and the city of Riga asked the merchant communities to embargo Russian goods until peace was made—which would adversely affect a mercantile center such as Novgorod. The master, however, was no longer fearful of a great defeat in Estonia. At last able to turn to the Archbishop, he acted vigorously. Realizing that Count Gunzelin represented the greatest threat to his order, Master Otto cut the ground from beneath the advocate's feet by writing to Gothland and warning its merchants not to have any dealings with Gunzelin on pain of great punishment. The city of Riga supported Otto, and Gunzelin, taking to heart the warning not to return to Livonia, sailed back to Schwerin that summer and forfeited his plans in the east. His plot had failed miserably.[30]

But what could the Teutonic Knights do with the Archbishop? His treasonous acts, dating over a period of three decades, indicated that he would also be dangerous in the future. The order therefore decided upon drastic action. The master sent knights to the cathedral, who in turn sent their servants into the church to kidnap the Archbishop and his prior in the midst of a religious service. Hastening to the order's stronghold at Segewold, they threw them into close confinement on bread and water, then turned on the episcopal vassals and forced them to take oaths of homage to the Teutonic Knights.

By December 1268 Albert Suerbeer saw that his position was hopeless and made a humiliating surrender to his enemies. He ceased his harassment of the order, formally dismissed Gunzelin, and promised not to complain to the Pope about his imprisonment or any mistreatment by the Teutonic Knights. Then the master stationed garrisons in several archiepiscopal castles and allowed the Archbishop to return to Riga. A broken man, Albert Suerbeer was an obedient puppet of the crusading order until his death several years later. These events came to light fifty years later, when a papal legate conducted an investigation and witnesses came forth to testify against the Teutonic Order.[31] The Teutonic Knights controlled the archbishopric of Riga through the canons, who soon acquired the authority so long denied them by Albert. Their agreement to prevent foreign princes from settling in the land should have precluded the schemes of another Count of Schwerin, but the Schwerin claims were revived two decades later.

The war with Russia also was concluded in 1268. Gathering a force estimated at 18,000 warriors and 9,000 sailors, the crusaders invaded Russia, burning Isborg and besieging Pskov. The Novgorodians' army relieved the city and pushed the crusaders back, and finally the master and a Russian delegation confirmed a peace treaty on board a ship on Lake Peipus. Satisfied, each army returned home.[32] Prince Henry of Mecklenburg, however, had caught the crusading fever and in 1270 joined an expedition to the Holy Land. Unfortunately, he arrived when a truce was in effect and attempted to visit Jerusalem in disguise, but was discovered by the Saracens and condemned to twenty-five years of captivity.[33]

It was not easy to persuade large numbers of crusaders to take the cross to Livonia in the future; nor was it easy to recruit men for the Holy Land. When larger and larger armies were needed, they did not appear, and it seemed that fewer and fewer men responded to the call each year. The revival-like atmosphere in which the crusades were preached failed to produce their customary scenes of mass hysteria and their fervid volunteers, and those who took the cross could redeem their vow with money. Prussia, however, retained its popularity because of its location; moreover, the Teutonic Knights organized an efficient crusade and raised the formality and pageantry of chivalry to unprecedented heights. The Livonian branch of the order shared in this to some extent, but it seems that many of its crusaders were of middle-class origin, whose religious enthusiasm still ran strong, and that this social difference was reflected in the subsequent history of the crusade: Prussia welcomed the large armies led by princes, and Livonia only a steady stream of individual middle-class crusaders.

Although the era of Albert Suerbeer ended with his humiliation and defeat, the difficulties of the Teutonic Knights were not yet resolved. The war with the Samogithians and Semgallians raged on as before, as the crusaders tried to pacify those areas and complete the land bridge between Prussia and Livonia.

NOTES TO CHAPTER TEN

1. *Reimchronik*, ll. 4159–4260.
2. Goetze, *Albert Suerbeer*, pp. 67ff; *Urkundenbuch*, 1: no. CCCXLI.
3. Olins cites the many accusations against the Teutonic Order as if the accusers were impartial, whereas they indicate the areas where Albert Suerbeer attempted to

exercise his authority rather than the difficult problems within the order. Peter Olins, *The Teutonic Knights in Latvia* (Riga: B. Laney, 1925).

4. *Reimchronik*, ll. 4552–4619.

5. Johansen, *Estlandliste*, pp. 168ff, 739–47.

6. Goetze, *Albert Suerbeer*, pp. 56–81.

7. *Reimchronik*, ll. 4653–4728.

8. Ibid., ll. 4915–4934.

9. Ibid., ll. 4935–5238.

10. Ibid., ll. 5541–5734; *Herman de Wartberge*, pp. 41–42.

11. *Reimchronik*, ll. 5941–5968.

12. Ibid., ll. 6006–6026.

13. Ibid., ll. 6041–6314.

14. The chronicler invented an interesting conversation between Mindaugas and the chief Samogithian leader in which the King is alternately entreated and threatened. (Ibid., ll. 6339–6426).

15. *Urkundenbuch* 1: no. CCCLXII. A knight or citizen of town would receive sixty Saxon Hufen, a family forty, a man with a horse ten, and a man with armor ten Hufen. A farmer would have freedom from taxes for six years and afterward would pay only the tithe and would retain his personal freedom. All applicants were directed to Memel.

16. Dahlmann, *Geschichte von Dännemark*, 1: 415; Bippen, *Aus Bremens Vorzeit*, 151ff; Adolf Gottlob, *Die Servitientaxe im 13. Jahrhundert* (Stuttgart: F. Enke, 1903), p. 81.

17. Karl Koppmann, "Chronologische Kleinigkeiten zur Deutsch-Dänischen Geschichte," *Mitteilungen des Verein für Hamburgische Geschichte* (March 1822), pp. 31f.

18. Johansen, "Die Bedeutung der Hanse für Livland," pp. 38, 41.

19. Münter, *Kirchengeschichte*, pp. 512ff.

20. *Reimchronik*, ll. 6599–6649.

21. Ibid., ll. 6891–6943.

22. Ibid., ll. 7121–7208; Thomas Chase, *The Story of Lithuania* (New York: Strafford House, 1946), pp. 15–18; Hellmann, *Das Lettenland im Mittelalter*, pp. 190–94; Constantine Jurgela, *History of The Lithuanian Nation* (New York: Lithuanian Cultural Institute, 1948), pp. 74–80.

23. *Reimchronik*, ll. 7209–7390.

24. Goetze, *Albert Suerbeer*, pp. 97–98.

25. *Urkundenbuch*, 1: no. CCCXCVI; *Herman de Wartberge*, p. 44.

26. *Reimchronik*, ll. 7421–7512.

27. Goetze, *Albert Suerbeer*, pp. 100–103; Paul Johansen, "Eine Riga-Wisby Urkunde," *Zeitschrift des Vereins für luebeckische Geschichte* (1958): 93–108; Witte, *Mecklenburgische Geschichte*, p. 170; *Urkundenbuch*, 1: no. CDVI.

28. *Reimchronik*, ll. 7604–7676.

29. *Chronicle of Novgorod*, pp. 101–3.

30. Johansen, "Eine Riga-Wisby Urkunde," pp. 97–100.

31. Goetze, *Albert Suerbeer*, pp. 103–7; *Zeugenverhör des Franciscus de Moliano (1312)*, ed. August Seraphim (Königsberg: Thomas and Opperman, 1912), pp. 6–7, 27, 29, 45, 62, 77, 128–29, 140 (hereafter cited as *Zeugenverhör*).

32. *Reimchronik*, ll. 7677–7768.

33. Witte, *Mecklenburgische Geschichte*, pp. 170–71.

11

Expansion into Semgallia

As the thirteenth century moved into its eighth decade, the relative isolation of Scandinavia and the Baltic area from the affairs of Europe continued; neither the loss of Jerusalem, the death of Conradin, nor the crusade of Louis IX had a noticeable effect upon the area. Perhaps some persons were moved by hearing how the aged King of France had died while on crusade in Tunisia, but leadership to turn such sentiment into action was lacking. General peace reigned in the Baltic area, so that crusaders could sail easily to Livonia, but this new generation was neither as forceful nor idealistic as its forefathers. The strong wave of eastward migration and colonization that had characterized the first half of the century had subsided, and the Princes who had sponsored it had so divided their lands among their numerous progeny that, instead of powerful princedoms, there was now only a collection of small and ineffective states. North German and Polish Princes were weak, and Denmark was exhausted by the quarrel between King and Parliament, so that in general the rulers, satisfied with maintaining the status quo, refused to involve themselves in ventures across the seas.

The only signs of vitality were found in the German cities along the southern shores of the Baltic Sea. The strongest of these was Lübeck, thanks to its city fathers who had procured trading privileges from Novgorod to Flanders and from Braunschweig to England. As the city on the Trave became the center of international trade in the north, its citizens assumed responsibility for protecting merchants from royal interference, piracy, and restrictive legislation. Wismar, Rostock, Stralsund, Greifswald, Stettin, Kammin, Danzig, Kulm, and Elbing followed their leadership, and Riga, Dorpat, and Reval depended heavily upon their assistance. It was not idle chance that caused the Rigans to allot Lübeck one of the towers in the ring wall and allow her merchants to build their own church within the city. Nor was it by random favor that the Teutonic Knights showered privileges upon Lübeck's merchants. As the years passed, the city continued to grow in wealth and influence, to become the most important market in the region. By overshadowing the trading center at Visby, Lübeck was preparing for a new era in Baltic history, the era of the Hanseatic League.

It was the cities that now provided most of the crusaders to Livonia. Members of the minor nobility still sailed east, but the major Princes who had led armies to Riga in earlier decades now remained at home, or journeyed to Prussia. The middle class, however, retained much of its enthusiasm—and presumably combined crusading and business by bringing western merchandise for sale in the Livonian markets and returning with goods purchased from Russian merchants.[1]

The city of Riga emulated Lübeck. Its councilmen had quarreled with Bishop Albert I, Bishop Nicholas, and Archbishop Albert Suerbeer, and their occasional triumphs won more and more autonomy from their episcopal lords. After Archbishop Albert Suerbeer had been humbled by the Teutonic Order, he could hardly resist the city's demands, and his successor was even weaker. John of Lune, who became Archbishop in 1273, gave way on numerous points, in effect granting the citizens self-government. Furthermore, the Teutonic Knights weakened the authority of that prelate by encouraging the citizens' independence, giving them various immunities and trading privileges throughout their vast estates and supporting them in disputes. Only later did the Teutonic Knights realize that the Rigans had become so powerful and wealthy as to constitute a real danger to their hegemony. The Archbishop was no longer a threat, but the citizens might well be. Riga, like Lübeck, seemed to be riding a rising tide, and her merchants, indispensable for transportation and supplies, were becoming aware of their new importance.

The position of Riga was enhanced by the weakness of the estates. The Archbishop had not been able to assume his post without appearing before a papal commission, and, bullied by the papacy, he contented himself with enriching his family, allowing the Teutonic Knights to supervise affairs of state for him. Many of the Bishops resided abroad, unable or unwilling to stay in Livonia, and their administrators observed the wishes of the crusading order. The cities, other than Riga, were small and poor and attracted few immigrants. A few Swedes settled in Estonia, and a few nobles took up residence on the lands, but most new settlements were merely the relocations of uprooted natives. As a result, Riga profited most by the influx of new blood and energy, and the other cities and bishoprics stagnated.[2]

Aware of the potential competition, the Teutonic Knights took steps to control the citizens. In 1274 they obtained supervision of Riga from the Emperor, Rudolf of Hapsburg, but similar opportunities meant little at that time because the master did not try to exploit them.[3] The order was too hard pressed in Semgallia to antagonize its allies in the merchant community—Riga contributed money, ships, and many good troops.

Master Otto, having made peace with the Novgorodians, thought he would be able to concentrate his efforts on the Semgallian front. For almost a year in advance, he had been recruiting for a winter expedition into Semgallia, and early in 1270 he assembled his force in Riga and advanced into the pagans' land. He had not gone far, however, when he received word that a large Samogithian army was gathered on the frontier, preparing to attack Livonia. He immediately took counsel with his brethren and, on their advice, hurried back to intercept the raiders; however, he was too late. The Lithuanians had penetrated to the sea, and then moved across the ice to Oesel, where they burned and plundered the rich native settlements. But Otto could hardly have been in a better situation: he had a large army, already assembled; more troops were coming in response to his summons; and he could intercept the Lithuanians' march homeward wherever he wished. His reinforcements—Danish vassals from Estonia, Bishop Frederick of Dorpat, and troops from Leal with their Bishop, Herman of Buxhoevden—and their native followers joined him as he moved north to the area of Wiek, where he planned to intercept and smash the raiders. Those who escaped the battlefield would have to cross Livonia or Kurland to return home—and die or be killed on the way. Looking forward to a great victory, Otto ignored the suffering of his men as they marched across the ice of the Gulf of Riga and the straits in the bitter cold. Finally, the two armies drew within sight of one another.

The Lithuanians dismounted from their sleds, lashed them together, and took refuge behind this barrier while, opposite them, the Teutonic Knights held council, moved into attacking position, and charged. The ice must have heaved and groaned from the weight of the two great armies clashing on the frozen sea, but it did not break, and the combat soon dissolved into scattered actions. Because their center formation attacked too early, the Teutonic Knights' main cavalry force became entangled in the sleds and were surrounded by the enemy. Their horses were cut down before the Bishops' men on the left, and the Danish vassals on the right were able to close with the enemy and relieve the pressure upon their flanks:

One could see a disorderly tumult of the two armies, Christian and heathen. The battle was hard fought, and the blood flowed onto the ice from either side. It was a fight in which many noble men were struck down. Slain in defeat was good Master Otto, and fifty-two good brothers. They spilled their blood for God. Also many outstandingly chivalrous warriors on both sides fell. Part of the natives fell. May God save their souls![4]

The Bishops' forces scattered their opponents, as did the Estonian nobles, but both forces unwisely forsook the main battle in pursuit of the fugitives. After long fighting, the Christian cavalry regrouped, formed one unit, and by repeated charges turned back the pagans' attacks on the main infantry force, saving the latter from massacre, so that by nightfall the crusader army was still intact. The pagans had lost 1,600 men and the Christians 600, but the Lithuanians held the field. Wounded, the Bishop of Leal ordered the retreat, and the Christians withdrew. The Lithuanians stripped the dead and returned home safely with their booty and, spreading the news of their victory, soon brought the other Lithuanians into the war alongside them.

Master Otto's authority passed to Vice-Master Andreas of Westphalia until an election could be held. Andreas, considering the defeat not only unnecessary but also costly and demoralizing, decided to regain the psychological advantage by winning a quick victory, and toward the middle of 1270 (just a few months later, in fact) he had his opportunity. Notified that the Lithuanians were raiding the order's territories, he gathered a small force and set off in ill-considered haste to counter and defeat the enemy. Having perhaps pushed his men too hard, he found it necessary to stop and rest, and while his soldiers lay at ease in the summer heat, probably with their armor laid aside, the pagans burst upon them from the forest and massacred Andreas and twenty knights.[5]

The newly elected master, Walter of Nortecken, was much more cautious than his predecessors. Realizing that raids alone were not sufficient to cow the Semgallians, he prepared expeditions against their major strongholds, planning to besiege, take, and garrison them and thereby gain control of the country.

Early in 1271 he brought a great army, composed of units from all the nearby regions, to Terwerten, the huge castle southwest of Mitau, and after a short siege stormed the citadel.[6] Then, returning to Riga, he began preparations for an expedition to Mesoten, the former seat of the Bishop of Semgallia. By Easter he had collected another army and sent it up the Aa River to Mesoten by ship, another indication of the importance of sea power. Instead of resisting, the natives surrendered and threw themselves on the master's mercy. Then he moved against another castle just upstream of Mesoten, where again the natives surrendered. In each case he imposed tithes and taxes on the natives and confirmed the settlement with treaties. Even so, many of the rebel tribes had not been subdued, and the struggle therefore continued.[7]

In 1273, wracked by illness, Master Walter returned to Germany and was relieved of his duties. (Climate and privation took a heavy toll in lives and health in the northeast, though we hear of this but rarely.) The chapter in Marburg heard his report, accepted his resignation, and elected Ernest of Rassburg as his successor. Grandmaster Anno, who congratulated Ernest, did not live to see the outcome of the struggle he once had led, but died that same summer. Anno was succeeded by another man who had once been connected with the Baltic Crusade, Grandmaster Hartmann, who had been present at the union of the Swordbrothers and the Teutonic Knights. Meanwhile the fighting had continued in Semgallia, with more Christian disasters, such as the massacre of a band of knights and their followers who, returning from a raid into Lithuania, were attacked in their camp.[8]

An interesting sidelight is the fact that the chronicler mourned a fallen Christian Lithuanian, a chivalrous warrior, who had often accompanied the knights on raids against his homeland, another indication that race and nationality were not all important in this crusade. Indeed, native Christians had always been considered as equals by the western Christians. The knights recognized and respected the courage and daring of their pagan opponents as well, characterizing their deeds as "chivalrous." Nobles, whether Christian or pagan, shared a common scale of military and social values apart from their religious values.[9]

The following summer, in 1274, before Master Ernest arrived in Riga, the Teutonic Knights overtook a Lithuanian raiding party, killed 600, and recovered the booty it had taken. This, a notable victory, gave Master Ernest another opportunity to repress the Lithuanians. Unable to make much progress in Semgallia, he planned to turn east and rebuild the castle at Dünaburg at the southernmost bend of the Dvina. Thus he would establish a base on the frontiers for raids into Lithuania and would also complete the chain of fortresses that sheltered the friendly Lettgallians from attack and secured the trade route to Polozk. Perhaps it would even provide cover for Selonia, the wild forest region between Dünaburg and Semgallia. In 1275, when the Lithuanians saw this castle restored on the bluff over the river, they understood its significance and knew that they must destroy it or face certain defeat. By rebuilding the castle, Master Ernest was able to threaten important settlements, and by putting pressure on the Lithuanians around Nalsen, he hoped to force them out of the war in Semgallia and Samogithia.[10]

The object was Samogithia, but only indirectly. By attacking the new

233

Grand Duke of Lithuania (as that monarch came to be known), the Teutonic Knights could assist their brethren in Prussia. The new monarch, who aided the Prussian rebels, often appeared in Prussia at the head of his army to assist the apostates. But by threatening the royal homeland, Master Ernest would as least distract him and force him to remain home, and perhaps would induce him to conclude a peace. The Prussian Knights could then attack Samogithia.

The Grand Duke could not ignore the mountain base; he had to destroy it. Although it would be a difficult task, the technology of native warfare had advanced far beyond that of his predecessors many years earlier, so that the Christians no longer had a monopoly on modern siegecraft. Moreover, the fortress was far in advance of the Christian lines.

> Thoreiden [the Grand Duke] came to Dünaburg with many heathens, planning to burn it. When he found the castle so strong, he ordered four large catapults built. Those in the castle were dismayed. Russian archers had come to serve King Thoreiden. They wounded many with their bows, but that was deceiving. Whoever was wounded in the castle was soon well again. Those in the castle fired back, felling many heathens below them in a short period, few of whom recovered. All four of the catapults began to operate, and they threw great stones day and night with all their might. The heathens brought up stones around the clock. I tell you that they knocked down many planks around the castle. The brothers became aware of that and filled in many places so they would not lose the castle. The assault lasted four full weeks, day and night.[11]

At length the Lithuanians and Russians began to drift away, their terms of commitment apparently expired. Thoreiden reluctantly gave up the attack. It was a hard blow to his prestige. The Lithuanians had been expanding into those areas of Russia devastated by the Tartars. Already he had difficulties with the nobles governing the newly captured Russian cities; now he could expect even less obedience.

The commander sent a full report to the master, who rejoiced at the victory. Flushed with hope of forcing the Grand Duke out of the war, he began plans for a great expedition against the Lithuanian homeland, assembling supplies at Dünaburg and collecting promises of participation from all parts of Estonia and Livonia. The expedition was delayed, however, by the situation in the east, for in 1277 it appeared that war with Russia was imminent. The merchants were very unhappy, complaining about the injustices they suffered at Russian hands—and everyone sought to please the merchants. The Archbishop and Bishops, the master, and the headman of Reval all wrote the trading centers and asked the merchants to abandon the mercantile post in Novgorod and replace it with a depot in Riga. This remarkable suggestion was not followed, but it may have been instrumental in bringing the Russians to terms. Whatever the reason, the embargo on Russian goods was soon lifted and the crisis passed, so that Master Ernest again turned to the Lithuanian problem.[12]

Later, in the winter of 1278–1279, Master Ernest summoned the Danish vassals, led by Eilard of Hoberg, the archiepiscopal vassals John of Thisenhusen and Henry of Franken, and the Kurs and Semgallians to join him in a daring raid on the castle of the Lithuanian Monarch at Kovno, deep inside the enemy homeland. In spite of the Christians' numbers, it was a risky venture, similar to that campaign that ended in disaster at Saule in 1236. Because the Teutonic Knights caught the Lithuanians unprepared, at first the enemy was unable to challenge them in open battle, and the crusaders plundered and burned many Lithuanian settlements and returned safely to the forest barrier not far from the Dvina.

Success and victory seemed to have gone to the daring master, but the Lithuanians had followed him at a safe distance, thereby preventing the Christians from dispersing and looting on a wider scale and undoubtedly saving many who had taken refuge in the forests. The Teutonic Knights apparently did not fear the shadow force, and when the master approached Ascheraden, he sent most of the native militias home with their share of the loot. After those native troops had dispersed, the Lithuanians rushed forward and challenged the smaller army of knights and militia that remained with the master to keep the Lithuanians from falling on Livonia in revenge. Master Ernest perhaps could not have avoided combat, but he had dismissed the militias, and he failed to take the initiative when he saw that the Lithuanians had not given up and returned home. His delay allowed numerous reinforcements to join the enemy without gaining any advantage to himself. Soon he was outnumbered. Not wishing to retreat into friendly castles and unable to summon the departed militias in time to help, he decided to fight with the troops on hand. Arranging his army in the traditional manner, he led the charge into pagans' ranks.

One saw on either side, both Christian and heathen, that many dauntless warriors, daring and outstanding men, fell in grim death. The snow turned red from blood. But the brothers' army drove the heathens completely out of their formation. Eilard, a good warrior who was hostile to all heathens, pursued them with his force and struck many dead. The heathens suffered from him. In this the brothers had truly fought manfully. However, it was too much for them. The heathen army rallied, with many men. It came to a melee of Christians and heathens. There was slashing and stabbing, and the blood flowed like a river down the steel rings of the armor. The brothers were defeated. The flag of Our Lady was cut down without mercy. A knight had it in his hand—he was named John—and he was killed. God help him from all distress. Thisenhusen was a warrior, and may the angels in heaven comfort his soul, for he was courageous. Even when all these men had been slain, one could still see the Master and his brothers undaunted, though they had suffered a terrible defeat. Meanwhile the Semgallians began to retreat. They did not leave one of their men there. This was not pleasing to the Christian army, and when the heathens became aware of it, they advanced with their force. The brothers' flag was down, and that was a blow to the Christians. Master Ernest fell, and with him seventy-one good brothers. They shed their blood for God. When Eilard had slain the heathens of whom you heard me speak, those he had pursued, he hurried back to his brothers. When he approached the battlefield he heard that the battle was lost. He was pained and angered, and he sorrowed greatly that the Master was slain. There was a large squadron of pagans to either side of the place through which he had to ride. That was the undoing to the hero. He spoke immediately to his knights: "It is my will that you remain by me faithfully, to triumph or die. I am completely exhausted." Some of the brothers had dashed off with him earlier and with these he now charged upon the heathen army. The heathens grasped up their arms. Lord Eilard's horse was shot from under him on the return, and he was mortally wounded. The others barely cut their way out of the heathens. Lord Eilard was dead, and we may mourn that. He had done his duty well. May his soul be comforted in eternal joy above. . . . The winter was so very cold that many men, Christian and heathen alike, froze. Many dauntless warriors, daring and outstanding men, froze. This book shall tell both friends and foes that this battle was fought earnestly and unstintedly in the year one thousand two-hundred and seventy-eight after God's birth, in mid-Lent, and not early, but very late in the day.[13]

The Christians had gambled by raiding so deeply into Lithuania, and the result was a great disaster. On that March day of 1279 the Teutonic Knights lost all the gains they had achieved during the preceding six years. Grandmaster Hartmann called together his masters at Marburg to hear the report from Livonia and to choose a new master. Then, after deciding to combine Prussia and Livonia into one administrative unit so that one master could direct the war against Lithuania, they chose Conrad of Fuchtewang and sent him to Prussia with numerous reinforcements.[14]

The secular nobility did not respond to the new call for crusaders. Brandenburg and Bohemia had not recovered from the defeat administered by Rudolf of Hapsburg. Mecklenburg, Saxony, and Holstein were involved in feuds, as was Lübeck, which had just suffered a terrible fire. Denmark was in disorder again. Except for a Baltic island prince, Wizlaw of Rügen, who came to their aid, the Teutonic Knights had to fight on alone, with only the help of individual middle-class volunteers.

Master Conrad traveled to Elbing in Prussia and summoned all the commanders to a great council. The representative from Livonia reported that the Semgallians had recaptured Terwerten by overrunning the outworks and capturing the arsenal and an archer, who had saved his life by training the pagans in the use of the crossbow. The garrison had not constructed sheltered battlements because the crossbow was thought to be a western monopoly, and by the skillful use of such weapons the pagan commander drove the garrison into the inner tower, which the knights were soon forced to abandon. Setting fire to the tower (a nun inadvertently perished in the flames), fifteen knights and their followers rushed out to attack the Semgallians arrayed before the gate, but the knights were captured to the last man, and were tried for their lives. The pagans formed a circle and thrust the knights, one by one, into the center to be accused or defended. Judged by the natives, the knights were either cut down immediately or sent to Lithuania to be held for ransom; many paid for their misdeeds, but most were spared. Occupied by the pagans, the castle became the major bastion of their defensive system, and much of Semgallia reverted to pagan control as a result. The report persuaded the council to provide the reinforcements the Livonian knight had requested.[15]

It was necessary for Master Conrad to remain in Prussia through the winter of 1279–1280, during which time the war continued in Semgallia. The Christian base for the war, after the loss of Terwerten, was the castle at Goldingen in Kurland, from which many raids were launched against the enemy's settlements. The exploits of its advocate and commander made them legendary figures in their own lifetime, as they carried the war deep into enemy country, literally to the gates of their castles. The advocate was unhorsed beneath the gate of Doblen, and several times routed hostile Semgallian forces.[16] But although these tales of knightly deeds and virtue were encouraging, they were insufficient to win the war. The knights wanted the master to lead them personally or at least visit Riga and Goldingen, and in the summer of 1280 Master Conrad left Prussia to the governance of a new master and sailed to Riga with a number of young knights who had been newly admitted to the order.

> It so happened that they arrived at Dünamünde on Saint Margaret's Day in two ships. The Dvina is the name of the well-known river that passes by Riga, as those know who live there. A messenger came running there to inform the brothers that the Master had come. Their horses were in the pasture and they sent for them quickly. The citizens were also informed. They were pleased over his arrival and rode out with the brothers to meet the Master on the beach. That field is well-known to many of you. They welcomed him gladly. He thanked commoner and noble, as was proper, all those who came to greet him. Then he rode with many escorts to Saint George's. That monastery lies within the city and the brothers live there. The Master bade the brothers sit down and they were served wine and mead. Then they rode back to their quarters. A few days after the brothers had ridden to meet him, they advised him to inspect the land, so he rode through Livonia. He found many good castles there, well-defended by brothers.[17]

This passage, though somewhat naïve, is a good description of the customary practices of Livonian ceremony. As elsewhere in Europe, pageantry and formal entertainment were very important. Wars would be interrupted, normal activities set aside, and of course no diplomacy could be conducted without extravagant pomp and ceremony. Thus Conrad's inspection of the castles, interviews with the bishops, and negotiations with the Danish vassals were long and festive occasions that extended through the next several months.

In the meantime, because the Christians' wide-ranging raids from Goldingen continued without interruption, the Semgallian commander, a famed warrior named Nameise, began to look for a means of distracting his enemies from Doblen, the pagans' principal castle just southwest of Mitau. If he could not defend the castle from attacks out of Kurland because of its exposed location, perhaps, by attacking across the Dvina he could force the Christians to shift their forces eastward and lessen the pressure from Goldingen. In the winter of 1280–1281 he gathered his warriors for a raid into Livonia and moved across Christian Semgallia, but scouts from Mitau discovered their presence and sent word to Riga, where Marshal Gerhard of Katzenellenbogen was waiting with a small force.

The marshal called up his men, sent word to the crusaders in the town, and ordered out a native militia of 100 men from Wenden, which was serving its turn as frontier guards. His plan was to locate and pursue the raiders the next morning, but during the night, the Semgallians captured a sentry who lied about the marshal's defenses. The Semgallians advanced until they saw the camp and realized their mistake, and fled so quickly, even dropping their shields in panic, that the sentry escaped and informed the marshal that the Semgallians were near. Marshal Gerhard immediately set out in pursuit with a small advance force, for several hours galloping in the tracks of the fleeing pagan horsemen; at last he saw some of the raiders far ahead of him, who soon disappeared into the woods.

Riding upon a frozen river, the raiders had followed its course until the ice gave way, plunging thirty horsemen into the freezing water. Abandoning their horses, the raiders scrambled out of the river and hid in the forest. Marshal Gerhard, however, rode past, intent on catching the main body of the enemy and not knowing that most of his followers had halted to rescue the horses. He had only nine men with him: five knights, three sergeants, and a crusader from Westphalia, who at last dropped out of the pursuit when his horse became exhausted. Still Gerhard rode on, not knowing where the pagans were but believing they were still ahead of him, whereas their commander was behind him with thirty men. They attacked the straggling knight and killed him and then set out in pursuit of Gerhard. Attacking by surprise from the rear, they overwhelmed the small band, killed three knights, and captured the others, including Gerhard. The rest of the Christian force advanced too late to rescue him, and he died in Lithuania in captivity, dueling for his life in a pagan ceremony.[18]

This incident, so typical of the bitter warfare along the frontier, did not deter Master Conrad from the campaign he was planning against Doblen. He amassed a great force and invited the knights from Estonia, Bishop Frederick of Dorpat, and many others to come to Riga. Arranging his forces under their various flags, Master Conrad led the army to Doblen, where he settled down to a siege, built a large engine, and advanced it to the ditch—when his scouts reported that a Samogithian army was approaching. After dismantling the machine and abandoning the siege works, the Christians deployed into battle formation. Master Conrad sought a fight but could not close with the enemy, who retreated into the swamps, using the thawing morasses as a protective buffer zone. At last Master Conrad gave up and returned to Riga, but he vowed to return in the summer for another try.[19]

The situation looked better in the spring of 1281, when a number of crusaders arrived in Riga, including Prince Wizlaw of Rügen and his Slavic followers, the Danish vassals under their headman, volunteers from all parts of Livonia, and, as usual, a large contingent of Riga citizens. Skirting the swampy lands southwest of Riga, the army boarded ships for transport to Mitau, where it camped outside the castle. In the morning, after the singing of Mass, Master Conrad led the army to Terwerten and besieged it. Soon an army of Kurs arrived from Goldingen, so that the total of Christian troops was almost 14,000. As soon as the siege tower was completed and the ditch was filled, the tower was moved forward under the cover of missile fire, and the wood in the ditch was ignited, so that fires blazed in many quarters. Nevertheless, the assault failed; but the Semgallians, who were not eager to risk another assault, called out and asked for peace. They offered to pay taxes and live quietly as neighbors of the Christians, but Master Conrad rejected their offer, saying they could not be trusted. Then the natives appealed to the Prince of Rügen and persuaded him to represent them. Prince Wizlaw spoke to the prior of Saint Mary's and to the friars and, after hearing their opinions, took them to Master Conrad, to whom they remonstrated, asking that he relent and grant the Semgallians fair terms. A peace with the Semgallians at Terwerten was soon confirmed, and the Christians returned to Riga.[20]

The expedition had reduced another Semgallian stronghold, but it had not subdued all of Semgallia; nor did the peace have the desired effect on the diehard pagans. The most famous war chief of the Semgallians, Nameise, would not accept the treaty and soon was in exile, fighting with the Lithuanians against the Teutonic Knights in Prussia. Soon the tribesmen would rebel again, and Terwerten would serve as their defensive bastion, shielding central Semgallia from Christian reprisals.

Master Conrad had meanwhile been relieved of his duties in Prussia and a new master, Manegold, had been chosen for that region; but Conrad suggested that a new master be appointed who would rule over Livonia under the direction of the master in Prussia. In the spring of 1282 it was decided that Master Manegold would coordinate Livonian affairs from Prussia, but first he should travel overland to Livonia to inspect the country and assist Conrad in supervising the election of a new master for the Livonian provinces. This was done, and the grand chapter met at Fellin to elect Willekin of Endorp. Manegold then returned to Prussia, and then was called to Acre for the elections of a new grandmaster. He obtained confirmation of Willekin's election shortly before his departure from the Holy Land, and while returning from Acre he was lost at sea. Conrad had sailed to Germany, and a decade later became grandmaster of the Teutonic Order.[21]

The master Willekin continued the debilitating war with Semgallia and Lithuania but without much success, for his responsibilities were almost too great for his resources. In addition to providing garrisons for his own castles, he now had to provide troops for the episcopal castles as well. The new Archbishop of Riga, moreover, was a weak man who abdicated his powers to the crusading order. He was not elected by the canons but was appointed by the Pope (a sign of episcopal weakness), and he did not hurry from Rome to Riga after his consecration in 1285 but spent a full year traveling through Italy and Germany before he took ship to his new post.[22] The eclipse of the Riga Church was almost complete. First the crusading order had taken over the direction of the crusade, then had seized most of the lands, and finally had humbled the Archbishop. What little authority remained was being usurped by the canons and the papacy. As a result, the Archbishop could no longer garrison his own castles. Theoretically his powers remained great, but in practice they were negligible. This weakness invited the Teutonic Knights to exert authority in areas that formerly were dominated by the Archbishop.

Only one estate was not subordinated to the will of the Teutonic Order: the burghers of Riga. Backed by the merchant communities of Visby and Lübeck and commanding great wealth, the patrician merchants of Riga resisted the encroachments of the Teutonic Knights upon their rights and privileges. The attitude of the Teutonic Knights was similar to that of other princes who were rebuffed by their "inferiors," but if the merchants' communities had hung together, the Rigans could have upheld their rights with greater success. The merchant communities of Germany failed to support the position of the Rigans because the developments of this era were favorable to them only at the cost of the merchants farther east. The decisions that the merchants made in the 1280s determined the politics of the next decade.

The 1280s were a decade of great merchant unity in which the Hanseatic League developed, and the cities resisted and defeated royal attempts to harm mercantile interests. It was the era when Lübeck led the cities—including Riga and Reval—to embargo Norwegian ports and obtain a monopoly on Norwegian trade. It was also the era when Lübeck worked very closely with Magnus, the King of Sweden, who was bent on expanding his kingdom at the expense of his neighbors and who curtailed the merchants' independence in the Baltic.

The Swedish monarch moved south into the Danish provinces, assisted by Hanseatic friendship and by discord in the Danish ranks. His chief opponent, King Eric Glipping, had faced a hostile nobility and rebellious prelates and suffered under papal censure. Repressive measures increased his opponents' resolution, and Eric's refusal to allow Parliament to meet had resulted in a civil war which prevented him from defending his lands against King Magnus. Eric might have done much better in future encounters if he had not allowed his arrogance to antagonize those nobles who supported him as well. On the pretext that he had seduced their wives, a number of nobles, dressed as monks, assassinated him in 1286. The remaining frontier defenses collapsed, and King Magnus seized provinces along the border. This sudden advance by the Swedes had a great impact on the merchant communities, because Magnus cast longing glances on Gothland and the wealthy city of Visby.

This was a serious threat for Riga. Visby was much more interested in Livonian affairs than was Lübeck, the former being concerned solely with Baltic trade and the latter already a center of international commerce, with ties to Flanders, England, and central Germany as well as to the Baltic. And it was all the more serious because Lübeck stood to profit from Visby's decline, especially if the merchant communities resettled in the city on the Trave. Lübeck had already persuaded her neighboring cities to exclude Gothlanders from the North Sea trade, just as the Flemings were excluded from the Baltic. In closing the narrow straits to all foreign vessels, Lübeck had overridden the Danish objections, which showed that its city council could determine the fate of that kingdom. At first the Rigans did not realize the importance of Visby to their own survival and prosperity; indeed, it was a Rigan vessel that first bypassed the customs inspection at Visby and sailed directly to Lübeck. But after King Magnus occupied Gothland in 1288 and the maritime court was moved to Lübeck, the Rigans began to complain; but it was too late. Riga's complaints merely antagonized the Lübeckers (perhaps there was jealousy between the cities as well) and close relations were never fully restored.[23]

Lübeck's ambitions were clear. Its councilmen were making themselves masters of the Baltic and the North Sea and whenever there were grounds for complaints, they complained, expecting quick action. A few examples from Livonia illustrate this development, the first of which occurred in 1286, when the Rigans found themselves in a controversy with the Lithuanians. The merchants had continued to trade with the Lithuanians and Russians up the Dvina in spite of war and religious differences. Rigan merchants visited Lithuania, and Lithuanians came down the river to Riga with their merchandise. This arrangement broke down, however, when the pagans imprisoned a Rigan ambassador and allowed him to die in captivity. In retaliation, the Rigans seized a number of Lithuanian merchants and held them against the payment of damages. When negotiations failed, war appeared to be imminent, and the Rigans warned all travelers that the Dvina was no longer safe. Two Lübeck merchants, confident that the reputation of their city would protect them, ignored the warning and were stopped by Lithuanians who took possession of their persons and their goods. Although the Rigans rescued them shortly, the Lübeckers were extremely angry. Blaming the Rigans, they demanded repayment for their losses, and even before they returned home they had written their city council about the behavior of the Rigans and their failure to guarantee safety on the Dvina.[24]

Another case involved a shipwreck and salvage rights. Lübeck's councilmen were seeking to recover the goods that had been taken from a cog that had been blown onto the shores of Estonia and wrecked. Visiting first Gothland and then Estonia, they asked for the return of the goods but had difficulty in tracing their whereabouts. Finally they visited two Danish vassals, who summoned their subjects to testify. They found that the goods had indeed been taken, but the natives who had taken them had fled their villages and were in hiding from the lord and his troops. Everyone refused to pay for the goods, and eventually the Lübeckers conceded defeat. But the efforts the councilmen had made indicate that they were accustomed to success in such matters, which again illustrates the power of Lübeck in the Baltic region.[25]

The formation of the Hanseatic League under the leadership of Lübeck did not help Riga as much as might be expected, because Lübeck was not interested in military adventures in the eastern Baltic. That did not matter so long as the Teutonic Knights were involved in war along the southern frontier of Livonia, but when the war ended, a long-brewing conflict broke out and Riga did not have the full unquestioning support of the Lübeckers.

Master Willekin, though fully occupied with border warfare, was less ambitious than his predecessors; he could not think about the land connection to Memel until Semgallia was reduced, and he could not subject Semgallia until he had captured its key castles in the interior. Nor had he resolved, as had the previous masters, to prevail by means of terror and intimidation. The earlier raids had failed to intimidate the stubborn pagans because the Semgallians were more warlike and more inured to hardship and suffering than their conquered neighbors, and because geography favored their resistance. Their numerous rivers and deep forests hindered attack by columns of knights but lent themselves to guerrilla operations by small groups of warriors. Overcoming geography and tribal patriotism was not an easy task.

Master Willekin, laying plans for a great operation in the winter of 1285–1286, brought supplies to Mitau by ship in the summer and stored them for transfer to Terwerten by sled after snow had covered the ground. When the time arrived, he gathered a large army from all of Livonia and Estonia, led it from Riga to Mitau and from there to Terwerten, hauling the laden sleds across the ice and snow. His plan was not to attack the castle, however (a tactic that had failed often enough before), but to build a castle nearby from which the garrison could harass the Semgallians in their homes and fields. Choosing a large hill, he constructed a timber and earth castle on it and named the castle Heiligenberg, "the Holy Mountain." He filled it with supplies, erected two stone-throwers on the walls, garrisoned it with 300 men, and returned home, leaving the fortress isolated deep in the enemy's land.

In the meantime the Semgallians had sent word to the Samogithians, who came to Heiligenberg with a great army. They arrived too late to engage the main army but just in time to join the attack against the new castle. The Christians had sallied out against the natives, clashing in the valley between the castles, fighting for control of the fields, and only now were they driven back within their walls. But if the Christians were confined within the walls, the pagans could not approach too close because of the deadly missile fire from the battlements. Meeting in council, the elders decided to besiege the castle, build a great tower, and assault the walls.

Their technology having improved as a result of contact with the westerners, the warriors brought wood to build towers and catapults and fill the ditches. Meanwhile the garrison built new bulwarks, dug new ditches, and strengthened its fortifications. For ten days and nights the armies' engineers competed, with survival at stake on each side. On the eleventh day of the siege the Samogithians pushed their machines toward the base of the wall to begin the great assault and thousands of warriors swarmed forward in the face of withering missile fire, filling the ditches and attempting to erect scaling ladders. The white snow reddened with the blood of the dead and the wounded. At last, propelled by hundreds of straining warriors, the catapults neared the battlements, but the opposing missiles pounded the machines and smashed the men with every shot or cut them down with volleys of arrows so that no one could survive.

Suddenly the attack was over. Many of the pagans fled, leaving the dead behind and carrying the wounded with them "like Germans carried their brides." The Samogithians burned the bodies they could recover and returned home. Three days later the Semgallians burned Terwerten and withdrew to Racketen. When the garrison soldiers came onto the field, they found 450 bodies along the base of the wall. The commander informed the master of the victory and then attacked the settlements around Racketen and Doblen. Throughout the spring his raiders cut down the natives in the fields and villages, and later repulsed another assault on the castle with bloody losses.[26]

The Semgallian elders, unable to defend themselves or their harvests against the raiders from Heiligenberg, resorted to their standard tactic: they would attack in another quarter. The castle's scouts, however, had discovered the enemy's intentions and notified the Riga garrison.

One lenten season it happened that the Semgallians were observed going toward Riga, planning on profit by raiding. It became known at Heiligenberg and they sent messengers immediately. The warning arrived at Riga, and when the Landmarshall heard that they intended to attack around Riga, he said, "We should prevent that." He ordered his brothers to arms, and they carried out his orders gladly. Very soon he and they were ready. After that they rode out before the city. Also some of the citizens came and a small force of crusaders. The Letts who had come to Riga were taken along. Some of the

Livs were there also, and they joined the force gladly. So in total there were five hundred and fifty in the army. They remained there most of the day, galloping and jumping, running and wrestling. When evening came, they still had not caught sight of the hostile army. The citizens rode into the city. The Marshall ordered his brothers to return to the stables. The natives came along. There was a compound which is well-known in Riga, named the Brothers' Stables. The Landmarshall ordered that the doors be left open. He said, "If God wills that they come to us here, we will fight. So prepare your spears manfully so that we will always be ready. If they wish to come to us here, we shall sally out against them." The gates remained open. The Marshall ordered watchmen to ride out, brothers and good soldiers. He thought that he would be well protected by so many men. But he was deceived, for all protection is in vain, if God does not shelter us. . . . Watchmen had been sent out, as you already know. But it was at a time when the nights was dark and cold, so that they did not see the army. All their precautions were in vain. The enemy arrived at Riga and no person saw them till they entered the stables. The brothers were sleeping everywhere, and all the natives were asleep. A servant saw them and cried loudly, "The enemy!" He awoke a few who were asleep. Had God not been watching over them, not one would have survived. The stable was filled with the enemy. They had not injured anyone yet when the Livs began to flee. They fled right upon awakening. That was the brothers' loss. The brothers fought against the pagans, and some spears were thrown at them, but the heathens were too strong. Eighteen were in the brothers' force. Everyone of the natives fled away. The brothers were left to fight alone. Five lay dead, and the others wounded seriously so that only three remained unhurt. Some of the servants were slain, for whom one later heard warriors sorrowing. The stables were immediately burned by the Semgallians.[27]

The warning and the preparations had been in vain. The reflection that God's will would prevail and that He had not chosen to protect the knights was small comfort; if He did not protect them, then all preparation was indeed futile. But they had suffered disasters before and expected to suffer them again, and they had little doubt that God nevertheless favored their cause. Though battles were lost, they usually inflicted more casualties than they received, and they could replace their losses easier than could their native enemies. Therefore, the Christians looked to the future optimistically.

Twelve days after the massacre Master Willekin called the commanders together in Riga to meet with representatives of the order from Germany and Prussia. As they were celebrating with their visitors, a report came that a Semgallian force was ravaging the islands of Uexküll in the Dvina River. Its castle was safe, but the settlement had been burned by the raiders. The master invited all his commanders and guests to participate in an expedition to relieve the island, and, leaving a lieutenant in his place, he rode out at the head of the force. Sixty crusaders and citizens and 200 native militia were waiting for him at Holm, which made a total of 500 mounted warriors. Assigning the men to the various banners, he hurried toward Uexküll, where he found the buildings still burning, and then set off in pursuit of the reported 1,400 raiders, but the enemy remained far out in front. Streams and pathless forests slowed both the pursued and the pursuer as the days passed, and on the evening of the third day the crusaders made camp in a thick wood alongside a stream. They built huge fires and fell into an exhaused sleep. Unknown to them, the Semgallians were nearby, and their spies had scouted the campsite. Sending their booty home, the Semgallians had turned back to fight their pursuers.

At dawn, after the master had assembled the army, the watch reported the Semgallian advance and everyone hurried to arms. The knights gathered around their banners, as did the citizens and crusaders, but their native allies were nowhere to be found; they had gone into the forest and, when the alarm was sounded, had taken to their heels, abandoning their horses and equipment. The master had to fight, despite the great numerical odds.

The two forces fell upon each other, the crusaders being led by their mounted commander, Volmar of Bernhausen, who represented the grandmaster. One of the Semgallians' formations engaged the knights, who were on foot, while others overran the camp and captured the horses. The opposed armies hacked away at one another until the dead were strewn through the forest. Finally the Semgallians prevailed, having cut down the last small group of knights around their battle flags. The commander was dead, as were Master Willekin and thirty-one knights of the Teutonic Order. While the Semgallians searched for the wounded and stripped the dead, a knight who had been wounded struck down a pagan horseman, seized his mount and fled through the forest, and evaded pursuit. Another wounded knight was beaten to death, one was burned alive, and four were carried away as prisoners.[28]

This second disaster of March 1287 was a costly one. It was not so much that so many knights had been killed; rather, the inner circle of leadership in Livonia had been destroyed. The commanders had been the most capable and experienced men in the country, and the visitors from Germany and Prussia were highly placed officers. The temporary master therefore called upon the second-rank officials to fill the various offices and to plan for the future. The council decided not to mourn the dead but to rejoice that they had slaughtered many enemies and had earned martyrdom—and they resolved to send to Germany for replacements, for Germany was a reservoir of knights, and continue the war. In response, the grandmaster rode to Prussia with reinforcements and, at a council in Elbing, supervised the election of the new master for Livonia, Cuno of Hazigenstein. Cuno was not a willing candidate; but the will of the grandmaster prevailed, and Cuno accepted the difficult and dangerous post.

Early in 1288 Master Cuno led his reinforcements along the sea from Memel to Kurland and was heartily welcomed in Goldingen. The route, though unsafe, was still open to large armies. Recovering from the despondency caused by the recent setbacks, the citizens and knights of Riga met Cuno outside the city, having prepared a great celebration. Only when the festivities were over did Cuno send his young knights from Franconia and Swabia to the various castles and began his inspection tour, a trip filled with grand formal entertainments in the most chivalrous tradition. It was only with the approach of winter that he was able to turn from parties and diplomacy to military affairs.[29]

The repeated Semgallian victories had endangered the castle at Heiligenberg because the natives, although they could not stop the raids or storm the walls, they could prevent supply columns from bringing in sufficient stores and could thereby starve the garrison into surrender.

By the winter of 1288–1289 its supplies had run low, and the commander had asked for more men, clothing, food, and equipment. The stores had been collected at Mitau, having been brought there by ships during the summer, but it was a difficult undertaking to transport them to the castle. Therefore Master Cuno summoned his allies and subjects from Livonia and Estonia, to Riga, ordering them to bring sleds that could carry the supplies. The force went overland to Mitau, where it loaded the supplies onto the sleds. Because it was a large army, safe from ordinary attack, the master felt secure in dispatching 600 men from the column to Doblen, who burned the outerworks of its castle and rejoined the supply column at Heiligenberg. After delivering the supplies, the army moved to Racketen and attacked its outer defenses. The outlying village was sacked and numerous Semgallians were killed, but the crusaders could not climb the icy hill to the castle against the enemy's resistance. The besiegers remained three days outside the castle before giving up and returning to Riga.[30]

The expedition had been a success—such a success that, in effect, it won the war. Worn down by the constant raids from Heiligenberg, the Semgallians could not survive much longer. Many had been killed, and the harvest had been so disrupted that many were starving. Having strength for one more great effort, the Semgallians sent for the Samogithians, asking their aid against the Christians.

The crisis came in the spring of 1289. A large force of Samogithians and Semgallians invaded the lands of the Archbishop and burned and robbed almost without resistance. Master Cuno was in Riga when the news arrived, and he sent summons to all his friends and allies, as his main striking force was in Semgallia. Troops arrived from Kurland, Mitau, Heiligenberg, and the garrisons around Riga. The episcopal force, a very small number, also came, as did the citizens and crusaders. But the total number of warriors was only 3,500. No one had come from Estonia, whose famous warriors were needed desperately.

When the army had been assembled and reviewed, the council met to discuss the campaign. No one advocated fighting, because there were too many pagans to oppose with any hope of victory, but Master Cuno reasoned that if pagan warriors were ravaging Livonia, there could be very few in Semgallia, and by such arguments he convinced his council to authorize an attack on the enemy's home ground. Dividing his army into two columns, he ordered an attack on the castles of Doblen and Sidobren, to the west of Mitau and Heiligenberg. Doblen barely escaped capture, and Sidobren suffered great casualties. (The knight who had served under Master Willekin, and had been the sole survivor of the master's last battle, almost carried the gate of the Sidobren castle. Carrying a banner among the fugitives from the nearby settlement, he had cut his way to the front of the castle and was storming the entrance when the garrison struck down the leading knights with rocks and missiles, wounded the banner carrier, and closed the gates.) The citadel of Sidobren withstood the assault, but very few natives were able to attain the safety of its walls; and of course they lost all their possessions to the booty-hungry Christians. The raids proved most successful, and soon another raid compounded the destruction.

Meanwhile the garrison at Heiligenberg also had been making life in

Semgallia impossible for the pagan tribesman. Sallies against fields and villages forced the natives to withdraw farther and farther, abandoning many ancestral homes and hearths. The knights ran off the cattle, cut down the grain, and pressed up to Doblen and Racketen so frequently that the capture of these forts was a constant possibility. In the end, the Semgallians burned Doblen, and when even Racketen proved untenable, the starving natives burned it down and moved to Sidobren. The raids from Heiligenberg had won the war. Only mopping-up operations remained.

The knights attacked Sidobren at all seasons, assisted by an expedition from Livonia and Kurland that thoroughly ravaged the land. Even the Archbishop sent his men to help.[31] By early 1290 the Semgallians' morale was so low that a group of warriors opted for surrender. Seizing the castle at Sidobren, they ordered those who wished to continue the fight to go to Samogithia, because they wished to parley in good faith. They sent to the commander at Mitau, informed him of their wishes, and asked him to send knights to make peace.

The commander was skeptical, but he accepted hostages and sent a mission. Master Cuno was no longer in Livonia, having sailed for Germany in late 1289 to resign his office, but his substitute called a council to approve the action. They rejoiced at the Semgallians' decision but insisted that Sidobren be burned to the ground so that it could not serve as a center for rebellion. The commander at Mitau thereupon rode to Sidobren with a large force, left his men in a nearby wood, and in the company of a small escort told the Semgallians of the harsh decision. They agreed to the terms and signed the treaty. Then the knights came up from the wood to supervise the evacuation of the fortress, after which it was burned to the ground. The natives moved to the neighborhood of Mitau, where they could be supervised more closely. Thus in 1290 the Teutonic Knights imposed a different peace from the one they had concluded a decade earlier. No longer would the natives be trusted to live in fortified settlements on their ancestral lands. They were moved back to Terwerten, Doblen, and Mitau and closely watched by the garrisons of those castles.

Master Holt, the new governor of Livonia, now had to deal with the Samogithians, who refused to agree to the peace settlements; but after a bloody campaign in the summer of 1290, even the Samogithians were exhausted. The Semgallians who refused to accept the verdict of battle withdrew into Samogithia, and the remainder, worn down by war, famine, and plague, lacked the strength to challenge German rule. The Semgallian war was over.[32]

The Teutonic Knights had fought and died for their Lady Mary and had completed the conquest begun nine decades earlier by Bishop Albert, but the subjugation of Semgallia presented them with the formidable task of occupying Samogithia and creating the land bridge to Prussia. They did not realize it, but the advance they made in 1290 was to be the last permanent conquest of their career. They would occupy Samogithia, but subsequent rebellions would soon force them back to the frontiers of 1290. So permanent was the stalemate that the modern frontier of Latvia and Lithuania follows the old line of division. Nor did the Teutonic Knights realize how bitter warfare had brutalized their sensibilities. They had never been known for their tender hearts, but the desperation of the wars in Livonia, Prussia, and the Holy Land had hardened them even more. As they turned to the arts of peace, they discovered that free men could not be treated in the same way as conquered subjects. Turning, at last, in knightly arrogance to the upstart citizenry of Riga, they provoked a conflict that ended all hope of permanent victory in Samogithia.

Notes to Chapter Eleven

1. Johansen, "Die Bedeutung der Hanse für Livland." See also Karl Pagel, *Die Hanse* (Braunschweig: Georg Westermann, 1965), pp. 58–66 and Philippe Dollinger, *La Hanse* (Paris: Aubier, 1964), pp. 42–46.

2. Herman Hildebrand, ed., *Das Rigische Schuldbuch* (St. Petersburg, 1872) has much to say regarding the growing importance of the Rigan merchant community and the means it adopted to assure continued growth and prosperity.

3. Arbusow, *Grundriss der Geschichte Liv-, Est-, und Kurland*, p. 52; *Urkundenbuch*, 1: no. CDXLV.

4. *Reimchronik*, ll. 7895–7912.

5. Ibid., ll. 7962–7994.

6. Ibid., ll. 7995–8030.

7. Ibid., ll. 8031–8071.

8. Ibid., ll. 8072–8106.

9. Ibid., ll. 8107–8120.

10. W. Newmann, in "Die Ordensburgen im sog. polnischen Livland," *Mitteilungen aus der livländischen Geschichte*, 14 (1899): 303–12, described this new castle; *Herman de Wartberge*, p. 48.

11. *Reimchronik*, ll. 8209–8241.

12. *Urkundenbuch*, 1: nos. CDLII, CDLVII.

13. *Reimchronik*, ll. 8398–8503. The correct year is 1279 (*Herman de Wartberge*, p. 49).

14. *Reimchronik*, ll. 8527–8604.

15. Ibid., ll. 8605–8812.

16. Ibid., ll. 8929–9192.

17. Ibid., ll. 8875–8911.

18. Ibid., ll. 9193–9404.

19. Ibid., ll. 9427–9507.

20. Ibid., ll. 9508–9667.

21. *Herman de Wartberge*, p. 50.

22. The Archbishops John I and John II accepted the subordinate role that earlier had been forced upon Albert Suerbeer. Their comparative poverty made it impossible to do without the assistance of the Teutonic Knights even in the garrisoning of their castles.

23. *Urkundenbuch*, 1: no. DV; 3: no. DXXIIIa.

24. *Urkundenbuch*, 1: no. DVII.

25. Ibid., nos. DXI–DXXIX.

26. *Reimchronik*, ll. 9899–10200.

27. Ibid., ll. 10201–10290.

28. Ibid., ll. 10329–10714.

29. Ibid., ll. 10745–10934.

30. Ibid., ll. 10935–11088.

31. Ibid., ll. 11089–11461.

32. Ibid., ll. 11462–11610; *Herman de Wartberge*, pp. 51–52.

12

The End of the Crusade

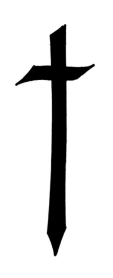

ALTHOUGH IT WAS NOT APPARENT AT THE TIME, THE END OF THE WAR with the Semgallians and Lithuanians marked the last expansion of Livonia and the beginning of new conflicts within the crusader states. Now that the most dangerous external enemies had been defeated, it seemed that a period of peace and prosperity would follow. The Teutonic Knights were confident of their ability to defend their possessions against attack from without and disorder within, for not only did they possess most of the land and key fortresses but they were supported by vast resources in Prussia and in the homeland. They dominated the Archbishop of Riga and occupied such parts of his lands as were necessary to assure a coordinated defense of Livonia. More independent than the Archbishop, perhaps—but also weaker—the Bishops of Dorpat and Oesel-Wiek offered little danger; and since the nobility in Estonia by and large supported their policies, the nobility could be counted upon to assist against any external foe. Only the cities remained outside the order's control, and only Riga had the strength to attempt to defend its liberties. As time passed, surely they would be able to dominate Riga, just as they had long dominated the cities in Prussia. Although the Rigans could expect some aid and comfort from their allies in the west, the quarrel over Visby had strained their relations with Lübeck. Moreover, the western cities, now forming into the Hanseatic League, had problems of their own.

Civil conflict in Denmark was to blame for much of the instability in the political situation. The murder of the last monarch had put a young boy, Eric Maenved, on the throne, who was confronted by ambitious and righteous prelates, some of whom were suspected of complicity in the assassination. The passing of the Archbishop of Lund, a foe of royal authority, was followed by the election of John Grand, a man who was even more closely implicated in the plot against the King. When the new Archbishop forbade Danish subjects to fight against the Norwegians, who were plundering the kingdom, the young King took up the challenge and incarcerated the Archbishop on charges of treason.[1] The effects of this new quarrel were eventually felt in Livonia.

North Germany was similarly upset by domestic quarrels. After young Henry of Mecklenburg returned home from crusade in Livonia, he soon set out for the Holy Land, where he fell into Moslem hands. When the

Egyptians refused to ransom him, his lands were governed by an uncle on behalf of Henry's young son, who came of age in 1285, at which time a feud began involving Saxony, Lüneburg, Holstein, and Schwerin. Although Henry's son successfully defended himself, the feud began a series of minor wars among these princes that lasted well into the next decade. It was in this latter period that the Teutonic Knights resumed the negotiations for Prince Henry's release. Princess Anastasia, his wife, raised 2,000 marks and delivered them to Lübeck for transfer to the Teutonic Order, but her hopes were dashed, after two years, when the order returned the money, explaining that the Moslems refused to ransom any prisoners at that time.[2]

Meanwhile the northern cities of Lübeck, Hamburg, Wismar, and Lüneburg were complaining of robber barons in Saxon-Lauenburg, a ducal territory that lay between these cities and controlled the roads and rivers. This state of affairs was particularly annoying to Lübeck because the city had hired the Duke of Saxon-Lauenburg as advocate, his primary duty being the suppression of robbery and piracy. Unable to end these depredations peacefully, the cities terminated the Duke's contract and hired the Princes in Mecklenburg, the Archbishop of Bremen, and the other Duke of Saxony (the lands had been divided) and attacked the castles from which the barons made their raids. By capturing and hanging several guilty nobles, the cities' army provoked feuds with the relatives and friends of the deceased barons and with the Duke of Saxon-Lauenburg, who believed his rights had been trampled on. A pitched battle resolved this feud in favor of the merchants, but it did not bring peace.

No sooner had one dispute been temporarily ended than another arose. The Prince of Werle in Mecklenburg, who had children from two marriages, made a grievous error in delaying the appointment of an heir. After he was killed by his eldest sons in an abortive kidnapping, his lands fell into turmoil, as the disputed inheritance was complicated by charges of patricide. All the neighboring princes mixed in the affair, and the surviving robber barons took advantage of the disorder to revenge themselves on the merchants' caravans.[3]

Even Lübeck had internal troubles. Its Bishop sought to rule or ruin, so that for a long time thereafter there was strife in the city as secular and ecclesiastical power vied for dominance. And in one of those periodic catastrophes so typical of the medieval period, the city had been destroyed by fire.

The international situation was just as troubled. The Moslems had stormed Acre in Palestine, ending the crusade in the Holy Land to all practical intents—and with that disaster ending crusading interest throughout western Europe. In Germany, a new dynasty came to the throne. It was a costly change for the Lübeckers, who had paid their taxes for several years in advance but were told that this payment would not be recognized. The princes, however, were largely indifferent, as the new Emperor was hardly more powerful than his vassals. Scandinavia was in turmoil, with Norwegian fleets ravaging the neighboring coasts and capturing German merchant vessels, and forcing the Hanseatic cities to raise fleets for their self-defense.

Throughout this trying period the city of Lübeck had been expanding in wealth and power. Its city council organized the league of princes and cities, paid for the mercenary troops, and commanded the fleets. Its armies won battles, its fleets swept the North and Baltic Seas; and therein lies the reason for Riga's isolation: the Lübeckers could not be everywhere at once. Victorious over their numerous enemies at home, the Lübeckers had to be careful not to overstrain their resources. Should they take on such a powerful foe as the Teutonic Knights? Or should they preserve their neutrality and attempt to negotiate an end to the conflict?[4]

The cities everywhere had risen in importance (Riga was no exception), and as the cities waxed, the nobles regarded them with fear and envy. Lübeck had faced and overcome the opposition; now Riga faced the trial. The Teutonic Knights understood the danger in burgher independence, and when they had both the opportunity and the excuse to suppress Riga's liberty, they tried to do so.

Because of the long and often disastrous Semgallian and Samogithian wars, the Teutonic Knights had ignored Riga, whose citizens had often proved to be reliable allies against the pagans and the Archbishops. Moreover, the citizens had developed a pride in themselves and their city—perhaps even arrogance—that offended the class consciousness of the noble knights. But the Rigans did not anticipate trouble, and its outbreak found them unprepared, as we shall see.

Riga had become a large and wealthy city thanks to the wise policies pursued by its burghers over the decades. From the very beginning the city fathers had decided that their city would be permanent and substantial, rather than merely a community of visiting merchants, such as Visby. With this in mind they had invited many varying groups to settle there, even admitting Russians to citizenship. Close and friendly relations with Visby and Lübeck, and a wise use of credit, stimulated trade. Moreover, their trade with the natives and with Russia and Lithuania proved immensely profitable. In summer their rivers filled with shipping, and in winter their sled trains crossed the snow and ice to distant markets.

Its citizens fought for their survival and for the advancement of Christianity, and fought almost as hard for their rights. Long ago, one of William of Modena's first acts had been the negotiation of civic privileges, when the burghers and Bishop Albert found themselves at loggerheads; another most serious civil rights conflict arose in the time of Albert Suerbeer, and again the burghers prevailed. Rich, numerous, and warlike, the citizens were aware of their power, and exercised it. Then in 1292 the city embarked on a new building program; the new city wall was to be twenty-four feet high, and all buildings within it were to be of brick or stone. The knights must have taken due notice of the civic attitude, although the Rigans may not have been aware of their unintended affronts to the nobles' pride.[5]

The Rigans also were becoming aggressive in foreign affairs. In the past there had often been difficulties with the Russians over robbery on the highways, and in each instance the Teutonic Knights had come to the aid of the Rigans; but now the Rigans could fend for themselves. Ambassadors from Riga, Visby, and Lübeck traveled to Novgorod in 1291 to protest such robbery and, after waiting fourteen days without obtaining an interview with the Prince, asked his brother for an explanation of the delay. Learning that the Prince was unable to stop the attacks because of political alliances and, therefore, was embarrassed to meet the ambassadors, they became incensed and sailed to Dorpat. Their report persuaded the merchant communities that they should embargo trade with Russia until their complaints were acted upon.[6]

Rigans also vigorously protested the removal of the maritime court to Lübeck, and although Lübeck's position prevailed, the protest illustrates Riga's good standing in the mercantile community.[7] The Rigans even sent a permanent representative of the papal Court to defend their interests. Such actions are signs that the city was acting independently, that is, in a spirit inimical to the interests of the Teutonic Knights. The knights began to wonder whether the situation might already be out of hand.

As the officials and knights of the order debated the situation, it may

have seemed that the present was the most favorable time for a showdown
with the upstart townsmen. The order had immense resources in Prussia
and Germany to back up its army in Livonia; there was peace with the
neighboring states; and the cities in the west were occupied with domestic
affairs, and usually were friendly toward the order. Riga, on the other
hand, was temporarily embarrassed by its quarrel with Lübeck and had no
other allies of importance. Reval had profited by Visby's decline and would
profit even more from Riga's disaster, therefore Reval looked to the King
of Sweden to protect its maritime route to Novgorod and ignored affairs
in Livonia. The Danish vassals, traditional allies of the Teutonic Order,
would remain neutral.

The Archbishop of Riga, John II, was so subservient to the master that
when he traveled to Germany in 1290 he had left his lands to his care and,
upon his return, had leased a number of strategic castles to the order. However, the new Archbishop was John of Schwerin—an ominous choice from
the view of the Teutonic Knights. It may not have been merely a coinci-
dence that a descendant of Henry the Black and Gunzelin of Schwerin was
elected in 1295, but it did not mean an immediate revival of archiepiscopal
authority. Archbishop John III had appeared in Rome to promise that his
election would not be a precedent that might hinder papal appointments
in the future. The canons may have chosen a strong man to defend their
interests, but he could not immediately undo past errors and reverses. Nor
could he revive the old claims against the order without long preparation.
More important, John III was not in Riga in the critical year 1296 but was
in Flanders, seeking treatment for a broken leg, and his property had been
left to the care of the master and the Riga city council.[8] If the Archbishop
could be of little help to Riga, the other Bishops would be even less helpful.
The Bishop of Dorpat, for example, was new in office and had lost control
of his territories.[9] Thus the city of Riga was weak and isolated vis-á-vis the
Teutonic Knights.

Tension heightened as the tenth decade of the thirteenth century passed.
City and crusading order quarreled on minor issues and competed for favor
in the western cities and kingdoms. The Teutonic Knights, moreover,
recognized the significance of Lübeck and sedulously cultivated its merchant community. Thus Riga profited very little by the passage of time. The
critical period came shortly after the Archbishop sailed west to Flanders.

The winter of 1295–1296 was more severe than usual, and the spring floods caused much trouble, so that ice floes dammed the Dvina below Riga, and the backed-up water threatened to flood the city. After the crisis passed, the citizens held a public meeting to discuss ways of avoiding floods in the future, and they were impressed by the plan of a visiting crusader. He suggested that the city construct a massive bulwark upstream that would prevent ice from flowing past the city, thereby protecting the city walls and lessening the danger of an ice jam downstream. The citizens approved the plan and chose a site where a small island facilitated the work. It was impossible to collect suitable materials—wood, stone, earth— on the northern bank of the Dvina, however, and therefore the Rigans built a bridge across the river near the site of the proposed bulwark, so they could obtain their supplies from the wilderness on the opposite bank.

The bridge was an expensive undertaking that cost more than 100 marks to complete. Wide and well built, it had a section that could be lifted to allow the passage of river traffic. It was no surprise, therefore, that the citizens soon announced that the bridge would be preserved—in addition to the proposed bulwark. The Teutonic Knights must have worried about that eventuality because the bridge could blockade upstream river traffic to and from the city in time of war. It could also isolate the Teutonic Knights in the interior and give the citizens of Riga control of the Dvina. The commander in Riga did not even notify the citizens but simply had his men demolish the almost finished structure.

The citizens immediately sent a delegation to the master, asking him to rebuke his men and give permission to rebuild the bridge, and the master indicated that he would look into the matter. Then, eight days later, he revoked all the privileges the citizens had held to wood, pasture, fishing, travel, and trade in the territories belonging to the Teutonic Knights. He followed this by arresting all the merchants in his lands and holding them as hostages. When the citizens threatened to appeal to the Pope, an officer replied that the Pope couldn't help them even if he lived in Riga, and in any case he was too far away. Only the intervention of Dominican and Franciscan friars averted war.

Each side then began preparations for a long conflict. The citizens of Riga wrote to Rome while the order brought in more soldiers and laborers and built two new towers on their convent, converting it into a fortress that garrisoned 500 men. When the master felt he was ready, he announced that the truce the friars had arranged would expire in one week, as provided for in the agreement. The alarmed Rigans wrote to Lübeck, explaining the origins of the dispute and asking for help.[10]

Fighting broke out in the city even before the truce expired. One citizen was killed and several were wounded by volleys of arrows from the knights' convent, and the knights set fire to the nearby houses. As the fire spread, the knights prevented the citizens from fighting it by threatening to massacre the populace. Later, angry citizens stormed the convent, destroyed it, and threw six captured knights into prison. The damage had been great, but the council was still in control of the city.

At this point Archbishop John returned to Riga. After arranging another truce, he investigated all the conflicting charges, but as he (and the Bishop of Dorpat) attempted to mediate with the Teutonic Order they discovered that the dispute about the bridge was no longer important—the knights claimed they had an old grudge to settle. In defiance of John's request that they refrain from military action until the papacy could investigate the matter, the knights ravaged the city's lands, burning manors, homes, and barns, cutting down fruit trees, driving off livestock, attacking fortifications, and killing the crusaders and merchants who tried to drive them off. On Christmas Eve they defeated a force from the city, killing nine crusaders and a number of burghers, and mocked the terrified citizens, shouting "Where is your Pope?"[11]

Archbishop John retired to his castle at Treiden to organize his defenses, but he was besieged by the Teutonic Knights, who attacked with ballistas and fire assaults, until after eight days the garrison could resist no longer. Taking the Archbishop prisoner, the knights transported him to their castle at New Mill and held him for thirty-three days on bread and water. They seized his treasury and church ornaments, valued at 6,000 marks, and used his seal to prepare documents that they forced him to sign. When the cathedral canons rejected their conditions for peace, the knights seized their lands. They also forced the archiepiscopal vassals to renounce their lord and swear homage to them.[12]

When news of all this reached the Bishop of Oesel-Wiek, he sent supplies to Riga and began to raise an army to rescue the Archbishop. His vassals, however, refused to fight, claiming they were too heavily outnumbered to have any chance of success. Then, when the vassals parleyed with the Teutonic Order at a peace conference, the knights violated the chivalric code by overpowering and disarming the vassals. Then they pursued the

Bishop to his castle at Leal, which they besieged, forcing him to surrender. The knights plundered and burned both the islands and the mainland, taking cattle and grain and destroying every house and church they encountered.

News of such actions could not pass unnoticed, and when the reports finally reached Rome the Pope was outraged. Boniface VIII, a strong Pope who was determined to emulate his greatest predecessors, summoned the Grandmaster, the Livonian master, and three commanders of the Teutonic Knights to appear in Rome within six months to explain their conduct, as well as the Archbishop of Riga and the Bishops of Dorpat and Oesel-Wiek. Unknown to the Pope, however, his intervention came too late to affect events in the northeast, where things had gotten completely out of hand.[13]

In March 1298 the desperate Rigans turned to the Lithuanians, those inveterate enemies of the Teutonic Knights, and signed an alliance with them. (It was stipulated, of course, that the pagans would adopt the Christian faith—a clause that was as necessary as it was meaningless.) Immediately the wild Samogithians broke into Livonia and inflicted several defeats on the knights, including one in June in which they killed the master and sixty knights. As a second string to their bow the Rigans signed an alliance with the King of Denmark, promising him some of the order's lands in Semgallia in return for his assistance. In short, by the time the Pope acted, the issue could no longer be limited to the Christians in Livonia.[14]

The Pope succeeded in obtaining the release of the Archbishop and the restoration of some of his property, and in July 1299 the Grandmaster and the Archbishop of Riga pleaded their cases before him. Again, the Teutonic Knights prevailed, and the arbitration left the archiepiscopal territories in the hands of the order until danger from the pagans had passed, which meant until Riga surrendered. Archbishop John did not return to Riga but remained in Rome until 1300, probably hoping to influence Boniface in his favor; then he traveled to Schwerin, where he died a short time later. Finally a number of Westphalian cities intervened in the dispute and arranged a truce between Riga and the Teutonic Knights.[15]

The real crusading era came to an end with the outbreak of this quarrel. The Rigans dared not give up their Lithuanian alliance, which would have meant their submission to the Teutonic Knights, and thus thirty years' war began in which the Rigans fought desperately but vainly for their liberty. The crusade ended, as had the first phase of the conquest, in civil conflict.

Notes to Chapter Twelve

1. Münter, *Kirchengeschichte*, pp. 525–27; Dahlmann, *Geschichte von Dänne-mark* 1: 421–23.

2. *Lübeckisches Urkundenbuch*, 1: 432, 471.

3. Fromm, *Chronik*, p. 49; Witte, *Mecklenburgische Geschichte*, pp. 174–76.

4. Hanseatic policy was always selfish and shortsighted, which provided strength at times but ultimately was ruinous. Riga was only the first great city to be denied support at a critical time.

5. *Das Rigische Schuldbuch*, pp. lxxii–lxxix.

6. *Urkundenbuch*, 1: no. DXLVI.

7. Ibid., 6: no. MMMLIII.

8. Fritz Schönebohm, "Die Besetzung der livländischen Bistümer," pp. 329–30.

9. *Urkundenbuch*, 6: no. MMDCCLVII.

10. Ibid., 1: no. DLXVII; *Zeugenverhör*, pp. 3, 8, 134; *Herman de Wartberge*, pp. 55, 149.

11. *Urkundenbuch*, 1: nos. DLXVIII, DLXXXIV, DLXXXV; *Zeugenverhör*, pp. 3, 8, 12–14, 114, 124–27, 140.

12. *Urkundenbuch*, 1: no. DLXXXIV; *Zeugenverhör*, pp. 6, 11, 26, 55, 99, 128–29, 141, 201.

13. *Urkundenbuch*, 1: nos. DLXXII, DLXXVIII, DLXXXVI; *Zeugenverhör*, pp. 4–20, 36.

14. *Urkundenbuch*, 1: nos. DLXX, DLXXII; *Herman de Wartberge*, pp. 54–55, 149.

15. *Urkundenbuch*, 1: nos. DLXXXI, DLXXXII, 6: nos. MMDCCLXIV, MMMCCVII; *Zeugenverhör*, pp. 7, 10, 12, 68.

Epilogue

To contemporaries—if we may assume that any were so long-lived—the fourteenth century did not appear very different from the thirteenth. Involved in her own difficulties and ambitions, Lübeck failed to assist Riga. Troubled by robber barons without and by their Bishop within, the Lübeckers were embroiled in increasingly complex problems, from which they would eventually emerge to lead the Hanseatic League to greatness. The King of Denmark continued his quarrel with the Archbishop of Lund, and when Pope Boniface VIII discovered that he could not settle it, he decided to transfer the Archbishop to another post. As Archbishop John III of Riga had since died, he offered Riga to the Dane, John Grand, who refused it, but later accepted the archbishopric of Bremen. Boniface's next choice for Riga, Isarnus, resigned the archbishopric after two years to transfer to Lund, after which two years almost elapsed before another Archbishop sat in Riga. This prelate, Frederick, also failed to come to terms with the Teutonic Knights, and for many years thereafter both he and his successors were to live in exile at the papal Court in Avignon.

Lest all this appear to be too depressing, it should be noted that Henry I of Mecklenburg was at last released by the Egyptians in 1298 and returned home to his faithful wife, Anastasia. Thus the last of the crusaders returned to Germany just as the crusading movement of this era was coming to an end.

The last of the important crusades (aside from those in Spain) was directed to Prussia, but Prussia served more as a showplace for the bored chivalry of Europe than as a theater for real crusading, and knights came to Prussia less to fight pagan tribesmen than to participate in the grandiose rituals of knighthood that had been invented and fostered by the Teutonic Knights. Nevertheless, it was an important outlet for the vestigial crusading fervor and deserves closer investigation than it has received.

One wonders what became of the ideals of the early crusaders. The Holy Land had not been liberated, nor had Constantinople been saved and returned to the bosom of the Church, nor had the pagans been converted—each success in these various endeavors proved transitory and eventually harmful. Saint Louis had no success in two crusades, and Saint Francis failed to convert the Saracens. Even the Templar Order would soon be dissolved amid shameful and embarrassing controversy. When people, mindful of such failures and tragedies, began to ask themselves if God really approved of crusaders, the crusades lost their popular appeal.

Why was the crusade to Livonia a moral failure? As Adam of Bremen wrote long before, the Slavs could have been converted more quickly by persuasion than by arms, but cupidity and avarice set the Christian cause back by many years. It was no different in Livonia. Christianity had triumphed; peace had triumphed; order had triumphed; but at what cost? War itself had become the greatest obstacle to conversion. Yet, it may be asked, if a crusade for the protection and extension of the faith, for the defense of rights and property, and for the liberation of entire peoples from slavery and superstition is unjust, what war is just?

The cause of the failure must be laid to avarice and fanaticism. Each sin alone is dangerous, but together they are deadly. How shocking to the modern mind is Henry of Livonia's admonition:

> Behold how the Mother of God, so gentle to Her people who serve Her faithfully in Livonia, always defended them from all their enemies and how harsh She is with those who invade Her land or who try to hinder the faith and honor of Her Son in that land! See how many kings, and how mighty, She has afflicted! See how many princes and elders of treacherous pagans She has wiped off the earth and how often She has given Her people victory over the enemy! Up to this time, indeed, She has always defended Her banner in Livonia, both preceding and following it, and She has made it triumph over the enemy. And what kings, whether of pagans or of Danes or of other nations, have fought against Livonia and have not perished? Consider and see, you princes of the Russians, or the pagans, or the Danes, or you elders of whatever people. Fear this gentle Mother of Mercy. Adore this Mother of God and give satisfaction to Her, Who takes such cruel revenge upon Her enemies.[1]

Brundage's translation requires two and a half pages for the chronicler's tirade, and ends, appropriately, with Henry's praise of the peace and justice the Virgin brought to her followers. The Virgin cult was very important to the crusade, its dedication to her honor being a primary attraction for the volunteers from the west, but the Virgin cult and fanaticism were European phenomena of that era and not special characteristics of the Baltic Crusade.

What, then, is noteworthy about the Baltic Crusade? First and foremost, it was a Baltic Crusade. Although most of the crusaders were Germans, as well as the entire membership of the Teutonic Order, and although German knights made up the majority of the secular vassals in Livonia and

Estonia, Frisians, Slavs, Swedes, and Danes participated in the crusade in large numbers. Moreover, it was in the period when the Danish Kings and their vassals were active in the crusade that the greatest successes were achieved. The Archbishop of Lund was personally active in Estonia for many years, and it was Scandinavian help that made the difference between success and failure in the early, critical days of the crusade. In short, the political situation in the west often determined the success of the crusade in the east, and when Danes and Slavs ceased to participate in the crusade the expansion slowed to a halt.

Second, the crusade was in great measure a mercantile adventure. At no time did the Teutonic Knights or the Bishops possess a fleet, yet never did they lack shipping or request aid from the merchants in vain. Middle-class crusaders were so important that they were admitted into the Sword-brothers and received privileges in the Teutonic Order. The Rigans served in all important campaigns and assisted in recruiting, transporting, and maintaining the crusaders, whose booty from the raids was sold through the merchants, who in turn provided for all the needs of the western occupiers of Livonia. Lübeck profited as much from the crusade as from the fishing industry, and the rise of German cities and the Hanseatic League must be attributed in part to the Baltic Crusade.

Third, there could have been no success without the natives' cooperation. "Divide and rule" was the motto, but the divisions were ready-made. The Christians merely stumbled onto a fortunate situation: in a backward, quarreling land they could side with the weaker tribes against the stronger tribes, until the whole country was conquered. Only the strongest natives, the Russians and the Lithuanians, could defend themselves against their traditional enemies when the latter were backed by the crusaders.

The blame for many of the brutalities in these cruel wars must be attributed primarily to the native irregulars, although the westerners committed their share of atrocities; but first, the former had to teach the latter how to hate. And native hatred was never able to focus upon the foreigners for more than a brief moment. If the natives had joined in a common effort against the crusaders, whose levies from abroad arrived irregularly and soon departed, the crusaders could never have maintained themselves permanently. However, many tribes rose in honor and wealth as Christians and as allies of the crusaders, at least for a brief period, and therefore assisted the completion of the conquest.

Fourth, superior military technology and tactics were vital to the crusaders' victories, but they were not permanent Christian monopolies. The knight was an efficient military machine, and the pagans soon copied his weapons and tactics. The crusaders' stone castles were impregnable at first, while the pagans' log forts could easily be taken by the skillful use of hurling machines, siege towers, and the like; but the pagans soon learned all the western techniques of building castles and conducting sieges. The mounted western cavalry, properly led, could ride down any infantry force in the open field, but soon the pagan cavalry, armored and led by skilled war chiefs, was countercharging or luring the knights into woods and swamps. The westerners' chain of command, so important in their early victories, soon was copied by the pagans and led to the formation of the Lithuanian state. Thus the only western advantage was money, collected by taxes, which could be used to hire more troops and build more castles, but revenues rarely equalled expenses, and by the time that the disputed lands were pacified and taxed, the crusaders were on the defensive and the era of expansion was over. Even then gifts and revenues from Germany were indispensable to the defense of Livonia.

Fifth, climate was important. When the knights learned to fight in winter, they gained a great advantage over their opponents. They could sally from their castles against the villages, travel up the frozen rivers on the ice, and better avoid ambush in forest and swamp. The cold weather was miserable, but was better—from the crusaders' standpoint—than fighting in the summer. Later, the most significant Russian and Lithuanian victories came in battles on the ice, after they, too, had learned the techniques of winter warfare.

Sixth, the crusade illustrates the role of the papacy in its greatest century. The Popes stood behind the crusade, encouraging and supporting it in every way. In their enthusiasm and impatience, they attempted to direct the crusade, which brought resistance and rebellion on the part of the Bishops and the crusading orders; but their zeal was more for the future of the Church than for the exercise of power. Nevertheless, the Popes were fallible men who made mistakes: Baldwin of Alna and Albert Suerbeer, both papal appointees, were no credit to the Church, though their goals may have been worthy. Fanatics, like their opponents, the crusading orders, they disturbed muddy waters. There were too few men like William of Modena, who followed the same papal instructions but to very different conclusions. The Popes, listening to the advice and counsel of ambitious experts, tried to exercise leadership, but their leadership too often resembled tyranny. Their offers to coordinate the crusade and to bring peace and justice to the region were rejected by men who had come to distrust and fear papal authority.

Last, because the memory of past victories and injustices lives on and has had a great effect on even twentieth-century Baltic politics, neither the exiled German Balts nor the nationalistic Latvians, Lithuanians, Estonians, or Russians have forgiven or forgotten. The true picture of the crusade has been distorted. One should not forget the evils of the past, but they should be seen in perspective. The crusaders were neither all good nor all bad; they were simply men. There were too many fanatics among them, but one rarely hears of the many simple, honest men who also crusaded in the northeast. One finds extremists of every type in mass movements, from those who are motivated by hate to those who are guided by love. Then as now, unfortunately, the former type prevailed.

The crusade was important for the countries known today as Latvia and Estonia, although a small German settlement, less than seven percent of the population, dominated their cultural, intellectual, and political life until its removal by the Hitler-Stalin pact of 1939. The western influence transmitted by these Germans has disposed these nations toward the west, and the russification processes of the nineteenth and twentieth centuries have not succeeded in turning these Baltic peoples from their national heritage, which is rooted in the Middle Ages. Unintentionally, the crusaders created the Latvian and, to a lesser extent, Estonian nations; and—for better or worse—the Baltic Crusade has had a permanent effect on all of northern Europe.

NOTE TO EPILOGUE

1. *Henry of Livonia*, p. 109.

House of Lippe

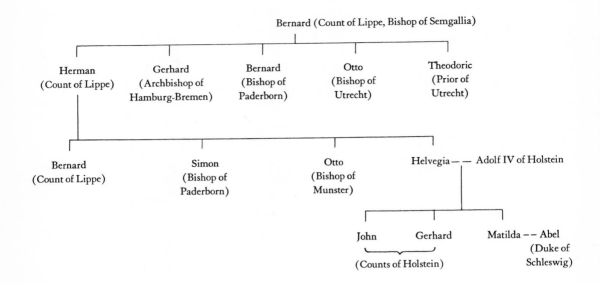

Bernard (Count of Lippe, Bishop of Semgallia)

- Herman (Count of Lippe)
- Gerhard (Archbishop of Hamburg-Bremen)
- Bernard (Bishop of Paderborn)
- Otto (Bishop of Utrecht)
- Theodoric (Prior of Utrecht)

- Bernard (Count of Lippe)
- Simon (Bishop of Paderborn)
- Otto (Bishop of Munster)
- Helvegia —— Adolf IV of Holstein

- John   Gerhard
- (Counts of Holstein)
- Matilda —— Abel (Duke of Schleswig)

Danish Royal House

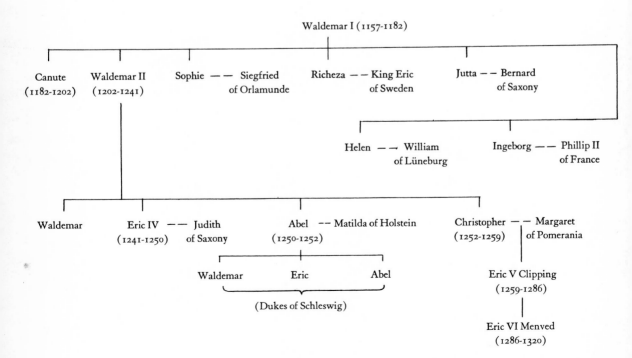

Waldemar I (1157-1182)

- Canute (1182-1202)
- Waldemar II (1202-1241)
- Sophie —— Siegfried of Orlamunde
- Richeza —— King Eric of Sweden
- Jutta —— Bernard of Saxony

- Helen —→ William of Lüneburg
- Ingeborg —— Phillip II of France

- Waldemar
- Eric IV —— Judith of Saxony (1241-1250)
- Abel —— Matilda of Holstein (1250-1252)
- Christopher —— Margaret of Pomerania (1252-1259)

- Waldemar   Eric   Abel
- (Dukes of Schleswig)
- Eric V Clipping (1259-1286)

- Eric VI Menved (1286-1320)

THE ASCANIAN FAMILY

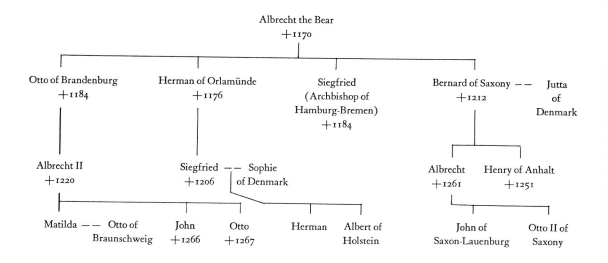

Albrecht the Bear
+1170

- Otto of Brandenburg +1184
  - Albrecht II +1220
    - Matilda —— Otto of Braunschweig
- Herman of Orlamünde +1176
  - Siegfried +1206 —— Sophie of Denmark
    - John +1266
    - Otto +1267
    - Herman
    - Albert of Holstein
- Siegfried (Archbishop of Hamburg-Bremen) +1184
- Bernard of Saxony +1212 —— Jutta of Denmark
  - Albrecht +1261
  - Henry of Anhalt +1251
    - John of Saxon-Lauenburg
    - Otto II of Saxony

THE WELF FAMILY

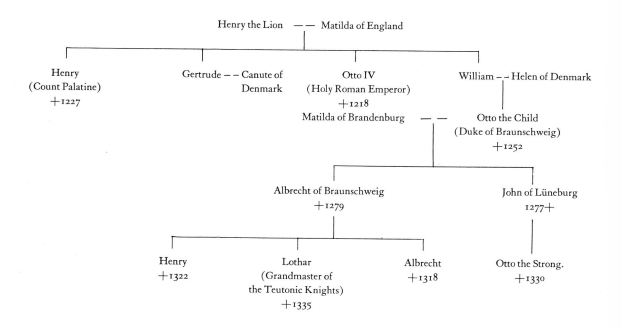

Henry the Lion —— Matilda of England

- Henry (Count Palatine) +1227
- Gertrude —— Canute of Denmark
- Otto IV (Holy Roman Emperor) +1218
- William —— Helen of Denmark

Matilda of Brandenburg —— Otto the Child (Duke of Braunschweig) +1252

- Albrecht of Braunschweig +1279
  - Henry +1322
  - Lothar (Grandmaster of the Teutonic Knights) +1335
  - Albrecht +1318
- John of Lüneburg 1277+
  - Otto the Strong. +1330

Buxhoeved Family

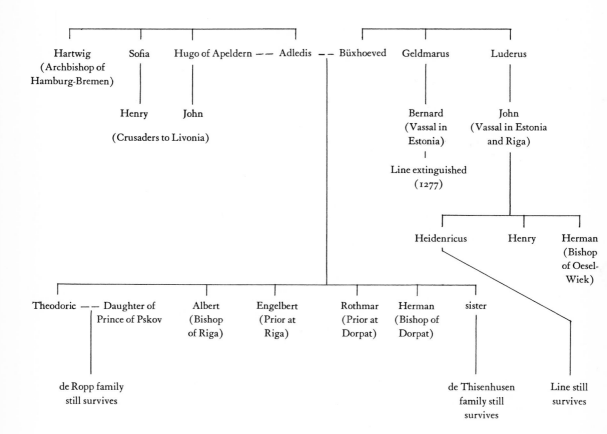

Each family provided numerous ecclesiastical officials to the Church in the diocese of Hamburg-Bremen who have not been listed.

Source: Gnegel-Waitschies, *Bischof Albert von Riga*.

MAJOR EVENTS IN EUROPE	MAJOR EVENTS IN LIVONIA
1175	
Fall of Henry the Lion	Mission to Livonia begins.
3rd Crusade Foundation of Teutonic Knights	
	Crusade to Livonia begins.
Civil War in Holy Roman Empire	
1200	
	Swordbrothers founded.
4th Crusade captures Constantinople	
5th Lateran Council	Crusade to Estonia begins.
5th Crusade fails at Damietta	
Emperor Frederick's Crusade recovers Jerusalem	William of Modena's legation.
Battle of Bornhoeved ends era of Danish greatness.	Baldwin of Alna's legation.
Beginning of struggle between Frederick II and Popes.	Battle of Saule ends Swordbrothers. Teutonic Knights invited in.
Jerusalem lost.	
Crusade of St. Louis	Battle on the Ice.
1250	
Death of Frederick II ends era of German greatness.	Battle of Schoden. Battle of Durben.
Constantinople lost to Greeks.	Loss of Sengallia, revolt of Kurs.
2nd Crusade of St. Louis	
Angevin Kingdom in Sicily.	Battle near Dorpat, peace with Novgorod.
	Battle near Ascheraden, Sengallia lost.
	Sengallia reconquered.
Loss of the Holy Land.	Civil War begins.
1300	

	POPE	EMPEROR	WELFS IN SAXONY
in 1175	Alexander III 1159 minor popes 1181	Frederick Barbarossa 1152	Henry the Lion 1144
		Henry VI 1190	William 1195
1200	Innocent III 1198	Phillip of Swabia 1197	
		Otto IV 1204	
		Frederick II 1211	Otto the Child 1213 (title of Duke of Braunschweig)
	Honorius III 1216		
	Gregory IX 1227		
	Innocent IV 1243		**BRAUNSCH- LUNE-** **-WEIG LINE -BURG LINE**
1250		Conrad IV 1250	Albert 1252 John 1252
	Alexander IV 1254	Interregum 1254-73	
	Urban IV 1261 Clement IV 1265		
	Gregory X 1271 minor popes 1276-	Rudolph of Hapsburg 1273	Otto 1277 Henry 1279
	Martin IV 1281 Honorius IV 1285 Nicholas IV 1288		and Albert 1279
	Clestine V 1294 Boniface VIII 1294	Adolph of Nassau 1292 Albrecht of Hapsburg 1298	
1300			

HOLSTEIN	DENMARK	ARCHBISHOP OF RIGA	MASTER OF ORDER
Adolph III 1164	Waldemar I 1157 Canute VI 1182		
		Meinhard 1186	
		Berthold 1196 Albert of Buxhoevden 1199	
title held by Albert of Orlamunde 1203-1226	Waldemar II 1202		SWORDBROTHERS Wenno 1204 Volquin 1209
Adolph IV 1223			
		Nicholas 1229	
			TEUTONIC KNIGHTS Herman Balke 1237
	Eric IV 1241		Andreas 1240 Dietrich 1242 Henry 1245 Andreas 1248
	Abel 1250 Christopher 1252	Albert Suerbeer 1253	Anno 1253 Burchard 1256
	Eric V 1259		
John 1261 Gerhard 1261 Gerhard II 1263			Werner 1261 Conrad 1263 Otto 1266
		John I of Lune 1273	Walter 1270 Welter 1270 Ernst 1274 Conrad 1279
	Eric VI 1286	John II of Vechten 1285	Willekin 1281 Cuno 1288
Henry 1290		John III of Schwerin 1294	Halt 1290 Henry 1295 Bruno 1296 Gottfried 1298

Selected Bibliography

The literature pertaining to the Baltic Crusade is very extensive, and the time and vast area covered by the crusade tend to give this literature a mosaic quality. No one historian, or collection of historical sources, covers every aspect of this complex era, and although certain works stand out, answers to many vital questions can be found only by reference to rather obscure and/or general historical works. Because the German historians provide exhaustive bibliographies, we have limited our list to a few key works.

Unfortunately for American students, there are very few books in English, and they vary considerably in quality. The most important are:

The Chronicle of Henry of Livonia. Translated by James A. Brundage. Madison, Wis.: University of Wisconsin Press, 1961. / This modern translation by a bright young American scholar could be improved by more extensive notes and maps, but it is accurate and literate. The *Chronicle* is a lively, intelligent account of the period 1180–1227 and ranks as one of the better medieval histories. Apparently written for the benefit of William of Modena, the papal legate who arrived in Riga in 1225, it is more thorough and more reflective than all but a very few medieval histories. It is a true classic and deserves the attention of the industrious student.

Chronicle of Novgorod, 1016–1471. Translated by Robert Michell and Nevil Forbes. Vol. 25 of the Camden Third Series. London, 1914. / Much less useful than the foregoing, and uneven in quality, but an indispensable account of the early history of this important Russian state.

Barraclough, Geoffrey. *Origins of Modern Germany.* Oxford: Basil Blackwell, 1957. / Excellent background historiography of medieval Germany. Recommended reading, although there is practically no information on the crusade itself.

Bilmanis, Alfred. *A History of Latvia.* Princeton, N.J.: Princeton University Press, 1951. / Written by a Latvian nationalist and retired diplomat, this work must be used with caution.

King, Wilson. *Chronicles of Three Free Cities: Hamburg, Bremen, Lübeck*. London: J. M. Dent & Sons, 1914. / Interesting reading but uneven in quality, although generally reliable.

Olins, Peter. *The Teutonic Knights in Latvia*. Riga: B. Laney, 1925. / Violently anti-German, this book must be used with great caution.

Spekke, Arnolds. *A History of Latvia*. Stockholm: M. Goppers, 1951. / Good, but has only a very short section on the thirteenth century.

Thompson, James Westfall. *Feudal Germany*. 2 vols. New York: Frederick Ungar, 1928. / Despite its Welfish viewpoint, this book is valuable for understanding Northern Germany in the period before the crusade.

Original sources have been assembled into a few great collections such as the first three titles listed below. Most of the individual chronicles or document collections derive directly from these.

Monumenta Germaniae Historica. Edited by Georg Heinrich Pertz, Theodore Mommsen, and others. Hannover, Berlin et al: Deutsches Institut für Erforschung des Mittelalters, 1826– . / Well-known to every medievalist, this giant collection includes correspondence, public documents, and chronicles. It is divided into several subdivisions. Under the subdivision *Scriptores rerum germanicarum in usum scholarum separatim editi* we find the following chronicles important: *Magistri Adam Bremensis Gesta Hammaburgensis ecclesiae pontificum*. 1st edition. 1846; 3d edition. Edited by Bernhard Schmeidler. Hannover: Hahnsche, 1876; *Annales Stadenses auctore Alberto*. Edited by Johann M. Lappenberg. Hannover: Hahnsche, 1859; *Helmoldi presbyteri Bozoviensis Chronica Slavorum*. 1st edition. 1868; 3d edition. Edited by Bernhard Schmeidler and Johann M. Lappenberg. Hannover: Hahnsche, 1937. There are also valuable chronicles in vol. 2 of the subdivision *Deutsche Chroniken, Scriptores qui vernacula lingua usa sunt*. Edited by Ludwig Weiland. Hannover: Hahnsche, 1877. Correspondence is found in the subdivisions: *Constitutiones et acta publica imperatorum et regum*. Hannover: Hahnsche, 1893–1919; and *Epistolae Saeculae XIII e. regestis pontificum romanorum selectae*. Berlin: Weidmann, 1883–1894.

Scriptores rerum Livonicarum; Sammlung der wichtigsten Chroniken und Geschichtsdenkmale von Liv-, Ehst-, und Kurland. Edited by A. Hansen. 2 vols. Riga and Leipzig: E. Frantzen's Verlag-comptoir, 1853. / Very carefully edited chronicles, but in an old edition. The basic works are available elsewhere.

Scriptores rerum Prussicarum. Edited by Theodore Hirsch and others. 2 vols. Leipzig: S. Hirzel, 1861–1874. / Contains important chronicles and collections of documents. Especially important for the latter part of the thirteenth century.

Annalles Danici medii aevi. Edited by Ellen Jørgensen. Copenhagen: G. E. C. Gad, 1920. / Basic collection of chronicles, some of which are included in MGH.

Heinrici chronicon Livoniae. 2d edition. Edited by Leonid Arbusow and Albert Bauer. Hannover: Hahnsche, 1955. / Relies on different manuscript than Brundage and is often considered superior. Notes are somewhat better also.

Livländische Reimchronik. Edited by Leo Mayer. Hildesheim: Georg Olms, 1963. Reprint of 1876 edition. / This rhymed chronicle covers the period 1180–1290. In middle high German and without notes. Very colorful description of battles, as one would expect in such a *chanson de geste*, but very weak on non-military affairs. Nevertheless, it is the principal account of the period 1227–1290.

Liv-, Est-, und Kurländische Urkundenbuch. Edited by Friedrich Georg von Bunge. 12 vols. Reval: H. Laakman 1853–1859; Riga and Moscow: 1867–1910. / Volumes 1, 2, 3, and 6 are very useful for the twelfth and thirteenth centuries. Must be used in conjunction with the following:

Liv-, Est-, und Kurländische Urkundenregesten bis zum Jahre 1300. Edited by Friedrich Benninghoven. Hamburg, 1959. / This is the index to all available documents on the Baltic Crusade in the thirteenth century. Benninghoven is the leading authority on the era, having succeeded his late mentor, Paul Johansen.

Regesta Pontificorum Romanorum (1198–1304). Edited by August Potthast. 2 vols. Berlin: Rudolph Decker, 1874–1875. / Contains short summaries of papal letters and bulls.

Das Rigische Schuldbuch. Edited by Hermann Hildebrand. St. Petersburg, 1872. / Explains the importance of surviving records of merchants of Riga.

Das Zeugenverhör des Franciscus de Moliano (1312). Edited by August Seraphim. Königsberg: Thomas and Oppermann, 1912. / A transcript of the inquiry by the papal legate into the feud between Riga and the Teutonic Knights.

Secondary accounts of the crusade in the German language are relatively numerous, and such articles are almost beyond counting. The most important are the following:

Arbusow, Leonid. *Grundriss der Geschichte Liv-, Est-, und Kurland.* Riga: Jonck and Poliewsky, 1918.

Benninghoven, Friedrich. *Der Orden der Schwertbrüder.* Cologne-Graz: Böhlau, 1965. / The most important new work on the Swordbrothers. Detailed investigation of their origin, activities, and downfall at Saule (1236) and Lake Peipus (1242).

Bunge, Friedrich Georg von. *Livland, die Wiege der deutschen Weihbischofe.* Leipzig: E. Bidder, 1875. / Important for ecclesiastical history.

————. *Der Orden der Schwertbrüder: deren Stiftung, Verfassung und Auflösung.* Leipzig: E. Bidder, 1875. / Excellent short account of the organization of the Swordbrothers.

Donner, Gustav Adolf. *Kardinal Wilhelm von Sabina, Bischof von Modena, 1222–1234.* Helsingsfors: H. Crohns and C. von Bonsdorff, 1929. / Minute investigation of the role of the papacy and papal legates in Livonia. Indispensable.

Goetze, Peter von. *Albert Suerbeer, Erzbischof von Preussen, Livland und Ehstland.* St. Petersburg: W. Gräff, 1854. / Best available account of this important figure, but outdated.

Gnegel-Waitschies, Gisela. *Bischof Albert von Riga: ein Bremer Domherr als Kirchenfürst im Osten.* Hamburg. A. F. Velmede, 1958. / A fine biography by another student of Paul Johansen.

Hausmann, Richard. *Das Ringen der Deutschen und Dänen um den Besitz Estlands bis 1227.* Leipzig: Dincker und Humbolt, 1870. / Good, but should be read in conjunction with Koch and Usinger.

Hellmann, Manfred. *Das Lettenland im Mittelalter: Studien zur ostbaltischen Frühzeit und lettischen Stammesgeschichte, insbesonders Lettgallens.* Münster: Böhlau Verlag, 1954. / A study of Livonia from the aspect of legal and social history. Investigates otherwise ignored questions related to the eastern area of Livonia.

Johansen, Paul. "Die Bedeutung der Hanse für Livland," *Hansische Geschichtsblätter,* 65–66 (1940–1941): 1–55. / Discusses relationship of merchant communities to the crusade.

————. "Eine Riga-Wisby Urkunde des 13. Jahrhunderts," *Zeitschrift des Vereins für lübeckische Geschichte,* 38 (1958): 93–108. / Provides new insight into the arrest of Archbishop Albert Suerbeer in 1268.

————. *"Die Estlandliste des Liber census Daniae.* Copenhagen: H. Hagerup, 1933. / Detailed investigation into Estonian tax lists for information about the mysterious period 1227–1238.

————. *Nordische Mission: Revals Gründung und die Schwedensiedlung in Estland.* Stockholm: Wahlström and Widstand, 1951. / Another look at the crusaders' policy in Estonia.

Koch, Friedrich. *Livland und das Reich bis zum Jahre 1225.* Posen, 1943. / Fine work by a young scholar who was killed in World War II. Especially good for North German and Danish influences on crusade.

Osten-Sacken, Paul von. "Der erste Kampf des Deutschen Ordens gegen die Russen," *Mitteilungen aus dem Gebiet der livländischen Geschichte,* 20 (1910): 87–124. / Account of the "Battle on the Ice" (1242). This journal is important for the many other interesting articles on the crusading era.

Rohkohl, Martin. "Albert Suerbeer, Erzbischof von Livland, Estland, und Preussen," *Zeitschrift der Gesellschaft für schleswig-holsteinische Geschichte,* 47 (1917): 68–90. / Important biography of this key figure, but outdated.

Schiemann, Theodor. *Russland, Polen und Livland bis ins 17. Jahrhundert.* Berlin: C. Grote, 1887. / Offers ideas that have been investigated further by more recent scholarship.

Toll, Baron Robert von. *Chronologie der Ordensmeister über Livland, der Erzbischöfe von Riga und der Bischöfe von Leal, Oesel, Wiek, Reval und Dorpat.* Riga, 1879. / Useful. Expert knowledge of German is not essential.

Usinger, Rudolf. *Deutsch-dänische Geschichte, 1189–1227.* Berlin, 1863. / A very helpful book. Contains list of extant documents referring to Albert of Orlamünde.

Wittram, Reinhard. *Baltische Geschichte; die Ostseelande, Livland, Estland, Kurland: 1180–1918.* Munich: R. Oldenbourg, 1954. / Good, but the section on the thirteenth century is short.

In Russian

Bassara, Artur and G. T. Naan. *Istoriia Estonskoi SSR.* Vol. 1. Talinn, 1961. / Excellent account of the Russian interest in Estonia and the military campaigns.

Index

Aachen, 183

Aa River: Livonian, 74, 82; Semgallian, 105, 218, 232

Abel, 130, 151, 161–62, 167, 175–77, 187–88, 212

Absalon, 12, 38, 42

Acre, 241, 257

Adalbert, Archbishop of Hamburg-Bremen, 5, 29 n

Adam of Bremen, 19, 29 n, 268

Adolf, Count of Dassel, 73, 110, 119

Adolf, Count of Holstein: II, 3, 4, 6, 13; III, 6, 9, 11, 13, 14, 36, 37, 39–42, 49, 72–73; IV, 119, 121, 130, 132–33, 135, 151–52, 162

Advocates: magistrates, 8, 10, 42, 57, 63, 68, 86, 104, 111, 113, 114, 136, 138, 156, 160, 169, 197, 198, 204, 206, 207, 237; of Archbishop of Riga, 137; of crusaders, 128; of Lübeck, 176, 256; of Riga, 221

Albert of Buxhoevden, 37–39, 43–45, 49–51, 54, 57, 60, 63, 67–70, 73, 76–77, 79, 81–83, 85–86, 90–92, 101–2, 104–5, 108–9, 110, 112–13, 119–20, 127, 129, 138

Albert of Orlamünde, 50, 60, 73, 90, 93, 99–102, 112, 119, 121–22, 133

Albert of Stade, 35, 41

Albert Suerbeer, 138, 179–80, 183–88, 191, 198–202, 204–6, 211, 218, 220–21, 223, 230, 270

Albrecht of Anhalt, 104, 106, 108, 130, 132–33, 141–42, 175

Albrecht the Bear, 3, 4, 6, 9

Albrecht, Duke of Braunschweig, 213–14

Aldenesch, Battle of, 154–55

Alexander III (pope), 6

Alexander IV (pope), 191, 194, 204

Alexander, Bishop of Dorpat, 219, 221

Alexander Nevsky, 165–68

Alna, 138. *See also* Baldwin of Alna

Amazons, 20

Ambassadors, 108, 142, 202, 243, 258

Amboten, 181

Anastasia, 220, 256, 267

Andreas: of Steierland, 183–86; Suneson, 42, 51, 67, 85, 104, 106, 108, 118; of Velven, 180; of Westphalia, 232

Angevin dynasty, 10, 35, 72, 87

Anno of Sangerhausen, 189–91, 197–98, 201, 211, 217, 219, 233

Armagh, Archbishop of, 179. *See also* Albert Suerbeer

Arnold: of Lübeck, 6; of Meiendorf, 50; a Swordbrother, 81

Arnstein, Count of, 146 n

Ascheraden, 182, 235

Assemblies. *See* Councils

Augustinian Order, 26, 61, 79

Austria, 4